Y0-CAO-969

The Soviet Treatment of Jews

Harry G. Shaffer

The Praeger Special Studies program—utilizing the most modern and efficient book production techniques and a selective worldwide distribution network—makes available to the academic, government, and business communities significant, timely research in U.S. and international economic, social, and political development.

The Soviet Treatment of Jews

PRAEGER SPECIAL STUDIES IN INTERNATIONAL POLITICS AND GOVERNMENT

Praeger Publishers New York Washington London

Library of Congress Cataloging in Publication Data

Shaffer, Harry G
The Soviet treatment of Jews.

(Praeger special studies in international politics and government)
Includes bibliographical references.
1. Jews in Russia—Political and social conditions—1917- —Addresses, essays, lectures. I. Title.
DS135.R92S48 301.45'19'24047 73-13338

PRAEGER PUBLISHERS
111 Fourth Avenue, New York, N.Y. 10003, U.S.A.
5, Cromwell Place, London SW7, 2JL, England

Published in the United States of America in 1974
by Praeger Publishers, Inc.

Printed in the United States of America

To my wife, Julie, and to our children,
Bernie, Ronnie, Lennie and Tanya

PREFACE

Even the most ardent pro-Soviet Western Marxists, and for that matter the Soviets themselves, would grant that there are individuals in the Soviet Union who harbor anti-Jewish feelings. It could hardly be otherwise. Age-old prejudices simply cannot be eradicated over night; stereotypes and myths implanted in the popular mind for generations during the era of the czars and recreated in more drastic forms than ever before during the days of the Nazi occupation are not easily extirpated. Some residues of personal feelings of anti-Semitism, especially among the older generation and among the less educated, are to be expected. But—and this is the all-important question—what is the position of the Soviet Government and of the Communist Party of the Soviet Union on the "Jewish question"? Are they intent on stamping out the remnants of anti-Jewish prejudice, or are they reinforcing it by word and deed? Are Soviet Jews treated as equals in the USSR; are the same opportunities extended to them as to the rest of the Soviet people; or are they overtly or surreptitiously discriminated against by the Soviet regime and by official Soviet policies? And if the latter be true, what is the extent, the degree, of such anti-Semitic discrimination?

There are many in the West who accuse the Soviet regime of discriminatory treatment of Soviet Jews, if not of outright, blatant anti-Semitism. Among those whose voices have rung out in protest are some of the recognized liberals of the Western world, individuals like Martin Luther King, Jr., and Bertrand Russell. Some Westerners equate the treatment of Soviet Jews with that of German Jews during the Nazi holocaust. Others, while labeling such comparisons absurd, still find varying degrees of discrimination, especially in regard to the rights of Jews to preserve and pass on to their children their religious and cultural heritage; yet others have words of high praise for the great opportunities extended by the Soviets to the Jewish minority and consider Western accusations propaganda, motivated by the desire to disparage Soviet socialism.

Official Soviet policy has always discouraged religion and has always been strongly anti-Zionist. It therefore condemns as anti-socialist certain views held and propagated, and at times even as criminal certain activities engaged in, by some Soviet Jews. But from the days of V. I. Lenin and Joseph Stalin to the days of Leonid Brezhnev and Alexei Kosygin, Soviet leaders have proclaimed that the complete equality of all is basic to socialist ideology and is a salient feature of Soviet policy.

Who is right? Who is wrong? Instead of attempting to furnish answers, this book exposes the reader to a large number of often diametrically opposed views of accusations and denials, of charges and countercharges, of evidence and counterevidence. In the process of becoming acquainted with different positions on this controversial, emotion-laden topic, the reader may well discover that the issues involved are much more complex and the conclusions by no means so clear-cut as they at first appear.

The book starts out with a prologue consisting of quotations reflective of the wide variety of divergent views on the subject. It is followed by a detailed account of the position and treatment of Soviet Jews in which I attempt to present a balanced view, taking account of conflicting evidence on the subject.

The rest of the book is devoted to readings intended to familiarize the reader with the whole spectrum of positions. The selections run the gamut from the writings by leaders of the militantly anti-Soviet Jewish Defense League to those of prominent members of the pro-Soviet Communist Party of the United States, and from statements representative of the official Israeli position to articles representative of the official position of the USSR. In the last selection of this volume, Soviet Jews from all walks of life give widely disparate reports on what it is like to live as Jews in the Union of Soviet Socialist Republics.

The problem of the position and treatment of Jews in the USSR has evoked much heat; if this book can contribute in a small way to diminishing this heat and shedding a little more light, it will have accomplished its goal.

I want to express my gratitude to Professor William Fletcher (University of Kansas) who went over the manuscript with a fine-tooth comb, and to Professors Thomas E. Bird (Queens College) and Jacob W. Kipp (Kansas State University) who also made valuable comments. I greatly appreciate the cooperation of those who gave permission to reproduce the selections contained in this volume: of authors, editors, and publishers in the West, of the Soviet Embassies in London and Washington, and of the Novosti Press Agency Publishing House in Moscow. For secretarial work, I am deeply indebted to Darlene Heacock, who worked cheerfully far above and beyond the call of duty to prepare the manuscript, and to Geraldine Rasmussen and Anita Williams.

Last, but by no means least, I want to thank my wife and most severe critic, Dr. Juliet P. Shaffer, who has given so liberally of her time and effort in reviewing several versions of this manuscript and who has offered countless invaluable suggestions and comments.

Harry G. Shaffer

CONTENTS

Chapter | Page

PROLOGUE: INTRODUCTION TO A WIDE DIVERSITY OF VIEWS

This prologue is intended to give the reader a bird's-eye view of the vast spectrum of widely divergent views on the subject of Soviet Jewry. To this end, a number of representative quotations from the writings and speeches of prominent individuals and from relevant documents have been selected. Western views include both Marxist and non-Marxist positions and run the gamut from the extremely anti-Soviet opinions expressed by a representative of the Jewish Defense League to the pro-Soviet position of a prominent member of the Communist Party of the United States. Soviet views are represented by quotes from Soviet leaders and government officials, past and present, and from documents reflective of the official Soviet position. (For representative statements by Soviet Jews, approbatory as well as critical of Soviet policies regarding Soviet Jewry, see "Soviet Jews Testify," pages 188-231 below.)

WESTERN NON-MARXIST VIEWS: A WIDE VARIETY OF OPINIONS

I do not believe that the Soviets can, in good conscience, deny the existence of widespread discrimination against their Jewish citizens. The testimony is in from too many sources, too many journalists, too many Soviet publications, too many emigrés to permit serious dispute over the nature and magnitude of this discrimination.

Arthur J. Goldberg, former associate justice of the Supreme Court and U.S. ambassador to the United Nations

The Jews of the Soviet Union . . . are sundered apart from the life-stream of Jewry. They are denied the right to national life and to religious and cultural expression—a right accorded to all other peoples in the Soviet Union. They are robbed of the right to come to their historic homeland.

Golda Meir, prime minister of Israel

The Jewish minority in the U.S.S.R. is subjected to singularly repressive treatment, special prohibitions are placed upon Jewish education, religious observance, and culture. Discrimination is practiced against Jews in employment and schooling. Anti-Semitism is inflamed by a stream of news articles, books, and cartoons from the government press.

Louis Rosenblum, Union of Councils for Soviet Jews

3 million Jews are being held hostage in a land which systematically denies them their rights and subjects them to harassment, outrage, and incarceration. . . .

Clarence D. Long, U.S. congressman from Maryland

There are two kinds of [Soviet] Jews. There are those who wish to renounce their Jewish traditions and blend into Soviet society; there are others who wish to maintain their traditions but are prevented from doing so by the Russian government.

Rabbi Richard Hirsch, director of the National Religious Action Center

The Soviet regime has persecuted the Russian Jewish Community to an unprecedented extent, seeking to gain by slow death what they dare not perpetrate openly before the world by massacre.

Frank J. Brasco, U.S. congressman from the State of New York

The world regards its [the USSR's] treatment of its Jewish citizens as sheer barbarism.

Philip Hoffman, president, American Jewish Committee

Those of us who remember the tragedy of the Warsaw ghetto uprising and the thousands of Jewish lives that were lost in that heroic encounter with the Nazis are fearful that history may repeat itself. God forbid.

Rabbi Zev Sega, chairman of the Essex County Conference on Soviet Jewry and past president and honorary president of the Rabbinical Council of America

Insofar as equating the holocaust in Germany with what is transpiring in the Soviet Union, insofar as Jews are concerned, there is no difference.

Bertram Zweibon, national vice chairman, Jewish Defense League

There can be no comparison with the terrible era of the Nazi holocaust or Stalin's blood purge of Jewish intellectuals. With respect to the majority, claims that Soviet Jews as a community are living in a state of terror seem to be overdrawn.

Richard T. Davies, deputy assistant secretary for European Affairs, U.S. Department of State (representing official view of U.S. Department of State)

I was a little offended by this drawback that the State Department was making in suggesting that some of the charges about a state of terror were overdrawn.

Benjamin S. Rosenthal, chairman, Subcommittee on Europe, of the Committee on Foreign Affairs, U.S. House of Representatives

I am appalled and aghast by Mr. Davies' statement on behalf of the State Department that Soviet Jews are not living in terror. The situation of Soviet Jews has worsened and Jews do live under intolerable conditions.

Rabbi Avriaham Weiss, board member, Committee on Russian Jewry

The question arises, is what the Soviet Union is doing to the Jews comparable to what Nazi Germany did? The answer is no, and no one in his right mind would make that comparison . . . .

The complaints, at least those that I have heard, are not that Jews are living in a state of terror as such, not that the Jews are being physically put into concentration camps, not that offenses are committed against them as occurred under the Nazis, but that the Soviet Union has embarked upon a campaign of long standing to make it more difficult for the Jews and for any other group to practice their religion.

Edward Koch, U.S. congressman from the State of New York

I am not suggesting that the Jews feel they are completely free, but I think the statement that they live in a state of terror is an exaggeration, based on my own personal experience.

Sol Polansky, first secretary of the U.S. Embassy in Moscow from September 1968, to July 1971

A picture has been created [in the West] of a community of almost 3,000,000 Jews under persecution [in the Soviet Union], living in daily misery and fearing for their lives. This picture is wrong. One can meet Soviet Jews every day whose reactions to the campaigns in their defense range from total bewilderment to sincere anger. . . . What has been persecuted throughout half a century of the Soviet system, persecuted almost to death, is the Jewish heritage: The religious practices and the culture through which Jews come together to acknowledge a common bond.

Peter Grose, Moscow chief of The New York *Times* from May 1965 to June 1967

If it had not been for the Soviet army, there would have been no Jews on earth at all.

Arthur Miller, American playwright

In the name of humanity, I urge that the Soviet government end all discriminatory measures against its Jewish community.

Martin Luther King, Jr.

A few non-Slavic peoples have a high susceptibility to Communism. The most prominent case in Eastern Europe (and in Russia as well) is that of the Jews. . . .

R. V. Burks, professor of History, Wayne State University, and former policy director, Radio Free Europe

WESTERN MARXIST VIEWS: NO ANTI-SEMITISM IN THE USSR

How should one actually regard the allegation of "Soviet anti-Semitism"? Is there any moral ground for this outcry? Can one adopt such an attitude to a country where Jews have been given the richest opportunities for living and developing? I myself did not see any manifestations of anti-Semitism in the USSR or any anti-Semitic literature of which we in the U.S.A., unfortunately, have more than enough; nor did I see any bandits with swastikas on their arms. In the U.S.A. they walk about in broad daylight.

Paul Novick, editor, Yiddish language New York City daily *Freiheit*

The Soviet government is not guilty of anti-Semitism: on the contrary, it is one of the few governments in the world . . . which illegalizes all expressions or manifestations of anti-Semitism or any other form of racism.

Dr. Herbert Aptheker, director, American Institute of Marxist Studies and member of the Communist Party of the United States

The myth of Soviet oppression of Jews is one of the greatest hoaxes of all times.

Young Worker, house organ of Young Workers' Liberation League of the Communist Party of the United States

SOVIET VIEWS:
EQUAL RIGHTS AND OPPORTUNITIES FOR ALL

Equality of rights of citizens of the USSR, irrespective of their nationality or race, in all spheres of economic, government, cultural, political and other social activity is an indefeasible law.

Any direct or indirect restriction of the rights of, or, conversely, the establishment of any direct or indirect privileges for citizens on account of their race or nationality, as well as any advocacy of racial or national exclusiveness or hatred and contempt, are punishable by law.

Constitution of the USSR, Article 123

The Prosecuting Office of the USSR combats any manifestations of anti-Semitism. Offenders are prosecuted. In many cases they are convicted and sent to prisons or camps. But in some cases public condemnation proves sufficient.

Gennady Terekhov, senior assistant of the USSR Chief Prosecutor

The Council of People's Commissars declares the anti-Semitic movement and programs a menace to the cause of the workers' and peasants' revolution and calls on all the working people of all the nations of socialist Russia to fight this menace by every means available.

Decree issued in 1919

Only the most ignorant, the most downtrodden people can believe the lies and slander that are spread about Jews. Shame on those who foment hatred towards Jews. . . .

The Jewish bourgeois are our enemies, not as Jews but as bourgeois. The Jewish worker is our brother. The Council of People's Commissars instructs all Soviet deputies to take uncompromising measures to tear the anti-Semitic movement out by the roots.

Vladimir Ilyich Lenin

Communists, as consistent internationalists cannot help but being the implacable and sworn enemies of anti-Semitism.

Anti-Semitism is a phenomenon profoundly hostile to the Soviet regime and it is sternly repressed in the USSR.

Joseph V. Stalin

The Jewish people in the Soviet Union are treated like everyone else. . . .

There has never been any policy of anti-Semitism in the Soviet Union.

Nikita S. Khrushchev, former first Party secretary and prime minister

Any kind of nationalistic survival—whether it be a manifestation of nationalism, chauvinism, racism, or anti-Semitism—is absolutely alien to and incompatible with our ideology. . . .

There never has been and there is not now any anti-Semitism in the Soviet Union.

Alexei Kosygin, prime minister

PART I

THE POSITION AND TREATMENT OF SOVIET JEWS: EQUALITY, DISCRIMINATION, OR RAMPANT ANTI-SEMITISM

CHAPTER

1

THE PRE-BREZHNEV-KOSYGIN ERA

THE JEWS UNDER THE CZARS

The pre-1917 history of Jews in Russia, in the Ukraine, in Lithuania, and in much of Eastern Europe was one of anti-Jewish prejudice, discrimination, hostility, and often outright hatred and persecution.

Jews have lived in parts of what today constitutes the territory of the USSR since the days of antiquity. Before the Christian era they had spread over the Caucasus; by the second century A.D. they had settled in Georgia, by the eighth in Kiev and surrounding areas and in Lithuania. By the time of the Tartar invasion in the thirteenth century, substantial settlements of Jews could be found along the banks of the Don, the Dnieper, and the Volga. When the Tartars destroyed the Grand Kiev Principality in 1240, most of the Jews fled to Poland. During the centuries that followed, the descendants of those who had remained were often subjected to official persecution, as illustrated by the infamous order issued by Ivan IV, the Terrible, crowned first Czar in 1547, to "baptize the Jews who consent to baptism and drown the rest."[1] In 1742, Queen Elizabeth "solved" the Jewish problem in Russia, at least for a time, by commanding the expulsion of Jews from the empire. In theory all, and in practice most, Jews were actually expelled.

The partitioning of Poland towards the end of the eighteenth century* changed the picture completely since it brought roughly 1

The first partition of Poland in 1722 gave the eastern provinces to Russia, the northern to Prussia, and the southern to Austria. More Polish territory was annexed by these three powers in the second million Jews, about one-half of the world's Jewish population at the time, under Russian control. The Czarist government thereupon established a "Pale of Settlement" in the Ukraine and adjacent areas and with relatively few exceptions Jews were not allowed to reside elsewhere in Russia. Official propaganda of church and state, strongly supported by much of the press and the theater, created in the minds of the Russian people a stereotype of Jews as crafty, wily, greedy, parasitical money-grabbers. Especially during the half-century prior to the Russian revolution such propaganda often went as far as accusing Jews of ritual crimes, including murder, allegedly perpetrated on non-Jews; and Jews were blamed for many of the ills that beset Czarist Russia. Zhid Idyot—Beware of the Jew†—became the slogan of the 1880s. After the murder of Czar Alexander II in 1881, his son, Alexander III, became Russia's new ruler. Described as "narrow-minded, limited, poorly educated . . . a confirmed anti-Semite,"[2] he superintended the enactment of anti-Semitic laws and the imposition of legal restrictions on Jews; and under his reign and that of his son Nicholas II, an anti-Semite like his father,[3] mass pogroms were tolerated and often even encouraged; by the time of the revolution, thousands upon thousands of Jewish men, women, and children had been brutally slaughtered, their houses burned, their property pilfered or destroyed. Pobedonostsev, chief prosecutor of the "Holy Synod," expressed the Czarist policy towards the Jews in a statement to the effect that one-third of the Jewish population was to be converted to Christianity, one-third was to perish, and one-third was to be

---

partition of 1793. And in the third partition in 1795, Poland disappeared from the map as an independent country until it was reestablished at the end of World War I.

*The Pale, originally along the northern and eastern boundaries of the territory annexed from Poland, was soon extended and in the nineteenth century encompassed all of Russian Poland, Lithuania, Byelorussia, most of the Ukraine, the Crimea, and Bessarabia. In the latter half of the nineteenth century, certain categories of Jews, including the wealthier merchants, those with higher education, and those who had completed their military obligations, were permitted to take up residence on Russian lands outside the Pale. But the census of 1897 shows that the then almost 5 million Jews residing inside the Pale accounted for 11.76 percent of its population, while the approximately 200,000 Jews in the rest of European Russia made up a mere one-third of 1 percent of the population there.

†Zhid is a derogatory word for Jew; yevrey is the proper Russian word; idyot literally means "is going," "is on the move," "is up to something."

compelled to emigrate.[4] At least the last part of Pobedonostsev's policy statement turned into reality: Between 1881 and 1914, one-third of the Jewish population of Russia emigrated. Among those who remained, a disproportionately large number, as compared with the rest of the Russian people, dedicated themselves to the struggle for a revolutionary reconstitution of society. By 1897, the year in which the Jewish revolutionary party, the Bund, was formed, Jews accounted for one-fourth of all political prisoners in Russia.

THE REVOLUTION AND THE YEARS OF LENIN'S RULE

To Russian Jews, the words of Vladimir Ilyich Lenin, foremost apostle of radical change, must have been particularly enticing. Outspoken on the issue of anti-Semitism, Lenin saw it as but a diversionary tactic of Russia's ruling classes intended to turn the anger of Russian workers away from their enemies, the wealthy "exploiters of the people." Here was a leader who emphasized the need for "complete unity" of Jewish and non-Jewish workingmen; who would publicly declare that "only the most ignorant and downtrodden people can believe the lies and slander that are spread about the Jews"; who asked Russian workers to raise their voices in protest against any form of national oppression; who called for the repeal of all laws that imposed restrictions on Jews in any sphere of social and state life and, in 1914, included that request in a bill of national equality introduced in the Fourth State Duma;* and who, once Soviet power had been established, had his Council of People's Commissars issue a decree calling on "all the working people of all nations of socialist Russia to fight the menace of anti-Semitism by every means available."[5] Here was the promulgator of an ideology that aimed at nothing less than brotherhood of all races and all nationalities (although not all classes within society); here was the proponent of the philosophy of "scientific socialism" whose founder, himself a Jew by birth, adjudged anti-Semitism a by-product of capitalist relationships inevitably destined to disappear under the new order. No wonder Jews in large numbers flocked to the revolutionary banner that was soon to fly over the new Soviet state. And the constitution of that new state was to contain the following sentence: "Equality of rights of citizens irrespective of their nationality or race in all spheres of economic, government, cultural, political, and other social activity is an indefeasible law."[6]

---

*The Duma was a parliament set up by Czar Nicholas II as a consultative body in 1905; it was terminated by the revolution in 1917.

During World War I, the persecution of Jews continued: They were accused of spying for the enemy; they were moved from areas near the Western front to the East; they were humiliated and tormented by contingents of the Czar's armies. And during the days of the civil war that followed, the White Armies, including units under the personal command of the "White" forces' supreme commander Anton Ivanovich Denikin, engaged in innumerable, widespread, and incredibly brutal pogroms. Literally hundreds of Jewish communities were wiped out, and estimates of Jews killed in these pogroms vary from 60,000 to 200,000.[7]

Among 2,160 names listed by the Soviets as heroes who gave their lives for the cause of the revolution in the years 1918 to 1921 there were 213 Jews.[8] And from the very outset, Jews played prominent roles. From the ranks of the Jewish people who had virtually no war tradition for two millennia came some of Lenin's chief military leaders, men such as Eydeman, Feldman, Gamarnik, Shtern, and Yakir, not to mention the architect and chief organizer of the Red Army, Leon Trotsky (born Lev Davidovich Bronstein). The first president of the new Soviet state, Yakov Sverdlov, was a Jew, and so were many of the top leaders, among them Kamenev, Radek, Yoffe, Zinoviev and, once again, Trotsky. In state administration, in public office, in education, in the arts, indeed throughout Soviet society, Jews were elevated to positions of authority and leadership in numbers far beyond their percentage in the total or even in the urban population. In 1927, one out of every ten civil service positions in Moscow, one out of every five in the Ukraine, and almost one out of every three in Byelorussia were held by Jews, in percentages roughly four times those of their respective percentages of the population in these areas.[9]

The lot of Jewish merchants and traders was less rosy. They were persecuted, and some were even executed as speculators, not because they were Jewish but because their old ways of earning a livelihood did not fit the ideological prescriptions of the new society. But when in 1921 the introduction of the New Economic Policy (NEP) called for an ideological retreat, permitting the temporary reintroduction of private enterprise into farming, trade, and small-scale industrial production, Jews once again turned to their old activities; five years later when Jews accounted for but 2 percent of the overall and 8 percent of the Soviet urban population, one out of every five tradesmen was Jewish and among craftsmen the percentage was twice as large.[10]

When Marx predicted that after the inevitable demise of the capitalist order anti-Semitism would gradually disappear, he also prognosticated the end of Judaism per se. In other words, to him the answer to the Jewish problem was assimilation, integration of Jews into the population at large. And this, precisely, was also what communist leaders of the era, Jewish and non-Jewish alike, opted for, from Lenin to Trotsky and from Rosa Luxemburg to Bella Kun.[11] Religion and Zionism were thus anathema to Marxist-Leninist ideology. While in the first four or five years of Soviet power about 50 Soviet publications were explicitly devoted to the eradication of anti-Semitism, with the declared purpose of freeing Soviet society from this "scourge of humanity" and making the Soviet Union the first state to abolish anti-Semitism completely, there appeared also numerous publications opposing the Jewish religion from an atheistic point of view.

To be sure, fierce campaigns were initiated under Lenin against all religions. To gain the full support of religious peasants and workers during the trying years of the civil war and the immediate postwar period, it became necessary to work out a temporary compromise with the formerly all-powerful Russian Orthodox Church; but the decree "On the Separation of Church from State and of School from Church," issued by the Council of People's Commissars and cosigned by Lenin in January, 1918, probably dealt a more damaging blow to that church than to any other, at least in the opinion of some scholars,[12] for it provided for the secularization of the state, the confiscation of property and funds of religious institutions, the discontinuation of the treatment of churches and church organizations as legal entities, and the prohibition of religious instruction in schools. The Jewish religion was detrimentally affected primarily by the prohibition of religious education for the youth. So as to stifle the voices of those who would decry acts against the Jewish religion as anti-Semitic, the enforcement of antireligious policies and the "enlightenment" of Soviet Jews in regard to the "correct" materialistic world outlook were generally placed in the hands of the Yevsketsia, the special Jewish section of the party in charge of Jewish affairs that operated until, with the increasing centralization of ideological, political, and economic life, it was abolished in 1930.

Throughout the 1920s, campaigns abounded to close down synagogues and religious schools; Zionists were branded as political reactionaries; and even Jews unwilling to work on the Sabbath or the high holidays were harassed. But until policies were changed under Stalin in the 1930s, a clear distinction was drawn between the Jewish religion and Zionism on the one hand and Jewish culture on the other. The former were relentlessly attacked; the latter was not. Hence, Hebrew was suppressed; but Yiddish (which 75 percent of Soviet Jews declared to be their native tongue) was not discouraged nor was the concept of the Jewish people as one of the more than one hundred peoples that entered into the composition of the population of the USSR. On the contrary, Yiddish-language theaters, schools, newspapers, and departments of Jewish study and research at institutions of higher learning were established or permitted to continue, albeit under the supervision of Jewish communists dedicated to the eventual elimination of the Jewish culture and the total assimilation of Jews.

Attacks against Jewish religion and culture, and even against Zionism, can be and often throughout history have been used to disguise what actually are anti-Semitic acts and policies; but to judge by all available evidence of the treatment and position of Jews and of the opportunities open to them, this was apparently not the case during Lenin's regime, nor during the early years of the Stalin era.

THE STALIN ERA

The NEP period was short-lived. By the end of the 1920s, when the Soviet Union, now under Stalin, turned once and for all to central planning and to the socialization of the means of production, private entrepreneurs—whether newly rich peasants (dubbed kulaks) or members of the "city bourgeoisie"—were declared enemies of the state. Although there were many Jews among the latter, their plight does not seem to have been related to their ethnic or religious background. Jews who grew up in the Soviet Union during the 1920s and early 1930s generally report that they were virtually unaware of any anti-Semitism.[13]

In 1928, the Birobidzhan region in the far eastern part of the Russian Republic was designated for Jewish settlement, and in 1934 it was given the status of a Jewish Autonomous Region. However, that distant and somewhat forbidding part of Russia has never attracted any large numbers of Jewish settlers. Estimated at between 13,000 and 25,000,[14] the Jewish population of Birobidzhan today accounts for only 5 to 10 percent of the total population there, and for less than 1 percent of the Jewish population of the USSR. Although, for a "people" to be designated a "nationality" in the Soviet Union, they must be of common ethnic background and have their "own" territory, it is by no means necessary that a majority of them reside there. But in the case of Birobidzhan, the percentage of Soviet Jews living in that "Jewish Autonomous Region" is so small that it hardly can be considered a home for Jewish nationals in the USSR.

The establishment of a Jewish National Region was probably intended primarily as an alternative to the Zionist goal of establishing a homeland in Palestine and as a gesture to lingering feelings of Jewish national identity. Occasionally, Westerners have asserted that it was primarily an attempt to rid the rest of the Soviet Union of most of its Jewish population. This latter interpretation seems highly questionable since the area selected was not such as could be expected to induce voluntary mass movements there and since no attempt was made to compel Jews to move to Birobidzhan.

Most Westerners who charge Stalin with rampant anti-Semitism believe that it began to develop and manifest itself in the 1930s, growing ever more vicious as time went on, interrupted only by a few years of national unity during and immediately after World War II. As late as November 1936, V. M. Molotov, one of the Soviet Union's leading statesmen under Stalin, would say warmly and with affection: "Our fraternal feelings towards the Jewish people are determined by the fact that this people gave birth to Karl Marx, to numerous great scientists, technicians and artists, and to many heroes in the revolutionary struggle."[15] But by that time the era of the great purges (1936-39), which brought with it the trials and execution of most of Lenin's Jewish associates, had already started; within less than three years a pact of friendship with Hitler had been signed; and from then on the picture became clouded by increasing uncertainties.

For no period of Soviet history have Western charges of anti-Semitism been stronger nor more thoroughly documented than for certain years of the Stalin era. The Soviets themselves have never confirmed these charges. Even during the height of the denunciation of the "personality cult," anti-Semitism was never mentioned in the Soviet press, in Soviet magazines or books, or in official Soviet documents as a motivating force for any of the numerous crimes with which Stalin was charged.

Stalin's official statements against anti-Semitism were similar to those made by Soviet leaders before and since, statements to the effect that "Communists as consistent internationalists, cannot help being the implacable and sworn enemies of anti-Semitism"[16] or that "anti-Semitism is a phenomenon profoundly hostile to the Soviet regime and is sternly repressed in the USSR."[17] While some scholars apparently feel that Stalin meant what he said, others have questioned the meaningfulness of such declarations; and in the minds of yet others, Stalin's actions simply gave the lie to his words.

It appears that Stalin discriminated against Judaism as a religion, that he was unwilling to grant Jewish religious congregations some of the concessions he was prepared to extend to others.[18] But Stalin seems to have concentrated his assaults even more on secular Jewish culture than on the Jewish religion.

During the 1930s and especially after the middle of the decade, Jewish schools and newspapers were shut down and Jewish cultural and religious life was severely curtailed. True, these steps must not necessarily be interpreted as anti-Semitic in nature. Since these were years of linguistic, cultural, social, and religious assimilation, of mass absorption of Jews into the mainstream of society, the reduction of Jewish institutions and activities was probably to some degree voluntary, the result of diminishing interest on the part of Jews, and especially younger Jews, in the traditions of their fathers; and to some degree the measures taken were undoubtedly intended to reinforce that trend. Still, the fact that most other nationalities could operate schools and newspapers in their own languages gives some credence to those who attribute ignoble motives to Stalin's actions. And the purges that cut so deeply into the ranks of Jews in positions of leadership certainly had nothing to do with assimilation. Moreover, during the era of the short-lived Nazi-Soviet pact, some Jews were dismissed from their positions, apparently because they were Jews. One could, of course, argue that the purges affected wide segments of the Soviet people and especially of the Party membership, Jews and non-Jews alike; that the restrictions of the Nazi-Soviet pact era can at least in part be explained in terms of diplomatic necessity; and that some Jews remained in high positions throughout the entire era. Yet, if there were no anti-Semitic motives involved, why, one wonders, were the many Jews in high positions who were victims of the purges replaced predominantly by non-Jews? Why, if the purges were not heavily weighted against Jews, did so few remain in high positions? And can diplomatic necessity really be accepted as more than a very inadequate, partial explanation of Soviet anti-Jewish actions during the Nazi-Soviet pact era?

During World War II perhaps a million Soviet Jews were slaughtered by the Nazi invaders. There is undeniable evidence that in some of the Nazi-occupied territories, and especially in Lithuania and the Ukraine, inhabitants aided and abetted in the extermination of Jews and the plunder of Jewish property.[19] Just how widespread such acts on the part of local residents were is more difficult to ascertain. While there are reports of wholesale collaboration with the Nazis in some localities, especially in the early days of the war, some distinguished Western scholars describe Nazi attempts to incite local inhabitants to pogroms as generally unsuccessful.[20] When the Soviets themselves report war crimes committed by Soviet citizens, they usually point out that Jews and non-Jews alike were victims of the "Fascists," and they consequently treat the actions of such Nazi collaborators as being directed against the Soviet people in general and not against Jews in particular. Moreover, as Soviet sources emphasize and Western sources frequently concede, there were many Soviet citizens who risked their lives for their Jewish neighbors, sharing with them their meager supplies of food and clothing, assisting them in various ways, and at times taking some of them, and especially children, into their homes for the duration of the war. Nevertheless, the long period of Nazi occupation had its impact on the non-Jewish inhabitants: Although, under the brutal treatment meted out by the

German occupation forces, most Soviet citizens grew increasingly hostile toward the invaders, the efficient Nazi propaganda machinery was not without success in rekindling the flames of age-old anti-Semitism, which even after the war seem to have smoldered on for years.

In the unoccupied parts of the USSR, the savage onslaught of the German armies and the news of the repression in the conquered territories united the Soviet citizenry. Soviet Jews soon found most restrictions previously imposed on them lifted. Consequently, Yiddish newspapers and publishing houses were reopened, and Jews who were so inclined resumed their cultural and religious activities.

The Soviet Jews' very survival hinged on the defeat of the Nazi invaders. More than ever before, their self-interest was tied to the victory of the Red Army. Once again, they did more than their fair share in the common cause.

Some 2 million Soviet Jews lived in or escaped to the unoccupied areas of the country. Of these, about 650,000 must have been male and of working age. Almost half a million, an extremely high percentage, served in the armed forces of the Soviet Union; they earned over 160,000 orders and medals during the war; several hundred of them were colonels and lieutenant colonels; more than 50 were generals;[21] more than 100 were awarded the highest Soviet military honor, the title of Hero of the Soviet Union.[22] And a Jewish Anti-Fascist Committee, officially established by the Soviets in April 1942, was to play a major role during the trying months that followed. Domestically, it was of some value in mobilizing and inspiring Soviet Jews; but infinitely more important, it proved instrumental in securing substantial aid for the Soviet war effort from Great Britain and the United States.

The Soviet Jews who survived the Nazi holocaust had no reason to suspect that their cordial relationship with the Kremlin would once again be reversed. But, alas, the honeymoon was not of long duration. Three years after the end of the war another dark half-decade began for Soviet Jews. Jewish cultural institutions, including Yiddish-language newspapers, publishing houses, schools, and theaters were once again closed down; Jewish authors, poets, composers, artists, and scholars were bitterly attacked in the Soviet press as "homeless bourgeois cosmopolitans," more than 400 were arrested or deported, some 25 among them who had held leading positions in Russian cultural life were sentenced to death and shot, while others died in prison camps; the Jewish Anti-Fascist Committee was disbanded, its chairman, Shlomo Mikhoels, was reportedly murdered by the KGB (Commission of State Security) on orders from Stalin,[23] and many of its former members were tried and executed; and shortly before his death, Stalin had nine distinguished doctors, six of them Jewish, arrested on charges of having assassinated several high Soviet officials and of having plotted the assassination of several others. At least some of these physicians, the Kremlin alleged, had been recruited by the American Joint Distribution Committee, a Jewish charitable agency dubbed an "international Jewish bourgeois national organization."[24] Stalin died in March 1953, before the trial; the so-called doctors' plot was soon exposed as a fabrication, the accused were exonerated, and the seven who had survived the ordeal were released.

Stalin's anti-Semitism, especially during the last five years of his life, appears well enough documented. And yet there are factors that, when taken into consideration, would seem to exclude a categorical conclusion that he was a fanatic anti-Semite. We do have the testimony of Stalin's daughter that years of struggle for power with Trotsky kindled in her father anti-Semitic feelings that gradually transformed themselves "from political hatred to a racial aversion for all Jews bar none"; yet, her first husband was Jewish, and although Stalin, she reports, was indignant about it and would say that "the Zionists put him over" on her,[25] he still gave his consent.[26] The wife of his son Yakov was also Jewish, and if Stalin didn't like it, neither did he stop the marriage. One of Stalin's sisters-in-law was Jewish; he had several half-Jewish grandchildren; he had many Jewish friends, some of whom were at times part of his household, such as Molotov's Jewish wife, Jan Garmanil's daughters, and a high foreign ministry official, Solomon Lozowsky;* Jews such as Maxim M. Litvinov and Lazar M. Kaganovich occupied some of the highest government and Party positions under Stalin;† and many Jewish intellectuals not only kept their positions throughout Stalin's lifetime but were even awarded the Stalin prize for their work, such as—to name but a very few—pianist Emil Gilels in 1946; film director Mikhail Romm in 1941, 1946, 1948, 1949, and 1951; film director Roman Karmen in 1942, 1947, and 1952; writer, journalist (and currently editor-in-chief of Literaturnaya Gazeta) Alexandr Chakovsky in 1950; symphony orchestra

---

*It should be pointed that, during a period when Stalin was turning against many of his friends, Molotov's wife was arrested and Lozowsky was executed.

†Litvinov was minister of Foreign Affairs until the 1939 rapprochement with Germany made his removal from that post virtually a diplomatic necessity; but he returned to public life in 1941, first as the Soviet ambassador to the United States and then as deputy minister of Foreign Affairs; and he was accorded a state funeral when he died in 1951. Kaganovich held many high posts under Stalin, including secretary of the Ukrainian Communist Party, member of the Politburo, secretary of the Moscow region, deputy premier, and member of Stalin's State Defense Committee.

conductor Natan Rakhlin in 1952; and writer Ilya Ehrenburg (who was also a deputy to the USSR Supreme Soviet at the time of Stalin's death) in 1952.[27] Moreover, Stalin's Soviet Union, at that time without much leverage in the Arab world, fully supported the foundation of the State of Israel in 1948. Originally welcoming it as an anticolonial development and hopeful that Israel would take a strongly anti-Western stance because of the West's earlier inaction in face of the extermination of Jews in Nazi-occupied territories (and, in any case, an anti-British position because of that country's resistance to the establishment of a Jewish state in Palestine), the Soviet Union was the first country to extend official recognition to the new nation,* took a strong pro-Israel position in the ensuing Arab-Israeli war that lasted until 1949, dispatched a Jewish Soviet army colonel to Tel Aviv to organize the Israeli artillery,[28] and was instrumental in having Soviet-controlled Czechoslovakia meet Israel's requests for substantial quantities of military hardware. But there followed in 1952 the infamous Slansky trial in Prague, where former Czechoslovak Party Secretary Rudolf Slansky and several others, most of them Jews, were accused of being British or Zionist intelligence agents, were found guilty, and were executed. Incredible as it may seem, the fact that Slansky, obedient to Stalin's bidding, had superintended the shipment of military supplies to Israel was used in the trial against him as "evidence" of his criminal actions on behalf of Zionism.

The difficulty of distinguishing anti-Semitism from other motivating factors can be well illustrated even in the case of the doctors' plot. While many observers have held that Stalin conceived of it as a prelude to more drastic action against Jews and while some have even reported that Stalin toyed with the idea of deporting, if not exterminating, all Soviet Jews,[29] others take the position of Paul Lendvai that even this, "Stalin's last anti-Jewish campaign, sprang less from anti-Semitism in the strict traditional sense than from consideration of policy, as a means to an end: the last great purge . . . of the old members of the Soviet Politburo. . . ."[30]

---

*In supporting the creation of the State of Israel before the United Nations in 1948, Andrei Gromyko said, "The fact that no Western European state has been able to ensure the defense of the elementary rights of the Jewish people, and to safeguard it against the violence of the Fascist executioners, explains the aspirations of the Jews to establish their own state. It would be unjust not to take this into consideration and to deny the right of the Jewish people to realize this aspiration." (Cited in Richard Cohen, ed., Let My People Go! [New York: Popular Library, 1971] p. 131.)

THE KHRUSHCHEV ERA

After a short period of "collective leadership," Nikita S. Khrushchev emerged as Stalin's successor. Judging by some of the statements made by the new leader, he would certainly appear to have harbored anti-Semitic feelings. He is, for instance, reported to have attributed the 1956 uprisings in Poland to the large number of Jews in high places,[31] and to have commented angrily on that occasion that there were too many Abramovitzes and Rabinovitzes, their names changed to end in "ski," in the Polish Party and government.[32] In an earlier incident in 1939, an interpreter correctly translated the Russian _Yevrei_ (Jews) in one of Khrushchev's speeches into the Polish _Żydzi_. However, this Polish word sounds like the contemptuous Russian _Zhid_ (yid). Khrushchev, assuming that this derogatory term was used in the translation, reportedly said on that occasion, "Oh Comrade, Comrade, I don't like them either . . . ," but he still admonished the interpreter for having used the word _Żydzi_ in public.[33] On the other hand Khrushchev continually denied the existence of any kind of anti-Semitism in the Soviet Union. He said to President Dwight D. Eisenhower in 1959 that "the Jewish people in the Soviet Union are treated like everyone else";[34] when replying to charges of anti-Semitism by Bertrand Russell he wrote to the late philosopher that "there has never been . . . any policy of anti-Semitism in the Soviet Union"[35] and that accusations of that kind were "a crude invention, a malicious slander, on the Soviet people";[36] and in a speech in March 1963, he reiterated that "no Jewish problem exists here and those who invent it are singing a foreign tune."[37]

In a sense, what Khrushchev said or even what feelings he held towards Jews—whether unprejudiced, tolerant, imbued with slight antipathy, or strongly anti-Semitic—is of much less import than what he did; what official actions he himself sponsored or superintended; what policies he instigated; and what private and semiofficial acts against Jews and what propaganda likely to stimulate anti-Semitism in the populace he ordered, encouraged, or tolerated. It behooves us therefore to pay more attention to what was done than to what was said.

With the death of Stalin, the era of mass political arrests, convictions, exile to Siberia, and execution, all involving a relatively high percentage of Jews among the victims, came to an end. Soon Khrushchev was to open the gates of Stalin's slave labor camps and release hundreds of thousands who had survived the ordeal, Jews and non-Jews alike. But if Stalin's acts had been anti-Semitically motivated, this was never officially admitted, nor was even the possibility of it officially conceded, by any of his successors. The doctors' plot was exposed in the Soviet press as a hoax within a month after

Stalin's death; three years later, in his secret address to the 20th Party congress, Khrushchev referred to it as the "ignominious case set up by Stalin," found to have been "fabricated from beginning to end";[38] and, as was pointed out above, some Western scholars see indications that Stalin intended to use it as prelude to a bloody purge.[39] Yet, nowhere was it even implied that the large number of Jewish physicians implicated and the charges of conspiratorial involvement of an American-Jewish agency—by then also proven to have been pure fabrications—might have been more than mere coincidence. And when Stalin's crimes were enumerated by Khrushchev at the above-mentioned 20th Party Congress in February 1956, and elaborated on in the subsequent years of de-Stalinization, persecution of Jews or even official discrimination against Jews was never mentioned among the dictator's faults. Only in the memoirs attributed in the West to Khrushchev[40] do we find references to allegedly anti-Semitic acts committed by Stalin and others under him.

The first three or four years after Stalin's death were years of greater religious tolerance; but beginning in 1957, with Khrushchev by then solidly in power, campaigns against Judaism as a religion were launched with renewed vigor. The Soviets emphasize that religious freedom is guaranteed in the USSR; and to the extent to which this means that religion has never been explicitly outlawed, such an assertion is correct. But the derision and vilification of the Jewish religion left no doubt as to official Soviet preference on the matter; and those reluctant to discard the faith of their fathers for philosophic atheism found themselves under additional pressure through harassment, diminished job opportunities at least in certain fields (such as teaching), great difficulty in being admitted to Party membership, and the virtual impossibility of rising in the Party hierarchy. Attempts to practice the Jewish religion and to teach it to the younger generation were further stifled by actions such as the wholesale shutting down of synagogues (estimated by some Western sources to have declined in number from 450 to 60 between 1956 and 1965)[41] and the interdiction of private prayer meetings. In 1962, the rabbinical seminary of the central synagogue in Moscow, the only institution of higher religious learning in the Soviet Union where kosher butchers, cantors, and rabbis had been trained, was reported to have been temporarily closed, and once reopened its student body was small enough to be counted on the fingers of one hand; and in 1964, the baking of matzoth—the traditional unleavened bread, the only kind of bread religious custom allows Jews to eat during the eight days of the Passover holiday—was prohibited.

Anti-religious campaigns, to be sure, were by no means limited to Judaism: Under Khrushchev assaults perhaps more intensive than ever before were launched against all religions and against religion per se. Some of the smaller religions were persecuted with particular vehemence, such as the Pentecostals and Jehovah's Witnesses, which forbade their youths to serve in the armed forces or to join communist youth organizations.[42] Yet the attacks on the Jewish religion became especially vituperative and abounded with charges not employed against other religions, charges that gave them a vitriolic flavor of their own. The Jewish religion was for instance depicted as particularly immoral since it allegedly made money the God of the Jewish faith, as particularly reactionary and proimperialist since it presumably promoted allegiance to Israel, and as particularly inflammatory since it promulgated the idea that the Jews were the chosen people,* which supposedly evoked in religious Jews feelings of hatred against other people.[43] Moreover, Jews were in a particularly vulnerable position because, in the case of Judaism, religion is so closely tied to the culture, traditions, and mores of the Jewish people and in part because attacks against Judaism as a religion, correlated as they were with attacks against Zionism and bolstered frequently by the age-old stereotyping of Jews, were hard to distinguish from attacks against Jews in general, and therefore tended to reawaken in the Soviet people lingering feelings of anti-Semitism.

While all this undoubtedly adds up to conditions highly unfavorable for Soviet Jewry in general and for all religious Soviet Jews in particular, the evidence of special discrimination against Jews, strong as it may be, is not quite so conclusive as one might think. Khrushchev would have been the first to verify that the eventual abolition of religion and its replacement by "scientific atheism" was part of the ideological undercoating of Soviet Marxist-Leninism† and that to this

---

*The phrase "chosen people," according to Jewish religion refers to the Jewish people having been chosen to disseminate the doctrine that there was only one God.

†The Soviet leadership's ideological predilection for scientific atheism dates back to Marx, who conceived of religion as the opium of the people (Karl Marx, "Contributions to the Critique of Hegel's Philosophy of Rights," Early Writings [London: C. A. Watts, 1963], p. 44), a narcotic that provided the masses of the poor with their only relaxation, their only joy, helping them to forget their otherwise miserable lives. Lenin seems to have given the concept of the "opium of the people" a slightly different connotation. To him, religion was like a narcotic in that it was used by the wealthy ruling minority to placate the exploited toiling masses by promising them eternal salvation if they but accepted their misery on earth, while threatening them with eternal damnation if they didn't. (The author is indebted to Professor William Fletcher for the observation that Marx and Lenin

end he openly and officially underwrote extensive antireligion propaganda campaigns; but he categorically rejected allegations that the Jewish religion was singled out for special repressive treatment.* For instance, the Soviets have maintained that synagogues were usually closed by their congregations of their own free will because of greatly diminished interest and attendance, especially on the part of the new generation of Soviet Jews. While there is evidence that higher authorities have taken the initiative in many cases and have exerted pressure on congregations in most others, there is undoubtedly some truth in Soviet assertions of diminishing interest since the trend away from religious pursuits appears to be a universal characteristic, according to some experts (see page 39 below), among Jews throughout the world, and probably this is even more so in a country in which all public means of communication and information have long been devoted to the propagation of scientific atheism. In the case of Moscow's rabbinical seminary, Soviet sources attribute the shortage of students also to a lack of interest and to the attraction that science and technology holds out to young Soviet Jews;[44] but Moscow's late Chief Rabbi Yehuda Leib Levin blamed the shortage primarily on the inability of prospective students to find living quarters in, or even to obtain a residence permit for, crowded Moscow.[45]

Rabbi Levin's point is well taken; it is difficult to understand why only five students, reportedly the total attendance in 1965,[46] should have emanated from Moscow's sizable Jewish population. Fear of official and unofficial disapproval and disdain for religion in general probably had their impact; but surely diminishing interest and the lure of other, attractive professions must have played their role also. And, finally, since the restriction imposed on the baking of matzoth coincided with the serious 1963 grain failure, it may perhaps not have been so anti-Jewish a measure as would at first appear. This,

---

attached somewhat different meanings to the concept of the "opium of the people.")

*Some Western scholars assert that the Jewish religion was not worse off, and may even have been better off, than some of the other religious denominations. Weinryb, for instance, points to the extremely bitter attacks on the Catholic and Uniate churches in the western Ukraine and Byelorussia in the immediate post-World War II period, and to all-out assaults in the late 1950s on the Muslim religion (with some 20 to 30 million believers), institutions, and clergy and on the Koran in Turkmen, Kirgiz, and the Azerbaijan SSR, and on Jehovah's Witnesses in Kazakhstan (Bernard D. Weinryb, "Anti-Semitism in Soviet Russia," in Lionel Kochan, ed., The Jews in Soviet Russia Since 1917 [London: Oxford University Press, 1970], p. 313).

at least, is the opinion of one non-Marxist Western expert, Peter Grose, who for many years was chief correspondent for the New York Times in Moscow. Since, under the circumstances, no Soviet citizen was allowed to buy flour,* it would have been difficult for the Soviets, Grose contends, to permit rabbis and synagogues to purchase it for what was ideologically considered an undesirable religious purpose.[47]

In areas other than religion, Soviet Jews would also appear to have received less than equitable treatment under Khrushchev's leadership: Jewish cultural institutions that had been shut down during the last few years of Stalin's regime were not reopened under Khrushchev. There was no permanent Yiddish theater, no Jewish schools, not even in Birobidzhan, and courses in Hebrew were virtually unavailable, even at institutions of higher learning (an issue discussed in somewhat greater length on pages 46-47 below). The bloody purges of the 1930s and the 1940s were condemned as vicious crimes, and it was contended that nothing similar had occurred in the Soviet Union since; but in his own way, subtly, nonviolently, and gradually, Khrushchev apparently removed Jews from positions of power, thus carrying on where Stalin had left off. By the time of Khrushchev's own removal as prime minister and first secretary of the Communist Party of the Soviet Union (CPSU) in 1964, there were very few Jews left in the Foreign Service, the top echelons of the Party or the Red Army. (On at least one occasion, in 1956, Khrushchev stated quite frankly that if Jews want to "occupy the foremost positions in our republics now" as they often had at the outset, "it would naturally be taken amiss by the indigenous inhabitants.")[48] And there were some reports, denied by the Soviets, of increasing discrimination against Jews in admission to institutions of higher learning.

In conjunction with anti-Zionist campaigns, the Soviets began to view and depict Israel increasingly as an antisocialist stronghold of Western imperialism. Relations between the Soviet Union and Israel had been deteriorating during the early 1950s, even before Stalin's death; but it was not until 1954 that the Soviets shifted to a definitely pro-Arab foreign policy. By 1955, the Soviets were supplying

---

*When the Western press attacked an earlier 1962 decree that prohibited the baking of matzoth, Western Marxist Herbert Aptheker countered the charges by explaining that the order banned only the use of state bakeries for the production of such ceremonial food items as matzoth or wafers used by the Orthodox Church in its religious services but did not prohibit their being baked in private homes or by private institutions. (See Herbert Aptheker, The Fraud of "Soviet Anti-Semitism" [New York: New Centuries Publishers, 1962], p. 15. Aptheker's article is reprinted on pages 101-102 below.)

aircraft and heavy arms to Egypt; during the Suez Canal crisis of 1956, they threatened the use of nuclear weapons, if necessary, in defense of Egypt and they subsequently replaced the weapons lost by Egypt during the confrontation with Israeli, British, and French troops. The Soviet Union also began to grant extensive credit to Arab countries, including that necessary for the initial financing of the Aswan High Dam, which was completed in 1964. To many Soviet Jews, and especially to those with strong religious or Jewish-nationalistic feelings, this shift to a pro-Arab, anti-Israel position must have been anathema. Increasing numbers wanted to emigrate to Israel; but few exit visas were granted—some 200, for instance, in 1960 and about the same number in 1963.

Campaigns against Jewish religion, culture, and customs and against Zionism would appear logical steps directed towards assimilating Soviet Jews completely into Soviet society and Soviet life. However, such measures of apparent discrimination as the removal of Jews from leading positions seem to be contrary to the ideological precept of assimilation prescribed by Marx and Lenin, and so, it would appear, was a new policy established under Khrushchev of identifying Soviet Jews in their internal passports as being of Jewish "nationality" (instead of the nationality related to their or their parents' birthplace such as "Russian" or "Ukrainian").* No son or daughter of Jewish parents could change this designation; only the children of mixed marriages were given the option, at age 16 (the age at which the internal passport is issued), to choose either the father's or the mother's "nationality" for identification in the passport.

During the early 1960s, Khrushchev launched an intensive campaign against so-called "economic crimes," which included such violations of the law as pilferage, bribery, and currency speculation. This campaign soon appeared to take on a strongly anti-Jewish character. According to official Soviet sources, the percentage of Jews convicted of "economic crimes" was smaller than the percentage of "criminals" of other nationalities.[49] Yet, the Soviet press reported cases involving defendants with obviously Jewish names all out of proportion to the number of Jews among those accused of such crimes, emphasizing the Jewish names of the defendants. And, whether justifiable or not,

---

*The Soviets and their Western Marxist supporters, it should be pointed out, would not agree with this interpretation. For a favorable account of the treatment of Jews under Khrushchev, see Herbert Aptheker, The Fraud of "Soviet Anti-Semitism" (New York: New Centuries Publishers, 1962); for a Soviet explanation of the rationale for the designation of Jewish nationality in the internal passport, see pages 101-102.

sentences imposed on Jews seem to have been especially harsh. Out of some 250 Soviet citizens executed for "economic crimes" between 1961 and 1964, more than half were reportedly Jews. (In December 1958, the death penalty had been extended to a number of "crimes against the state," both economic and noneconomic in nature; in May 1961, capital punishment was extended to additional law violations, primarily in the sphere of "economic crimes.")

Manifestations of what appeared to be anti-Semitic tendencies soon drew the attention of Soviet authors and poets, among them some who regretted the development and others who added fuel to the flames. Best-known among the former was the young Soviet poet Yevgeny Yevtushenko, then about 30 years of age.

At Babi Yar, a ravine on the outskirts of Kiev, virtually the entire Jewish population of the city—tens of thousands of Jewish men, women, and children—had been slaughtered by the Nazis. In September 1961, Yevtushenko published a poem entitled "Babi Yar" in Literaturnaya Gazeta, wherein he decried the fact that no monument to the Jewish victims of Nazi brutality had been erected at Babi Yar. He identified himself with the victims, implied strongly that anti-Semitism had not yet disappeared in the Soviet Union, and pledged to fight unrelentingly against it. Wrote Yevtushenko:[50]

> Every old man who was murdered here
>   is I;
> and I am every child who was murdered here.
> No part of me
>   will ever forget this call.
> Let the International
>   above us sweep
> when earth's last antisemite of them all
> for all eternity is buried deep.
> No Jewish blood runs in my blood, it's true;
> and yet the antisemites, every one,
> with bitter rancour hate me
>   as a Jew.
> And therefore
>   of Russia I'm a trueborn son.

For his stand, Yevtushenko was taken to task by Khrushchev himself, who charged the young poet with displaying "ignorance of historical fact" and asserted that the poem conveyed the impression that only Jews had been victims of "fascist crimes" while in reality the "Hitlerite executioners" had slaughtered Russians, Ukrainians, and other Soviet people as well. Moreover, Khrushchev emphasized once again there was no need to raise any doubt concerning the treatment of Jews in the Soviet Union since "from the days of the October Revolution, Jews in our country have had equality with all other people of the USSR in all respects."[51]

To the Western world, Khrushchev's assertions of equal treatment for Jews became increasingly unconvincing as literature began to appear that, although purportedly directed not against Jews per se but against the Jewish religion and against Zionism, was nevertheless in substance, tone, and design reminiscent of the viciously anti-Semitic publications of Nazi Germany. One of the worst of these, and the one that aroused the most resentment in the West, was Trofim K. Kichko's Judaism Without Embellishment (Iudaizm bez prikras) published in 1963 in Kiev under the auspices of the Ukrainian Academy of Sciences, presumably as a work in scientific atheism. In this book one can find cartoons depicting Jews stereotyped in looks (hook-nosed and so on) and actions (swindlers), and other cartoons linking Zionism to Nazism. (See examples of two such cartoons on page 22 and others of a later period on pages 35-36 below. The allegation that Zionists assisted in exterminating Jews can be found in Soviet anti-Zionist literature to this very day and is discussed on pages 30-31 below. For an explicit Soviet view on the topic, see pages 175-181).

An incensed West flooded the Kremlin with protests. Among those who appealed to the conscience of the Soviet leaders were some of the renowned liberals of the Western world, individuals such as Bertrand Russell, Martin Luther King, Jr., Albert Schweitzer, and Linus Pauling. And a leadership no longer insensitive to world opinion began to respond: Judaism Without Embellishment was condemned as "crude and offensive" by the Ideological Committee of the Party Central Committee and ordered withdrawn from circulation; the printing of Jewish religious calendars in editions of a few thousand was resumed; and after two decades of silence on the matter, the names of Jews who had been awarded the title of Hero of the Soviet Union during the days of World War II were at long last officially published,* apparently to show how large a part Jews played in Soviet life and in the war effort and how much their deeds were appreciated and recognized.

Apart from any discrimination against Jews by Soviet authorities, anti-Semitic acts were ostensibly committed by private Soviet citizens and groups of citizens in the late 1950s and early 1960s. Accounts in the Western press have run the gamut from reports of anti-Semitic

---

*There are reports that as early as 1943, Ilya Ehrenburg had been officially instructed to "play down the exploits of Jews in the Red Army" (William Korey, "The Origins and Development of Soviet Anti-Semitism: An Analysis," Slavic Review, March 1972, p. 117).

"All sorts of swindlers and cheats find refuge in the synagogue." (From Trofim K. Kichko's 1963 book, **Judaism Without Embellishment.**)

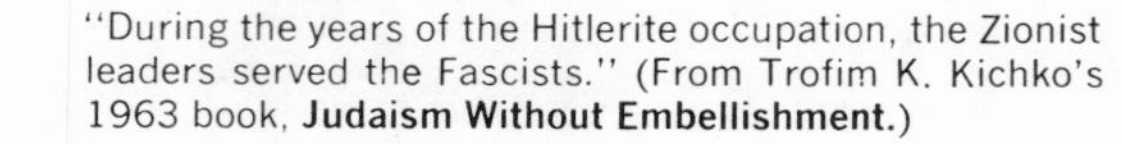

"During the years of the Hitlerite occupation, the Zionist leaders served the Fascists." (From Trofim K. Kichko's 1963 book, **Judaism Without Embellishment.**)

From Richard Cohen, ed., Let My People Go! (New York: Popular Library, 1971), insert between pages 128 and 129. Reprinted by permission.

literature being distributed and of schoolchildren being called "dirty Jews" and being beaten up by gangs of non-Jewish children, to reports of fires allegedly set at synagogues in Georgia and near Moscow and of anti-Jewish riots in Uzbekistan following Muslim charges that Jews were using blood for ritual purposes.[52] Such reports, more often than not, were scorned by the Soviet leadership as untrue "imperialist" or "Zionist" propaganda intended to discredit the USSR. Yet, on rare occasions, Khrushchev would admit that anti-Semitic sentiments still existed in the Soviet Union; but he would dub such sentiments "remnants of a reactionary past" and would emphasize that Soviet leaders were not anti-Semites.[53]

Evidence and counterevidence of anti-Jewish discrimination in the area of religion during the Khrushchev area was discussed above. Overwhelming though the evidence of discrimination in other areas may be, there is, once again, counterevidence pointing in the opposite direction. For example, only a handful of books in Yiddish may have been printed during the Khrushchev era (as compared with none at all during the last five years of the Stalin regime), but with Jewish schools closed during much of the 1930s and after 1948 most Jewish children reared with Russian as their basic language, the Soviets' assertion that relatively few Jews were interested in or even capable of reading books in Yiddish did not sound completely unreasonable (an issue taken up in greater length as it applies to present times on pages 44-45); a special 40 kopek stamp with Sholem Aleichem's picture was issued on the occasion of the centennial of his birth in 1959; Soviet Jews were recipients of awards, honors, and medals including the coveted Lenin Prize and were elected to the Soviet Academy of Sciences in numbers far exceeding their percentage in the Soviet population;* newspapers and magazines, while periodically launching attacks against religion, Zionism, Israel, and against Jews charged with economic crimes, also frequently discussed sympathetically the suffering of Jews during the Nazi period, on occasion defended individual Jews, and often published positive items showing contributions of individual Jews to Soviet society; and even if it were true that Jews were being discriminated against in admission to institutions of higher learning, they still constituted a percentage of university students far greater than their relative proportion among the Soviet people. (See also Table 1 and discussion, pages 49-51 below.)

---

*In 1964, for instance, 16 percent of those elected to full membership and 7.5 percent of those elected to corresponding membership were Jews (American Jewish Yearbook 66 [New York, 1965], p. 429).

Khrushchev's policy of removing Jews from positions of authority and power is perhaps the clearest single example of his regime's anti-Semitism. One may give him the benefit of the doubt and assume that he agreed with Ukrainian authorities that "the anti-Semitism with which the population has been infected by the Germans can only be uprooted gradually,"[54] assume, in other words, that he was motivated primarily not by hatred of or hostility towards Jews but by a pragmatic desire to placate latent popular anti-Semitism. Still, his action was highly discriminatory; it would find little approval in the West; it could not be defended in terms of Marxist-Leninist ideology; and one would have to accept a most narrow definition of anti-Semitism not to call it anti-Semitic. However that may be, so few Jews were affected that job discrimination was hardly ever complained of. Actually, many Soviet Jews, including emigrants from the Soviet Union, while lamenting the lack of religious and cultural facilities for Jews in the USSR, reported that they had encountered no anti-Semitism in the Soviet Union and that, for instance, most pressure against the exercise of the Jewish religion came not from the Soviet Government or Party but from "Jewish atheists."[55] No wonder that some Western Jewish scholars, such as Hans Lamm, when attempting to resolve whether or not the Soviet system was to be regarded as anti-Semitic, expressed their "conviction that this question cannot be clearly answered one way or another."[56]

NOTES

1. Jacob Frumkin, Gregor Aronson, and Alexis Goldenweiser, Russian Jewry (1860-1917) (New York and London: Thomas Yoseloff, 1966), p. 17.
2. Ibid. pp. 16-17.
3. Encyclopaedia Britannica (Chicago, 1969), vol. 19, p. 797.
4. See, for example, Shmuel Ettinger, "Russian-Jewish Relations Before and After the October Revolution," in Richard Cohen, ed., Let My People Go! (New York: Popular Library, 1971), p. 151. The same statement can also be found in Soviet sources; see, for example, Solomon Rabinovich, Jews in the USSR (Moscow: Novosti Press Agency Publishing House, n. d. [1971?]), p. 14. This book is a second, revised, edition of Rabinovich's Jews in the Soviet Union, published by Novosti, Moscow, in 1967.
5. See, for example, Soviet Jewry, U. S., House of Representatives, Subcommittee on Europe of the Committee on Foreign Affairs, Hearings, 92d Cong. 1st sess., November 9 and 10, 1971 (Washington, D.C.: Government Printing Office, 1972), p. 275; also, Soviet Jews: Fact and Fiction (Moscow: Novosti Press Agency Publishing House, 1970), pp. 14-15.

6. Article 123 of the Constitution of the USSR.

7. See, for example, Bernard D. Weinryb, "Anti-Semitism in Soviet Russia," in Lionel Kochan, ed., The Jews in Soviet Russia Since 1917 (London: Oxford University Press, 1970), p. 298.

8. To the Memory of Fighters for the Proletarian Revolution (Moscow, 1928).

9. Paul Lendvai, "Jews Under Communism," Commentary, December 1971, p. 72.

10. Ettinger, op. cit., p. 157.

11. Lendvai, op. cit., p. 71.

12. For example, Joshua Rothenberg, "Jewish Religion in the Soviet Union," in Kochan, op. cit., p. 162.

13. Peter Grose, "The Kremlin and the Jews," in Harrison E. Salisbury, ed., The Soviet Union: The Fifty Years (New York: Harcourt, Brace and World, 1967), p. 424.

14. The lower figure comes from Guy Vinatrel, "The Plight of Soviet Jewry," The American Zionist, December 1970, p. 33; the higher figure from Rabinovich, Jews in the USSR, op. cit., p. 24.

15. Pravda, November 30, 1936.

16. Quoted in Grose, op. cit., p. 424.

17. Quoted in New York Times, January 15, 1931.

18. For this widely held interpretation see, for example, Rothenberg, op. cit., p. 174; also Walter Kolarz, Religion in the Soviet Union (New York: St. Martin's Press, 1961), p. 388.

19. See, for example, Ettinger, op. cit., pp. 161-162; or Weinryb, op. cit., p. 305.

20. See, for example, Donald W. Treadgold, Twentieth Century Russia, 2d ed. (Chicago: Rand McNally, 1964), p. 364.

21. For a list of over 50 Jewish Red Army generals, one Red Air Force marshal, and two Red Navy admirals, see Rueben Ainsztein, "Soviet Jewry in the Second World War," in Kochan, op. cit., pp. 276-277.

22. Ibid., p. 275.

23. See, for example, Ilya Ehrenburg, Post-War Years: 1945-54 (Cleveland and New York: World Publishing Company), p. 125; also Svetlana Alliluyeva, Only One Year (New York: Harper and Row, 1969), pp. 148-149.

24. Pravda, January 13, 1953.

25. Alliluyeva, op. cit., p. 162 and 148

26. Svetlana Alliluyeva, Twenty Letters to a Friend (New York: Harper and Row, 1967), p. 197.

27. Prominent Personalities in the USSR and Who Is Who in the USSR, both compiled by the Institute for the Study of the USSR (no longer in operation), Munich, Germany and published by the Scarecrow Press, Metuchen, N.J., in 1968 and 1972, respectively.

28. Jean Riollot, "Israel's Twenty-fifth Anniversary," Radio Liberty Dispatch, April 4, 1973, p. 2.

29. For example, Alexander Werth, Russia: Hopes and Fears (New York: Simon and Schuster, 1969), p. 223.

30. Lendvai, op. cit., p. 70.

31. A. Flegon and Yu Naumov, Russkii Antisemitism i Evrei (London: Flegon Press, 1968), p. 70.

32. Werth, op. cit., p. 225.

33. For more details, other examples, and additional source references on the subject, see Bernard D. Weinryb, "The Concept of 'Anti-Semitism' and Its Meaning in Soviet Russia: A Study in Soviet Semantics," Grantz College Annual of Jewish Studies 1 (1972), pp. 91-92.

34. Cohen, op. cit., p. 10.

35. Pravda, February 28, 1963.

36. Pravda, March 30, 1963.

37. Pravda, March 8, 1963.

38. The full text of Khrushchev's address to the 20th Party Congress in February 1956 can be found in English translation in the Congressional Record, 84th Cong., 2d sess., vol. 102, part 7, pp. 9389-9402; and also in Basil Dmytryshyn, USSR: A Concise History (New York: Charles Scribner's Sons, 1965), pp. 401-444; the quote is from Dmytryshyn, p. 431.

39. Dmytryshyn, op. cit., p. 263. See also page 14 above.

40. Khrushchev Remembers (Boston: Little, Brown, 1970), esp. pp. 258-269.

41. Weinryb, "Anti-Semitism in Soviet Russia," op. cit., p. 316.

42. Ellsworth Raymond, The Soviet State (New York: Macmillan, 1968), pp. 17-18. For other religions that came under special attack, see also footnote p. 17 and text pp. 41-42.

43. Rothenberg, op. cit., p. 177.

44. See, for example, Rabinovich, Jews in the USSR, op. cit., p. 79.

45. Associated Press report, April 21, 1965.

46. Maurice Friedberg, "The State of Soviet Jewry," in Paul Hollander, ed., American and Soviet Society (Englewood Cliffs, N.J.: Prentice-Hall, 1969), p. 304.

47. Grose, op. cit., p. 431.

48. S. Levenberg, "Soviet Jewry: Some Problems and Perspectives," in Kochan, op. cit., pp. 36-37. Also, Moshe Decter, "Jewish National Consciousness in the Soviet Union," Perspectives on Soviet Jewry (New York: Academic Committee on Soviet Jewry and the Anti-Defamation League of B'nai B'rith, 1971), p. 14.

49. Gennady Terekhov, senior assistant to the USSR Chief Prosecutor, in Rabinovich, Jews in the Soviet Union, op. cit., p. 22.

50. From a translation by Jack Lindsay, originally published in the Anglo-Soviet Journal, Spring 1962, pp. 15-16 and reprinted in Harry G. Shaffer, ed., The Soviet System in Theory and Practice (New York: Appleton-Century-Crofts, 1965), p. 380. Reprinted by permission.

51. Pravda and Izvestia, March 10, 1963.

52. Reported from several sources in Weinryb, "Anti-Semitism in Soviet Russia," op. cit., p. 315.

53. See, for example, his remarks made to a delegation of the French Socialist Party in 1956, reported in Levenberg, op. cit., pp. 36-37.

54. Weinryb, "Anti-Semitism in Soviet Russia," op. cit., p. 307.

55. Quoted from Hadoar 45, 31 (1966): 510-511 in ibid., p. 317.

56. Hans Lamm, "Jews and Judaism in the Soviet Union," in William C. Fletcher and Anthony Strover, eds., Religions and the Search for New Ideas in the USSR (New York: Praeger Publishers, 1967), p. 109.

CHAPTER

2

THE BREZHNEV-KOSYGIN ERA

Since the fall of Khrushchev in October, 1964 and especially since the six-day Arab-Israeli war of 1967, there has been mounting concern in the West regarding the treatment and well-being of Soviet Jews. Once again, there is a wide spectrum of views, running the gamut from the position of the extremist Jewish Defense League, which sees no difference between "the holocaust in Germany" and "what is transpiring in the Soviet Union,"[1] to the position of Western Marxists who describe the "myth of Soviet oppression of Jews [as] one of the greatest hoaxes of all times."[2] Most observers appear to have adopted intermediate positions, similar to the one taken officially by the U.S. Department of State to the effect that there is indeed discrimination but that there can be no comparison with the horrors of the Nazi holocaust or even of Stalin's bloody purges of Jewish intellectuals.[3] Yet, many in the West view the alleged plight of Soviet Jewry as serious enough to warrant action. To this end, special international conferences (such as the World Conference of Jewish Communities on Soviet Jewry held in Brussels in 1971) have been convened in recent years, special organizations have been founded, mass rallies called, and hearings held before committees of the U.S. Congress. Countless appeals have been made to Soviet leaders to stop all discrimination against Soviet Jews, to permit them to follow freely their religious convictions and cultural traditions, and to allow those who want to emigrate to do so. And many tens of millions of dollars collected by the United Jewish Appeal have been set aside to aid those Soviet Jews bent on emigrating to Israel.*

---

*There have also been occasional acts of violence such as the burning of Soviet cars and the bombing of the Aeroflot office in New York and of the Soviet Embassy in Washington. But with the exception

In response to this veritable outpouring of Western sentiment for Soviet Jews, numerous publications in Western languages (some of them written by Soviet Jews) have come off Soviet presses, trying to prove by argumentation and by the presentation of official documents, of figures, and of actual examples that "the Jews in the Soviet Union enjoy both de jure and de facto equality with all other nationalities and . . . are not discriminated against,"[4] and asserting that charges of discrimination are nothing more than "imperialist-Zionist" propaganda intended to discredit socialism and the USSR.

ANTI-SEMITISM OR ANTI-ZIONISM?

In the West, allegations that anti-Semitism is a conscious policy of the Soviet leadership have abounded in recent years. At the extreme, one can even find comments to the effect that by now the communist countries have "the greatest program of organized anti-Semitism since Hitler."[5] Soviet anti-Semitism has been attributed to numerous factors such as traditional anti-Semitism long inherent in Russian culture; the desire to exert influence on the Arab world; the presence of 30 million Muslims in the Soviet Union as an impetus towards a pro-Arab stance; the occasional need for scapegoats; the utilization of popular prejudices to detract attention from other problems; and a general suspicion of Soviet Jewry, linked by religion, culture, and tradition to "bourgeois" world Jewry and to Israel.

The Soviets do not deny that there are still "isolated instances of "anti-Semitism," especially among older people who are "culturally backward," often in the form of disrespect, insulting remarks, or parents opposing the mixed marriages of their children, but the Soviets hold such incidents to be nothing but ideologically unacceptable and often illegal legacies of the Czarist past that are rapidly fading from the Soviet scene.[6] Kosygin dubbed "any kind of nationalistic survival—whether it be a manifestation of nationalism, chauvinism, racism or anti-Semitism—" as something "absolutely alien to and incompatible with our ideology";[7] and, as other Soviet leaders before him, he proclaimed that "there never has been and there is no anti-Semitism in the Soviet Union,"[8] a statement surely intended to refer

---

of Rabbi Meir Kahane's militant Jewish Defense League, such acts of violence have been deplored by both Jews and non-Jews virtually throughout the Western World. (For greater elaboration on the use of violence on behalf of Soviet Jewry and on Rabbi Kahane and his Jewish Defense League, see pages 110-113 below.)

to official Soviet policy and ideology and not to isolated acts of individuals. Soon after Khrushchev's regime had come to an end, manifestations of anti-Semitism were explicitly attacked in the Soviet press[9] and Party members were admonished not to follow such "modes and mistakes of the masses."[10] Moreover, the Prosecuting Office of the USSR presumably brings the force of Soviet law to bear on perpetrators of anti-Semitic acts. "Offenders," we are told by the senior assistant to the Soviet Union's chief prosecutor, "are prosecuted. In many cases they are convicted and sent to prisons or camps. But in some cases public condemnation proves sufficient."[11] In extreme cases, authors or editors of outrageously anti-Semitic publications have been even removed from their positions and expelled from the Party.

Anti-Semitism may be repugnant to Marxist ideology, contrary to the teachings of Lenin, and incompatible with the proclaimed goal of the brotherhood of all mankind, to be achieved in the era of perfect communism, but all this certainly does not hold true for anti-Zionism.

Since the Israeli victory in the six-day war in 1967, Soviet attacks on Zionism have proceeded relentlessly and with unprecedented vituperation. No effort has been spared to disparage, debase, and vilify Zionism. In recent years, Zionist ideology has been described as "a mixture of Judaistic mysticism, nationalistic hysteria, shameless social demagogy and racialist concepts of the superiority of 'God's chosen people' over all other peoples,"[12] and Zionism has been linked with "American imperialism" and "West German revanchism" in portrayals of a gigantic plot aimed at the overthrow of communist regimes, primarily by means of ideological subversion from within.[13] Especially since 1967, reports have been carried in the Soviet press asserting that there are 20 to 25 million Zionists, Jews as well as non-Jews, in the United States, including 60 percent of all American lawyers and 43 percent of all American industrialists, that 56 percent of the big publishing houses serve the aims of Zionism, and so on.[14] Zionists have been depicted over and over as criminals, fully comparable to the Nazis, who would unhesitatingly kill Arab men, women, and children to further their nationalistic ambitions. Ascribing to Theodor Herzl, founder of Zionism, a statement to the effect that anti-Semitism was the catalyst that would induce Jews to leave their country of residence and found a state of their own,[15] the Soviets have accused the Zionists of having collaborated, during the civil war that followed the Russian Revolution, with viciously anti-Semitic counterrevolutionary forces, responsible for killing tens of thousands of "working class" Jews, because Zionism, allegedly, "needed the anti-Semitism of the counter-revolution to compel working Jews to rush from pogroms into the bosom of Zionism and emigrate to Palestine."[16] In the same vein, Zionists have been accused in literally hundreds of Soviet articles, pamphlets, and books of collaboration with the Nazis. "Zionists counted on Hitler's anti-Semitism to bring persecuted Jews to their fold," states a recently published Soviet article.[17] An English-language Soviet pamphlet charges that in Soviet-occupied territory there were many known cases of overseers of death camps and of special "police" empowered to "keep order" in Jewish ghettos who were recruited by Gestapo men from the "ranks of Zionists."[18] "There is plenty of proof," asserts a Jewish retired Soviet Lieutenant General, G. Plaskov, "that the Zionist leaders, in effect, encouraged the fascists to persecute Jews in Germany."[19] Veniamin E. Dymshits, highest-ranking Jew in the Soviet government and Party (see pages 55-56), to give one more example, asks where the Zionists were and what they were doing when World War II was on, and he takes them to task for forgetting that "it was the Red Army that saved millions of people, including Jews, from fascist slavery."[20] And in their publications, the Soviets give countless examples of alleged deals worked out between Zionist agents and the Nazis.[21]

Some Western sources assert that an anti-Zionist, anti-Israel position is a time-tested cover for anti-Semitism,[22] that socially and ideologically unacceptable anti-Semitism is easily masked as anti-Zionism,[23] and that, in any case, "the average Soviet . . . reader of the by now daily diet of 'anti-Zionist' literature would have to make an almost superhuman effort to remember that the stereotypes apply only to the nebulous Zionists and the far-away Israelis, not to the Jew who may happen to live next door."[24] Such Western non-Marxist views have been given strong support by Senator Umberto Terracini, the most eminent Jew in Italy's Communist Party, chairman of the communist group in the Italian Senate and former president of the Constituent Assembly. In an interview granted in November 1972, to Carlo Casalegno, reporter for the non-communist Italian _La Stampa_, Terracini contended that anti-Semitism in the Soviet Union was reawakened after the six-day war. For simple people, not to speak of the ill-intentioned, he warned, it was in fact very difficult to distinguish between condemnation of Israel, a struggle against Zionism, and an anti-Semitic campaign. And the men responsible, he charged, "have not always done what was needed to avoid or dissipate confusion." Terracini denounced particularly what he called "openly anti-Semitic" pamphlets distributed especially in the Ukraine, Moldavia, and the Baltic territories; and he showed the interviewer the Italian edition of a Novosti bulletin in which the author, one Nikolai Rebrov, asserted that Jews prayed every Sabbath "for the extermination of Christians and heretics," adding that some of them "put it into practice."[25]

In another more recent, and in some respects more severe, accusation, the French League Against Anti-Semitism brought suit against the Soviet Embassy in Paris for inciting racial hatred. The suit charges that an article that appeared in the embassy's _Bulletin_ of September 22, 1972, was an almost exact replica of a piece published before the pogroms of 1906 by the Russian anti-Semitic association "The Black Hundreds" under the title "The Jewish Question: The Impossibility of Extending Rights to Jews." Allegedly, the only difference between the earlier piece (which was bitterly denounced by Lenin) and the one published in the fall of 1972 by the Soviet Embassy in Paris was that in the latter the word "Zionist" or "Judaist" was substituted for the word "Jew."[26]

The Soviets deny that their resolute stand against "reactionary" Zionism—a stand that dates back to the days of Lenin—is in any way anti-Semitic.[27] They maintain that it is the Zionists who desire nothing more than "to raise an impenetrable wall between Jews and non-Jews"[28] and who would like to give the impression that "Jew" and "Zionist" are synonymous terms so that all Jews could be classified as Zionists,[29] even though Zionism "has never been the ideology of the Jewish working people."[30] The entire so-called question of the position of the Jews in the Soviet Union, Soviet sources have it, is "nothing but a concoction . . . a provocation fabricated from beginning to end";[31] and this kind of anti-Soviet, anticommunist propaganda, they argue, purposely overlooks the fact that hundreds of thousands of Jews are members of the Communist Party of the Soviet Union and 9 out of every 10 young Jews between the ages of 14 and 28 (at least one-third of all Soviet Jews) are members of the Young Communist League.[32]

Once again, it is no simple task to evaluate objectively these charges and countercharges, for there is much contradictory evidence. Surely, Soviet charges of "fabricated provocations" are given some credence by statements such as one recently attributed to Moshe Dayan to the effect that Israel, for its own survival, needs events such as the rescue of Soviet Jews.[33] But, on the other hand, no matter how sincere the intentions of the Soviet leadership to draw a clear demarcation between anti-Zionism (which they openly profess) and anti-Semitism (which they publicly denounce), there is no denying that in much that has appeared in print since 1967 on matters Jewish in the Soviet Union, both fiction and nonfiction, the distinction between "good Jews" and Zionists and between decent, honest, loyal Jewish comrades and the age-old stereotypes of Jews created by anti-Semites of past generations seems to have gotten lost in the shuffle.

For instance one can find it said in recent Soviet publications that the goal of Zionism is not merely the revival of a Jewish state in Israel but the "establishment of an empire from ocean to ocean which is to rule the entire world,"[34] and that to accomplish these ends Zionism "secretly infiltrates the life cells of all the countries in the world, undermining from within all that is strong and healthy . . . grasping all that is important in the administrative, economic, and spiritual life of each country."[35] In spite of subsequent official Soviet condemnation of the book from which the latter quote was taken[36] and even though in that particular novel there is a "good Jew,"* such frightening portrayals of the goals and tactics of Zionism must surely tend to make Soviet non-Jews apprehensive; and they are likely to become even more suspicious of all their Jewish countrymen when they are told that through Trotsky, "a typical agent of Zionism," the worldwide Zionist conspiracy even entered into the leadership of the Communist Party of the Soviet Union;[37] that in 1968 Zionists played a major role in the attempt to lure Czechoslovakia from the socialist fold,[38] with such leading Czechoslovak communists as O. Sik and E. Goldstuecker† collaborating with international Zionism in this endeavor;[39] and that in the absence of a personal disavowal "every Jew is a Judaist (i.e., a Zionist) and every Judaist an Israeli."[40] And latent anti-Semitism is hardly placated nor suspicion of Jews put to rest by recent novels that cast Jews in the roles of degenerate archvillains. For instance in one of them, Ivan Shevtsov's Love and Hate[41] (by now also officially condemned in the Soviet Union), the devil incarnate is the Jew Nachum Holtzer, a fiendish, perverted sadist who murders his own mother for her inheritance, turns a beautiful teen-age Russian girl into a drug addict, seduces her, kills her, and dismembers her body. Often, publications such as these also feature cartoon-style illustrations of stereotypic Jews, short, fat, hook-nosed, wide-mouthed, and ugly, showing them to be unsavory, greedy, evil characters; many of these cartoons consist of caricatures of Zionists portrayed as ideological offsprings of Nazis and as bloodthirsty allies of American imperialism. (A few examples of such cartoons, published during the Brezhnev-Kosygin era, are reproduced on pages 35 and 36.)

In the Soviet Union, there are no privately owned and operated newspapers, magazines, or publishing houses, free to publish whatever they desire. Nothing adjudged as violating Soviet law, Marxist-Leninist ideology, or socialist morality—nothing adjudged as putting in jeopardy the socialist foundation of Soviet society—is supposed to appear in

---

*The "good Jew," Aaron Hertsovich, disagrees with the view that Zionism serves American imperialism. On the contrary, the novel's author, Shevtsov, has him assert, it is American imperialism that serves the aims of Zion.

†Ota Sik was head of the Economic Institute of the Czechoslovak Academy of Sciences, member of the Party's Central Committee, deputy prime minister under the Dubcek regime, and chief architect of Czechoslovakia's "New Economic Model"; Goldstuecker headed Czechoslovakia's influential Writers' Union. Both men have been in voluntary exile in the West since the August 1968 military intervention by the Warsaw Pact nations.

print.* But since more than 40,000 book titles are published each year,[42] not to speak of millions of newspaper, magazine, and journal articles, it would obviously be impossible for one individual, or even for one central office, to censor everything before it goes to press. The responsibility for approving material for publication rests therefore with the editors of periodicals and with the persons in charge of such matters in the case of publishing houses. Under the circumstances, the central authorities in Moscow cannot be held responsible for every offensive line published in the land. But when many books and articles come out, all slanted in a certain direction, when they are published in editions of many tens of thousands, and when the Party does not take a stand against them until after all copies have been sold (and then only when indignation abroad, even within large communist parties, and at times among the Soviet intelligentsia has reached a high level), one suspects that they are published with at least the unofficial consent of the Soviet leadership.† And in many cases even such belated disassociation has not occurred. Particularly disconcerting in this connection is the rehabilitation of Trofim Kichko. Exposed in 1953 in Literaturnaya Gazeta as a war-time Nazi collaborator in the Ukraine,[43] his Judaism Without Embellishment officially condemned[44] and withdrawn from bookstore shelves, Kichko was ousted from the Party. But before the 1960s had come to an end, he was given a highly prestigious award by the Presidium of the Supreme Soviet of the Ukraine for an article published in a Ukrainian youth organ in which he denounced a plot of "international Zionist bankers," and in 1968 he brought out a new book, the above-cited Judaism and Zionism, in an edition of 60,000. Apart from its savagely anti-Zionist orientation and its admonition that every Jew is a potential Zionist (both referred

---

*For instance, advocacy of the Maoist interpretation of Marxism-Leninism is taboo and so is "war-mongering" (which does not include the backing of "national liberation movements"). On the other hand, "constructive criticism," by which is meant criticism aimed at improving certain operations (for instance enhancing enterprise efficiency) but that does not alter the socialist framework of society is encouraged.

†The two books by Ivan Shevtsov, discussed above, were published in large editions: his In the Name of the Father and the Son in March 1970 in an edition of 60,000, his Love and Hate the following month in an edition of 200,000. On July 12, 1970, Pravda denounced both novels as "ideologically vicious and artistically weak." (For more details and a Zionist view on these and other recent Soviet publications, see, for example, William Korey, "The 'Protocols' in Soviet Literature," The American Zionist 41, 1 [September 1970]: 14-17.)

"Dayan to Hitler: 'Move over!' " (From **Kazakhstanskaya Pravda,** Alma Ata, June 21, 1967.)

"Position of invading aggressor." (From **Krasnaya Zviezda,** Moscow, June 15, 1967.)

"The aggressor's relay baton." (From **Bakinski Rabochi,** Baku, June 23, 1967.)

From Richard Cohen, ed., Let My People Go! (New York: Popular Library, 1971), insert between pages 128 and 129. Reprinted by permission.

"A link in a criminal chain." (From **Agitator**, Moscow, May 1970.)

"Tel Aviv rickshaw." (From **Krasnaya Zviezda**, Moscow, March 18, 1970.)

From Richard Cohen, ed., Let My People Go! (New York: Popular Library, 1971), insert between pages 128 and 129. Reprinted by permission.

to above), the book's claim to fame lies in its analysis of Judaism as a singularly vicious and contemptible religion.

JUDAISM AS A RELIGION

After interviewing Jews in the Soviet Union and Jewish emigrants from the USSR in Israel, U.S. Congressman Edward Koch of Manhattan testified before a congressional subcommittee concerned with Soviet Jewry that the complaints he had heard from Soviet Jews he had talked to were not that they lived in terror or that offenses were committed against them in any way comparable to those perpetrated by the Nazis; what they lamented, rather, was that the Soviet Union was embarked upon a campaign of long standing to make it more difficult for Jews as well as for adherents of other faiths to practice their religion. "It is not easy," Representative Koch concluded, "to be religious in the Soviet Union."[45]

The Soviets have been steadfastly open and outspoken about their antireligious orientation and their intention to propagate atheistic beliefs. But they deny that their propaganda is directed against any one religion in particular. "Anti-religious literature in the USSR," the Jewish Soviet journalist Rabinovich* tells us, "pursues solely the aim of enlightenment and shows the harmful effect of _any_ kind of religion." And he avows that "no one in the Soviet Union" singles out the Jewish or any other religion for special attack.† This, however, is simply not so. In recent years especially, some Soviet publications

---

*Rabinovich, veteran Jewish Soviet journalist, decorated three times during World War II for valor in battle and author of books on Soviet Jews written in Russian and Yiddish, has been labeled in the West an "official [Soviet] functionary and government propagandist" (Hans Lamm, "Jews and Judaism in the Soviet Union," in William C. Fletcher and Anthony J. Strover, eds., _Religions and the Search for New Ideas in the USSR_ [New York: Praeger Publishers, 1967], p. 117).

†Solomon Rabinovich, _Jews in the Soviet Union_ (Moscow: Novosti Press Agency Publishing House, 1967), p. 85. Emphasis added. In the second edition of the booklet, published under the title _Jews in the USSR_ (see Chapter 1, note 4 above) the sentence "No one in the Soviet Union attacks either the Jewish or any other religion" has been omitted; however another sentence is retained that states that "Soviet anti-religious propaganda is based on scientific reasons and therefore it does not permit any tendentious or subjective approach to a particular religion, let alone discrimination against any religion" (pp. 85-86 in the 1st and p. 80 in the 2d edition).

have focused their attacks on the Jewish religion, depicting its tenets as a threat to non-Jews everywhere. Trofim Kichko's Judaism and Zionism, referred to above, is an outstanding, although by no means unique, specimen of such publications. Its general drift and orientation can be readily perceived from the following two passages:

> Isn't the anti-humanism of Judaism best illustrated by the morality of the prophet Moses himself? About this "most meek and holy man" it is said in the Torah that by his deeds he had brought about the loss of thousands of Egyptians. . . . Under the banner of religion he inculcates the Israelites with poisonous hate for all other peoples . . . he orders them to usurp the land of the Canaanites, persuading them that God had promised these lands to their forefathers.
>
> The ideologists of Judaism through the Holy Scriptures teach the observant Jews to hate people of another faith and even destroy them.

In another recent Soviet publication, to give one more example, it is charged that the theory that the Jews are "God's chosen people"* bears a close resemblance to the "superior race" concept of the Nazis.[46] And there are other works, both fiction and nonfiction, that portray synagogues as places in which swindlers, black-market racketeers, and Zionist agents carry on their shady business, some of these works featuring the rabbi as being in charge of such illegal operations.†

What Soviet officials proclaim and what Soviet authors and journalists write on the subject of religion is certainly of great importance But, once again, the analyst must be concerned not only with opinions and statements but also with actions. It therefore behooves us to take a careful look at what has happened to Jewish religious practices and to compare the treatment meted out to the Jewish religion with that accorded to other religious denominations.

In 1926, there were more than 1,100 synagogues in the USSR; by 1973 their number has diminished to perhaps 40 to 60.[47] The smallest of three remaining synagogues in Moscow was ordered by

---

*The article actually says the "Zionist theory"; but it is according to the Jewish religion that the Jews are supposedly the "chosen people." (See footnote, page 16 above.)

†One recently published novel with such a main theme was set in the late 1930s, thus enabling the author to incorporate Nazi-Zionist cooperation into the plot (Yuri Kolesnikov, "The Promised Land," Octiabr, no. 9, 1972).

the authorities to shut down as of November 1, 1971, leaving the metropolis's quarter-million Jews with only two, the large Choral Synagogue (often referred to as the Moscow Central Synagogue) and the small Marina Rosha—this latter without a rabbi since 1964;[48] and the last synagogue in Kiev was reported to have closed its doors early in 1972.[49] There are only a handful of functioning rabbis left in the Soviet Union;[50] the average age of Jewish clergymen (rabbis, slaughterers, ritual circumcisers) is above 70;[51] and there are conflicting reports as to whether the Moscow yeshiva (college for the training of Jewish religious functionaries, the only one in the Soviet Union) was in operation in the late 1960s and the early 1970s.* In any case, the yeshiva was open in 1972; 6 students were reported in attendance; and Shulem Royzen, chairman of Moscow's Jewish congregation, expressed hope of seeing the number of students increase to 25.[52]

The Soviets do not deny the considerable decrease in the number of synagogues and rabbis.† However, they ascribe this state of affairs not to steps taken by the authorities but to diminishing interest in religion among Soviet Jews, a well-nigh universal phenomenon among Jews everywhere, they maintain, including even Israel. Moreover, the Soviets maintain that there is no difference, in regard to the diminution of religious institutions and practices, between the Jewish and other religions in the USSR.‡ Such views find at least partial

---

*In 1965, a group of New York rabbis visiting Moscow found that the seminary had been reopened (Albert Boiter, Major Trends in Soviet Development Since Khrushchev, [Munich: Radio Liberty, November 1965], p. 44); and five students were reported in attendance (See page 15 above). According to Rabbi Elovitz, the seminary was still open in November 1971 (Soviet Jewry, U.S., House of Representatives, Hearings Before the Subcommittee on Europe of the Committee on Foreign Affairs, 92d Cong., 1st sess., November 9 and 10, 1971 [Washington, D.C.: Government Printing Office, 1972], p. 12); but other Western sources report it as "no longer in operation" (for example, "Fact Sheet on Anti-Jewish Discrimination in the Soviet Union," in Richard Cohen, ed., Let My People Go! [New York: Popular Library, 1971], p. 146; also Rabbi Charles Sheer in Soviet Jewry [Hearings], p. 231.) A 1970 Soviet publication states simply that "the Moscow Central Synagogue has a theological school—the Yeshiva—training rabbis, shoshets (sic.; ritual slaughterers), etc." (Soviet Jews: Fact and Fiction [Moscow: Novosti Press Publishing House, 1970], p. 28).

†The Soviet Census of 1970 gives the number of synagogues remaining in operation in the USSR as "under one hundred."

‡Moscow, for instance, had reportedly over 1,500 Russian Orthodox churches at the time of the revolution, but only 44 in 1970 (Solomon

support among Western scholars. Joshua Rothenberg, research associate of East European Studies at Brandeis University, for instance, attributes the sharp decline of religious practices in the USSR primarily to administrative measures and official pressure; yet he does not deny that the position and influence of the Jewish religion would "undoubtedly" have weakened in the Soviet Union, "even if repressive measures against religion had not been implemented," since over the past half-century an erosion in religious practices has been noticeable "in most Jewish communities throughout the world."[53] And Alexander Werth finds religion in general on the decline throughout the Soviet Union. Jews, he reports, are becoming more and more voluntarily assimilated, largely through intermarriage; and in cities such as Moscow or Leningrad, he contends, "nearly all" Jews are already assimilated.[54]

Unwilling to accept the theory of equal, if unsympathetic, treatment of all religions in the Soviet Union, some Western Jewish sources point out that other religious groups are permitted to conduct church conferences, organize religious committees, and attend seminaries and religious schools abroad, while Jews are not. Non-Jewish religious groups are also allowed to manufacture crucifixes, candles, and at least in the case of the Orthodox Church even icons for religious use; and they may prepare and instruct clergymen and print prayer books, hymnals, and religious pamphlets. Jews, on the other hand, are not permitted to manufacture prayer shawls, phylacteries, or other devotional items, and training facilities for Jewish clergymen as well as the publication of religious Jewish literature are at best minimal. Hence, such Western sources tend to conclude, "religious discrimination is self evident."[55] A few years back, a similar conclusion was reached by the above-mentioned Jewish-Italian veteran communist, Senator Umberto Terracini. In a book published in 1966, Terracini charged that there had been no restoration of legality in the field of Jewish culture and religious activity after the "violent suppression" of the Stalin period. "Correspondingly," Terracini concluded, "the organization of the Jewish religion and the exercise of its worship remained extremely restricted <u>in comparison with other churches and cults existing in the USSR</u>"; and he argued that even if it were true that most Jews had assimilated, there still was "no justification for denying to the Jewish community the means for developing further its cultural and religious life."[56] Since Terracini wrote these lines, there appears to have been some liberalization of Soviet attitude towards the Jewish religion, so slight however that no conclusions as to general trends can be drawn therefrom at this time. The baking of matzoth

---

Rabinovich, Jews in the USSR [Moscow: Novosti Press Publishing House, n.d.], p. 78).

for Passover, for instance, has been generally permitted since 1966;* a new Jewish prayer book (the first since 1958 and only the second since 1917) was published in 1968 in an edition of 10,000; and the ban against presents or shipments of religious items was partially lifted in the same year. A religious calendar, the Soviets report, is published every year by the Moscow Central Synagogue.[57]

Even if some religious groups in the Soviet Union at present enjoy certain privileges not extended to followers of the Jewish faith, it should be pointed out in all fairness that this does not necessarily mean that Soviet Jews are worse off in their religious pursuits than _all_ other religious denominations. One of the West's experts on religion in the Soviet Union, William C. Fletcher, while not asserting equal treatment of the Jewish religion, has arrived at the conclusion that "on balance, Judaism has received par treatment from Soviet antireligious policy—a bit worse than some (Orthodox or Baptists), a bit better than others (Pentecostals or Buddhists)."[58]

Fletcher's point is well taken. There have been reports of frequent harassment, persecution, and arrests of clergymen in the Lithuanian Catholic Church;[59] the Soviets have obviously looked unfavorably upon religiously inspired practices of polygamy or even of selling daughters as wives to the highest bidders; and as can be expected, there has been little patience with religious sects that instruct their members not to serve in the country's armed forces. But while _some_ religious denominations have been much more disadvantaged in their religious pursuits than the Jews, religions comprising the overwhelming majority of adherents in the Soviet Union (and among them especially the Orthodox Church) appear to be in the "a bit better off" category.

JEWISH CULTURE

Many Western observers and emigrants from the Soviet Union have charged the Soviets not with mistreating Jews as individuals but primarily with having instituted policies that have stifled Jewish cultural pursuits in the USSR. Peter Grose, former Moscow chief correspondent of the New York _Times_, for instance, very emphatically asserts that the picture often painted in the West of Soviet Jews being persecuted or living in daily misery and fearing for their lives is utterly wrong and that "one can meet Soviet Jews every day whose reactions to the campaigns in their defense range from total bewilderment to sincere anger." However, Grose goes on to explain, "What

---

*According to Soviet sources, the mechanized bakery connected with the Moscow Central Synagogue baked about 100 tons of matzoth in 1969 (_Soviet Jews: Fact and Fiction_ [Moscow: Novosti Press Publishing House, 1970], p. 28).

has been persecuted throughout half a century of the Soviet system, persecuted almost to death, is the Jewish heritage: the religious practices and the culture through which Jews come to acknowledge a common bond."[60] More specifically, critics such as Grose charge primarily that there is a purposely contrived dearth of Yiddish-language newspapers, magazines, books, theater performances, and the like in the USSR.

There is only one Yiddish-language newspaper in the Soviet Union, the Birobidzhaner Stern, published three times weekly in editions of 1,000 in the Jewish Autonomous Region, Birobidzhan;* and there is only one Yiddish-language magazine, Sovietish Heimland, that comes out in a monthly edition of 25,000.† A mere handful of Yiddish-language books are published (as compared with 300-400 published annually in the 1920s and 1930s);‡ and there is apparently no regular, full-time, stationary theater group performing in Yiddish in the USSR, although such amateur Yiddish theater troupes as those of Vilnius and Kishinev attract enthusiastic audiences as do traveling theater groups and periodic Yiddish music and literary readings.[61]

The Soviets deny any suppression of Jewish culture in the USSR. They point out that by the early 1970s, there were more than 100 members of the Union of Soviet Writers writing in Yiddish;[62] that books in Yiddish are published regularly** (one recent one, an anthology

---

*As with newspapers elsewhere in the USSR, the Birobidzhaner Stern is posted in public places in Birobidzhan; but it apparently does not accept outside subscriptions and is hard to come by beyond the borders of the Jewish Autonomous Region.

†Between 17,000 and 18,000 copies of the magazine are sold each month in the Soviet Union, a third of these at newsstands, the rest by subscription. The other 7-8,000 copies are circulated abroad in 30 countries (Soviet Life, October 1972, p. 48).

‡One Western source gives the number published between 1959 and 1970 as 22 (Guy Vinatrel, "The Plight of Soviet Jewry," The American Zionist, December 1970, p. 48); another as 8 for the years 1960-68 and as having "increased" in 1969 and 1970 "largely as the result of the pressures of world opinion" ("Fact Sheet on Anti-Jewish Discrimination in the Soviet Union," in Richard Cohen, ed., Let My People Go! [New York: Popular Library, 1971], p. 145). During the preceding decade, however, there was reportedly not a single book in Yiddish published in the USSR (Ben Tzion, "The Jewish Question in the Soviet Union," New York Times Magazine, May 3, 1970).

**A recent Soviet publication lists 10 Jewish authors whose books it reported as having been published in Yiddish in 1968-69 (Soviet Jews: Fact and Fiction [Moscow: Novosti Press Publishing House, 1970], p. 24).

in Yiddish of modern prose, contained contributions of over 50 writers); that in Birobidzhan (where less than 1 percent of Soviet Jewry lives), one finds daily Yiddish-language radio broadcasts,* frequent literary evenings at the Sholem Aleichem Library, and a Jewish (as well as a Russian) theater that puts on performances in the region's capital (also called Birobidzhan) and in outlying areas; that in addition to the amateur theater companies of Birobidzhan, Vilnius, and Kishinev (which for their high standards of acting and production have been classed as "people's theaters") there are other companies such as the Jewish Drama Company of Moscow directed by Veniamin Shvartser, the Leningrad Jewish Drama Company directed by Esther Roitman, Sid Thal's group from Chernovtsy, which presents musical skits and sketches mainly in the Ukraine and Moldavia; and that at least half a million people annually attend the Jewish professional and amateur drama companies, in addition to well-attended recitations of Yiddish literature and concerts of Yiddish songs.[63]

While thus asserting that Jewish culture continues full of life and vigor in the USSR, the Soviets would be the last to deny that it is nevertheless gradually declining, particularly as regards the use of the Yiddish language in literature and in the performing arts. This, however, is attributed not to any pressure by the authorities but to the gradual assimilation of Soviet Jews who can no longer "imagine their life without Russian books, the Russian theater, music and painting."[64] How, the Soviets wonder, can the West talk about suppression of Jewish culture when, for instance, Sholem Aleichem has been honored by a postage stamp with his picture on it, by streets named after him (for instance in Peryaslav in the Ukraine, where he was born, and in Kiev), by celebrations and special meetings in many cities and towns throughout the USSR on the occasion of the 50th anniversary of his death in 1966, including one held in Moscow's Central Writer's Club that attracted 2,000 people, and by publication of his works in editions totaling many millions of copies[65]—all attestations corroborated by Western observers.[66] The monthly edition of Sovietish Heimland and the number of books published annually in Yiddish may not be very large; but this is so, the Soviets explain, simply because relatively few Jews can or want to read Yiddish-language magazines and books. Surely nothing but artificially contrived anti-Soviet propaganda, the Soviets insist, can possibly interpret this as suppression of Jewish culture in light of the fact that during the past three

---

*Western sources report only "isolated broadcasts in Yiddish" (Jerry Goodman, "Will the Soviet Union 'Revive' Jewish Culture?" in Richard Cohen, ed., Let My People Go! [New York: Popular Library, 1971], p. 223).

years Sovietish Heimland has featured a "teach-yourself-Yiddish" column in the last two pages of each issue and that between 1965 and 1970 a total of 175 books by 72 Jewish writers and 7 collections and anthologies (each containing contributions from 10 to 50 authors) were published in the Soviet Union in editions totaling more than 20 million copies in Yiddish, Russian, Ukrainian, Byelorussian, Lithuanian, Latvian, Moldavian, Georgian, Kazakh, Uzbek, Turkmenian, Kirghiz, French, English, and Spanish.[67] (Note that this is actually a relatively small number since during those six years close to a quarter of a million titles in editions totaling over 5.5 billion copies were published in the USSR).[68] And, they ask, how can there be talk of "suppression" when during some of the high holidays of the Jewish religion large numbers of nonreligious, nonworshiping Jews gather freely at their synagogues to celebrate their festivals in keeping with their national traditions, making merry, singing, and dancing in the streets. (Western Jewish observers also report vigorous celebrations, attended by large numbers of Soviet Jews; but many of these observers attribute this phenomenon to a reawakening of Jewish spirit in the Soviet Union that is exhibited in defiance of Soviet pressures.)

What has been said is not necessarily evidence that Jewish culture is permitted to flourish freely and undisturbed in the USSR; but on the other hand, assertions of total suppression of Jewish cultural life would surely appear to be gross exaggerations. And there is undoubtedly much truth in Soviet explanations of waning interest in Yiddish among Soviet Jews. In the Soviet census of 1970, 17.7 percent of Soviet Jewry listed Yiddish as their native tongue, as compared with 21.5 percent in 1959, over 70 percent in 1926, and 97 percent in Czarist Russia at the beginning of the twentieth century. But even this figure of 17.7 percent is somewhat misleading. On the one hand, there are surely Jews in the Soviet Union who still speak and perhaps even read Yiddish although they give another language (for example, Russian) as their native tongue; but there are probably many others who give Yiddish as their and their children's "native language," although at least some members of their family may hardly ever speak it outside the home and may not even be able to read it at all (just as in the United States there are many immigrants and children of immigrants, including this author, whose native tongue may be one other than English but who rarely if ever speak or read their native language). In any case, there can be no doubt that Soviet Jews are being increasingly assimilated into the mainstream of Soviet life and that ever fewer speak Yiddish at work, on the street, or even in their homes. So much has the use of Yiddish dwindled among Soviet Jews that Sol Polansky, first secretary of the U.S. Embassy in Moscow from 1968 to 1971, testified before a congressional subcommittee that he was "not at all persuaded that there are enough Jews in the Soviet

Union who know and speak Yiddish to make it worthwhile [for the Voice of America] to broadcast in Yiddish [to the USSR]."[69]

DISCRIMINATION IN EDUCATION?

Western critics contend that the absence of public schools in which instruction is carried out in Yiddish is discriminatory. Such critics often emphasize that in the 1920s and 1930s some 100,000 children studied in Yiddish schools in the Soviet Union; that as late as 1940 the number was reportedly still between 85,000 and 90,000; but that at present there is not a single public school in all the land in which Yiddish (not to speak of Hebrew) is the language of instruction, and that there has been none for a quarter of a century. As examples of discrimination, such critics point to the Ukraine, where three small minorities each numbering fewer than 400,000 (the Moldavians, the Hungarians, and the Poles) have schools in their native tongues while some 1 million Jews do not; or to the Russian Federated Republic, where there are special schools for the 12,000 Chukchi and the 6,300 Koraks, but none for almost 1 million Jews. Even worse, these critics charge, there isn't a single course in Yiddish or Hebrew taught in any public school in the USSR although there are such classes in 59 other languages.[70] Other Western observers, however, see the nonexistence of Yiddish schools merely as an extension of or a parallel to general trends, pointing for instance to 3 million Ukrainians living in the Russian Federated Republic who have no Ukrainian-language schools for their children either.[71]

The Soviets ascribe the discontinuation of Yiddish-language schools not to arbitrary or discriminatory action by the authorities but, once again, to changing conditions and waning interest on the part of Jews themselves. After the revolution, they point out, a network of Jewish schools was set up throughout the USSR because there were many poor Jewish families whose children spoke only Yiddish. Through these schools, the Jewish youth was prepared for life in the new society. But the situation has changed. Jews from the small Jewish settlements have moved to urban areas until today somewhere between 95 and 98 percent of Soviet Jews live in cities and towns.[72] What a handicap it would be for the present generation of Jewish schoolchildren to study physics or mathematics in Yiddish when afterwards on their jobs or at the universities all their work and instruction would be in one of the main languages, such as Russian or Ukrainian! "Can we say now," asks the Jewish Soviet journalist Solomon Rabinovich, "that there is a real objective need for Jewish schools in any part of the country?"[73] And to illustrate the lack of interest that would make it injudicious for the Soviet state to reopen Yiddish-language public schools at this stage of Soviet history, a Jewish Soviet professor told how a few years back the Lithuanian minister for Education learned about some Lithuanian Jews who wanted a Yiddish-language school and thereupon announced that such a school would be started. But even those who had first requested it reconsidered and very few applications were received. "You would hardly open a school if no more than three or four children were going to attend," commented the professor. "Surely," he went on, "you would not want children of Jewish nationality to be forced to study in Yiddish."[74]

Thus, the Soviets base their case against the reestablishment of Yiddish-language instruction in public schools on what they see as an objective lack of need. On the other hand, the right of Soviet citizens to educate their children in their own language is guaranteed in the Constitution of the USSR (Article 121), in the constitutions of all the union and autonomous republics, and in the 1961 Party Program,[75] and it has been proclaimed over and over by Soviet authorities in recent years.* This does not necessarily mean that the Soviet state is obligated to open a new special-language school on demand anywhere and at any time, no matter how small the number of prospective pupils involved. What it does mean is that Soviet law allows any 10 parents to make private arrangements for educational classes for their children in their own language. While the Soviets ascribe the general absence of such instruction in Yiddish to a lack of interest, some Western sources argue that it can be "only fear and apprehension that keep [Soviet Jews] from requesting what they are legally entitled to."[76]

A few years back, Maurice Friedberg, then director of the Russian and East European Institute at Indiana University, charged that

---

*For example, the USSR ratified the UNESCO (United Nations Educational, Scientific and Cultural Organization) Convention Against Discrimination in Education in August 1962, which bestowed upon national minorities the right "to carry on their own educational activities, including the maintenance of schools and . . . the use or the teaching of their own language" (Doc. E/CN.4/Sub.2/210, January 5, 1961, p. 6; emphasis added); the Soviet Government subsequently reiterated to UNESCO that every Soviet citizen could have his children taught "in any language he wished" (Periodic Reports on Human Rights Covering the Period 1960-62, Commission on Human Rights, Doc. E/CN.4/861/Add.2, December 20, 1963, p. 42). And in 1968, to give one more example, Soviet Minister of Education Mikhail Prokofyev reiterated that "peoples of all nationalities inhabiting the USSR . . . are entitled to receive an education in their native language" (Education in the USSR [Moscow: Novosti Press Agency Publishing House, 1968] p. 9).

in the Soviet Union Hebrew was taught only in Christian theological academies and that, except as part of abstruse programs in philology or archeology open only to advanced students, "not one Soviet University offers a course in Yiddish or Hebrew or in Jewish History."[77] While such courses may indeed have been rare exceptions, Soviet writers point out that at that time Leningrad University offered a course in Hebrew grammar, a course in modern Hebrew, and a course of lectures in Jewish history, and that students could become acquainted "with the fundamentals of Jewish poetry and the beauty of the mediaeval poetry of Yehouda Galeva, Moses ibn Ezra, and Salomon ibn Gabirol."[78] More recently, the New York Times published a letter over the signatures of such well-known individuals as Theodore M. Hesburgh, Arthur Miller, Hans J. Morgenthau, Bayard Rustin, and Telford Taylor, which asserted that a secret police action was conducted in the Soviet Union against militant Jews who dared to study Jewish history or Hebrew.[79] A Soviet publication retorted bitterly that "this letter appeared at a time when Professor Isaac Vinnikov was lecturing at Leningrad University on Semitic and Hebrew studies and discussing biblical texts with his students, and when a team of Soviet scholars were preparing a Russian-Hebrew dictionary for press in a large edition."[80]

Western critics in general are not concerned as much with the number of courses in Hebrew, Yiddish, and Jewish history offered at Soviet universities as they are with alleged discrimination against Jewish youths attempting to enroll in institutions of higher learning in the USSR. Most of these critics will readily acknowledge that, due to their traditional emphasis on learning, Soviet Jews have benefited "more than any other nationality" from the immense expansion of education under the Soviet regime,[81] as indicated by figures that show that some 15 percent of all Jews in the USSR now have a "higher or specialized secondary education," compared with a national average of 5 percent.[82] But other nationalities are catching up; and this is widely attributed in the West to "discrimination both in educational enrollment and professional appointments."[83]

Some Western sources report that since Khrushchev left office Soviet students of Jewish extraction have encountered "enormous difficulties" in registering at universities.[84] Stalin's daughter Svetlana Alliluyeva said at a New York news conference in 1967 that she personally knew of Soviet universities and institutions that, although they do accept talented young Jews, sometimes give preference to less talented students of other nationalities;[85] and she charged that for Jews enrolling at the University of Moscow a "percentage quota was, in essence, reinstated" after the war.[86] Western sources also have it that there is some kind of quota system, but precisely what that system is or what its effects are is unclear. The American expert on Soviet Jewry William Korey, for instance, cites Western scholars who reported the existence of such a quota system in the post-World War II Stalin era and through the early 1960s and one Soviet source that acknowledged it in 1963, yet he concedes that "the extent to which the quota system continues to affect deleteriously the admission of Jewish youngsters, especially in major universities, cannot be determined."[87] But the Bibliothèque Juive Contemporaine of Paris, an "authoritative source of information concerning the status of Jews in the USSR," tells of annual preferential admission quotas to Soviet colleges and universities that are supposedly granted to each union republic but not to Soviet Jews since these latter do not have such a republic of their own and of a sharp decline in the relative number of Jewish students, who represented 13 percent of all Soviet university students in 1935, 3.2 percent in 1960, and 2.5 percent in 1970.[88] And Alexander Werth, while stating categorically that "there is no official numerus clausus against Jews anywhere" in the USSR, reports "persistent rumors" that Moscow University tends to limit the percentage of Jewish students so as not to exceed the percentage of Jews in the population of Moscow (about 5 percent). That such restrictions actually exist at some particularly famous universities is suggested, Werth submits, by the extensive migration of Jewish students, teachers, and scientists to the new cities and institutes of higher education in Siberia.[89]

The Soviets, once again, adamantly deny all charges of discrimination. According to official Soviet sources, out of a Jewish population of under 2.2 million (less than 1 percent of the total population of the USSR),* 105,000 were enrolled as students at Soviet institutions of higher education in 1970, which comes to approximately one Jewish student for every 21 Soviet citizens of Jewish origin;[90] in comparison, they point out, there is only one Russian student for every 47 Russians,

---

*Unless otherwise stated, numbers of Jews in the Soviet Union are based on Soviet Census figures, such censuses having been taken in the USSR in 1920, 1923, 1926, 1939, 1959, and 1970. For census purposes, nationality in the Soviet Union is determined by asking citizens what their nationality is. As has been mentioned before, Soviet citizens of Jewish "nationality" are also identified as such in their internal passports, where "nationality" cannot be changed at will. (See page 17 above.) Israeli sources hold that in 1970 there were about 1 million more "passport Jews" (including their children under 16) in the Soviet Union than the number indicated in the census ("The Problem of Soviet Jewry," Answers and Questions, Pamphlet No. 7 [Jerusalem: Information Division of the Ministry for Foreign Affairs, December 1972], p. 3).

one Ukrainian for every 65.5 Ukrainians, and one Byelorussian for every 69 Byelorussians.[91] They ascribe the large percentage of Soviet Jews attending institutions of higher learning—more than two and a half times that of the over-all average of the Soviet population—to the fact that virtually all Soviet Jews live in towns and cities,[92] whereas the proportion of urban dwellers among the Soviet population at large is only somewhat above 50 percent.[93] In any case, they affirm and reaffirm, peoples of all nationalities in the USSR have an "equal right to enter educational establishments";[94] nationality does "not in the least affect admission" to any educational facility;[95] and the attitude towards Jews in this respect is "the same as towards any other nationality."[96]

It is an undeniable fact that the number of Jewish students enrolled in Soviet institutions of higher learning has increased steadily over the years, both in absolute numbers and as a percentage of the Jewish population of the USSR. But on the other hand, as the proportion of total enrollment in Soviet institutions of higher learning, the Jewish student body declined considerably from the 1930s to 1960 and has continued to decline during the 1960s; in other words, the number of non-Jewish students has increased more rapidly than that of their Jewish fellow students. (For absolute numbers and percentages, see Table 1.) This, the Soviets emphasize, must not be ascribed to any alleged discrimination. In part, it can surely be accounted for by a decrease of the Jewish population—in the early 1940s brought on by Nazi extermination policies in the occupied areas and, more recently, presumably the result of low birth rates, intermarriage, and assimilation.* But the Soviets attribute it primarily to the ascent of the less

---

*See footnote, page 48. There is no evidence that Soviet Jews tried to conceal their Jewish nationality for the 1970 census, and surely none that a larger percentage tried to conceal it for the 1970 census than for the 1959 census. But, granted that such a possibility exists, there could surely be some Soviet citizens of Jewish parentage who are identified in their internal passports as Jews but have given another nationality for the census. Moreover, children of mixed marriages, who can choose the nationality of either parent at age 16, can be listed until then under the nationality of either parent; but there seems to be a tendency to list them as having the nationality of their mother—and it is estimated that twice as many Jewish men marry non-Jewish women as Jewish women marry non-Jewish men—and to list them as having the nationality of the non-Jewish parent, especially if he or she is of Russian nationality. Once again, however, there is no reason to assume that either of these tendencies was greater in 1970 than in 1959. While the official number of Soviet Jews could therefore be an understatement

TABLE 1

Jewish Students at Higher Educational Institutions

	1935	1960	1965	1970
Total pop., USSR (thousands)	176,000[a]	212,400	229,600	242,000
Jewish pop., USSR (thousands)	2,900[b]	2,268[c]	2,210[d]	2,151[e]
Total students, USSR (thousands)[f]	563.5	2,395.5	3,860.5	4,580.6
Jewish students, USSR (thousands)[f]	74.0	77.2	94.6	105.8
Total students, USSR, as percent of total pop., USSR	0.3[g]	1.1	1.7	1.9
Jewish students, USSR, as percent of Jewish pop., USSR	2.6[h]	3.4	4.3[i]	4.9
Jewish students, USSR, as percent of total students, USSR	13.3	3.2	2.5	2.3

[a]Rough estimate based on population figure of 165.7 million for 1932 (from Fulfillment of Second Five-Year Plan, p. 269, as cited in Alec Nove, An Economic History of the USSR [London: Allen Lane, The Penguin Press, 1969], p. 180) and of 194.1 million for 1940 (Narodnoe Khoziaistvo SSR, 1970, p. 7).

[b]Rough estimate, based on figure of 2.68 million Jews in the USSR in 1926 and 3.02 million in 1939 as cited from Soviet census figures in Alec Nove and J. A. Hewth, "The Jewish Population: Demographic Trends and Occupational Patterns," in Lional Kochan, ed., The Jews in Soviet Russia Since 1917 (London, New York: Oxford University Press, 1970), p. 136.

[c]Due to incorporation of Poland, Bessarabia, and the Baltic Republics into the USSR and due to some eastward migration from these annexed territories and to a lesser extent from some other parts of East Europe, the Jewish population of the Soviet Union increased to 4.8 million in 1941. By 1960, it was less than half the number (the figure of 2.268 million, taken from the census of 1959 is for 1959; for the pre-1939 territory it was actually only 2.047 million.)

[d]Rough estimate based on census figures for 1959 and 1970.

[e]Based on census data.

[f]Enrollment figures are for 1935 and for school years 1960-61, 1965-66, and 1970-71, respectively.

[g]Based on rough estimate of 1935 total population, USSR.

[h]Based on rough estimate of 1935 Jewish population, USSR.

[i]Based on rough estimate of 1965 Jewish population, USSR.

Sources: Natsionalnaya politika VPK(b) v tsifrakh, 1935; Sotsialisticheskoe stroitelstvo, 1936; Narodnoe Khoziastvo SSR, SSSR, 1963, 1965, 1970; Soviet Census, 1959, 1970. See also other sources in footnotes.

developed areas where few Jews live. (For Kazhakstan and the Central Asian republics, for instance, the Soviets list 103 institutions of higher learning with an enrollment of 554,000 students, while before the revolution there was none.)[97] And, comments the Jewish Soviet journalist Rabinovich, "one has to be extremely biased not to be pleased by such a happy fact as the tremendous growth of the cultures of all nations and nationalities in the Soviet Union, including those that were backward and downtrodden in the past . . . . (Their progress) naturally means that increasing numbers of representatives of new sections of the population become students."[98] This latter conclusion does not seem unreasonable since students from the formerly underdeveloped parts of the USSR have been encroaching on the percentage of students not only of Jewish but also of Russian and Ukrainian nationality. *

DISCRIMINATION IN JOB OPPORTUNITIES?

Most Western charges of job discrimination against Soviet Jews point to the relative dearth of Jews in the Soviet Union's diplomatic corps and in the highest echelons of the Party, government, and armed forces. There is only one Jew, Veniamin E. Dymshits, among the 241 full members of the Party Central Committee, and only a handful of Jews among the more than 1,500 deputies to the Soviet Union's highest legislative body, the Supreme Soviet;† in recent years, Western

---

if a definition other than self-determined nationality for adults and parent-determined for children were used, the growth rate of Soviet Jewry, positive or negative, might not be affected in any case.

*Between 1962/63 and 1970/71, the percentage of Russians among Soviet students enrolled in institutions of higher learning dropped from 61.3 to 59.5 percent, that of Ukrainians from 14.5 to 13.6 percent (from figures in Narodnoe Khoziaistvo SSR; 1970 [Moscow, 1971], p. 651). While this percentage drop was not as large as that of Soviet Jews (from 2.7 to 2.3 percent for the same period [ibid]), it should be noted that in terms of total population of each nationality, the percentage of Soviet Jews attending institutions of higher learning in the USSR is still more than twice that of the Russians and more than three times that of the Ukrainians (roughly 4.9 percent of Soviet Jews, 2.1 percent of Russians, and 1.4 percent of Ukrainians being currently enrolled).

†The Supreme Soviet consists of two houses, the Soviet of the Union, based on population with one deputy per 300,000 people, and the Soviet of Nationalities, based on territorial and national units with 20 deputies from each of the 15 union republics, 11 from each autonomous

sources have it, it has become virtually impossible for a Jew to rise to one of the top ranks in the Soviet Union's armed forces, although during the days of World War II there were substantial numbers of Jewish colonels, lieutenant colonels, and generals in the Red Army (see page 11 above); and the Soviet Foreign Office and diplomatic corps (in the days of Lenin so heavily staffed with Jews that the former was often jokingly referred to as "the Synagogue") are virtually bereft of Jews today.*

In regard to positions in areas others than the ones mentioned above, Western charges, if levied at all, are usually much more guarded. Some Western observers actually see marked improvement since the days of Khrushchev, find the Foreign Ministry and the diplomatic service the only fields from which Jews are virtually excluded (a situation that "is substantially also true of Britain, France, and many other countries"), agree that allegations to the effect that certain Jewish scientists are slower to be appointed to top jobs at the Soviet Academy of Sciences than Russians or Ukrainians are probably correct (but "does not some similar discrimination or prejudice exist in most European countries?"), go as far as asserting that, except in some parts of the Ukraine, there is no more discrimination against Jews in the USSR than there is in most "civilized" countries, and conclude that it is becoming less and less of a problem as assimilation progresses.[99] Others, such as the renowned Western Sovietologist Alec Nove and his younger coauthor J. A. Newth, express personal views that "discrimination in various forms undoubtedly makes life difficult for many Jews in many walks of life," but they caution that the

---

republic, 5 from each autonomous region, and 1 from each national area. The members on the Supreme Soviet elected in 1966 who are known to have been Jewish were Veniamin G. Dymshits, the late Ilya Ehrenburg, both referred to previously, and lathe operator Raphail Khersonsky, academician Yuri Khariton, and editor in chief of Literaturnaya Gazeta Alexandr Chakovsky. For names of seven Jews elected to the Supreme Soviet in 1970 see the first seven names on the list that begins on page 55. (Soviet Life, July 1971, p. 39, lists five—all but Veniamin Dymshits and Riva Vischikina—as "among the Jews elected to the USSR Supreme Soviet at the last election," thereby implying that there are others.)

*Stalin's daughter Svetlana Alliluyeva, for instance, charges that when in 1966 a talented young man with special diplomatic education had been singled out for a position with the Soviet Embassy in Washington, Minister Andrei Gromyko turned him down for one single reason: because he was a Jew. (Alliluyeva, Only One Year [New York: Harper and Row, 1969], p. 170.)

existence of such discrimination "cannot be proved by any of the official statistics to which we have access," and that "endeavors to use these statistics for this purpose would expose the users to devastating and deserved counter-attack."[100]

The official Soviet position has always been that the personal success of Soviet citizens, their social standing, their career, depend on skill, ability, diligence, patriotism, and loyalty; nationality or race do not matter. Two decades ago, this position's applicability to the Jewish minority was spelled out clearly in the Soviet Encyclopedia in a statement to the effect that in the USSR Jews can engage in all occupations and professions and take part in building communism.[101] In recent years, numerous statements by prominent Soviet Jews have appeared in the press, eloquently reaffirming official Soviet proclamations on the issue. As one example, Pravda not long ago published a letter signed by 70 veteran Bolsheviks of Jewish extraction who had joined the Communist Party in the years 1903-20. The letter reads in part: "The Soviet Union has granted all nationalities, including Jews, every right and possibility to work, to enjoy all the benefits of science, culture, education and art, the right to take part on a broad scale in all aspects of the operation of the state, and the right to elect and be elected to all organs of government."[102]

There is no doubt that the "Jewish occupations" of yesteryear—tradesmen, small shopkeepers, and the like—have long since virtually ceased to exist in the USSR. Under the Soviet regime a true socio-economic transformation of Jews has taken place. Many today are laborers, factory workers, truck drivers; but disproportionately large numbers are in medicine, law, theater, film, newspaper work, and the sciences—the white-collar professional occupations in general. Jews account for a percentage of the membership of the Soviet Academy of Sciences, several times their percentage in the population at large, and even in such "sensitive" fields as atomic research or aircraft design there are unusually high concentrations of Soviet Jews.[103] Exceptionally large numbers of Jews can be found among the annual recipients of state prizes for scientific and artistic achievements. The percentage of Jews among "scientific workers"* in the Soviet Union has been falling; but it is still seven times as large as the proportion of Jews in the population, and the number of Jewish scientific workers has increased rapidly in absolute terms and also as a proportion of Soviet Jewry, both about doubling during the decade of the

---

*"Scientific workers," nauchnye rabotniki in Russian, include individuals in all fields who have professional appointments at institutions such as universities, research institutes, or the Academy of Sciences.

1960s (see Table 2).* Even in government there are, according to Soviet sources, no fewer than 8,000 Jewish deputies to the Supreme Soviet, USSR, the Supreme Soviets of the republics, and the local Soviets (although the Soviet sources have failed to report what percentage of the total these deputies constitute); and among them are at least seven deputies to the Supreme Soviet, USSR, apparently an increase of at least two since the previous election in 1966. And the Soviets affirm, "there are quite a few generals, colonels and other officers of Jewish nationality in the professorial staffs of Moscow's military academies. Some of them were schooled on the battlefields of World War II, others come from the young galaxy of Soviet military leaders."[104]

After examining Western charges and Soviet contentions, one cannot help but conclude that Jews—so numerous and influential in the sciences—are indeed underrepresented in (but not completely missing

TABLE 2

Jewish "Scientific Workers"

	1960	1965	1970
Total scientific workers, USSR	354,158	664,584	927,709
Jewish scientific workers, USSR	33,529	53,067	64,392
Jewish scientific workers, USSR as percent of total scientific workers, USSR	9.5	8.0	6.9
Jewish scientific workers, USSR, as percent of total Jewish population, USSR[a]	1.5	2.4	3.0

[a]For population figures see Table 1.

Source: Narodnoe Khoziaistvo SSR, 1965 and 1970.

---

*In other words, as in the case of students in Soviet institutions of higher learning, the total number of scientific workers has increased relatively even more rapidly than the number of Jewish scientific workers.

from) the top echelons of the Soviet Government, Party, and armed forces. Yet, taken as a whole, the list of prominent Jews in the Soviet Union is so impressive that it reads like a series of pages of a Who's Who in the USSR. The following lists some of the Soviet Union's most prominent Jewish citizens.

CROSS SECTION OF PROMINENT JEWS IN THE USSR*

In the Government and High Public Office (All-Union Level Only)

Veniamin Dymshits, deputy, Supreme Soviet, USSR
Yuli Khariton, deputy, Supreme Soviet, USSR
Vladimir Peller, deputy, Supreme Soviet, USSR
Riva Vischikina, deputy, Supreme Soviet, USSR
Mikhail Abelman, deputy, Supreme Soviet, USSR
Kostas Glikas, deputy, Supreme Soviet, USSR
Alexandr Chakovsky, deputy, Supreme Soviet, USSR†

---

*This selected list includes only individuals who, as far as could be ascertained, were still alive and held the positions listed at the time this was written.

Sources: Soviet Life, July 1971, pp. 39, 40; Soviet Life, July 1972, p. 53; Zionism: Instrument of Imperialist Reaction (Moscow: Novosti Press Agency Publishing House, February-March 1970) pp. 24-25; Zionism: Instrument of Imperialist Reaction (Moscow: Novosti Press Agency Publishing House, March-May, 1970) pp. 19, 25, and 43; Solomon Rabinovich, Jews in the USSR (Moscow: Novosti Press Publishing House, n.d.) pp. 50-56, passim; Alexander Werth, Russia: Hopes and Fears (New York: Simon and Schuster, 1969), p. 225; Prominent Personalities in the USSR (compiled by the Institute for the Study of the USSR [no longer in operation], Munich, Germany, and published by the Scarecrow Press, Metuchen, N.J., in 1968).

†In the USSR, elected public office is, as a general rule, not a full-time, year-round job. The Jewish deputies to the Supreme Soviet, USSR, hold a variety of jobs: Peller is chairman of a collective farm in the Jewish Autonomous Region, Birobidzhan; Abelman is chairman of the Executive Council of the Lenin District Soviet of Working People's Deputies and Vischikina of the executive committee of a village Soviet, both in Birobidzhan (and they both probably hold other jobs also); Glikas is chairman of a collective farm in Lithuania; and Dymshits, Khariton, and Chakovsky hold important positions and are noted elsewhere in this list.

Veniamin Dymshits, vice chairman, USSR Council of Ministers; chairman, State Committee on Material Technical Supplies; member, Central Committee, CPSU (also listed above as deputy to the Supreme Soviet, USSR)
Lev Volodarsky, deputy chief, Central Statistical board, USSR
Yuli Bokserman, deputy minister, Gas Industry, USSR
Iosif Ravich, deputy minister of Communications, USSR
Leonid Glikman, deputy minister, Chemical and Oil Engineering, USSR
Abram Levinsky, deputy minister, Electrical Engineering, USSR
Aaron Gindin, member, State Committee for Science and Technology
Semyon Ginsburg, chairman, Board of Stroibank (Construction Bank), USSR
Isaac Kaganovich, prosecutor, Investigation Department, Chief Prosecutor's Office of the USSR
Valentine Zorin, deputy minister of International Affairs

General Staff, Armed Forces

Colonel General David Dragunsky, head of one of the Soviet Union's military academies
Lieutenant General Matvei Vainrub, commanding general, Kiev Military District
Major General Isaac Rabinovich, head of Chair of Engineering and Technical Branch, Kuybyshev Military Engineering Academy; corresponding member, USSR Academy of Sciences
Major General M. I. Schraiber, professor; D.Sc., Medicine
Colonel General A. D. Tsirilin, D.Sc., Military Science
Major General M. L. Shtern, "Honored Builder of the Russian Federation"
Major General Zinovi Kontsevoi
Lieutenant General Shimon Krivoshein

Eminent scientists:

Yevsey Liberman, professor of Economics, Kharkov University; popularizer of "economic reforms"
Isaac Mints, head, Chair of History of USSR, Lenin State Pedagogical Institute, Moscow; full member, USSR Academy of Sciences
Bentsion Vul, physicist; corresponding member, USSR Academy of Sciences
Israel Gelfond, Mathematician; corresponding member, USSR Academy of Sciences

Yuli Khariton, physicist and physical chemist; full member, USSR Academy of Sciences (also listed above as deputy to the Supreme Soviet, USSR)
Lev Gatovsky, director, Economics Institute, USSR Academy of Sciences
Gersh Budker, physicist, director of Institute of Nuclear Physics, Siberian Branch, USSR Academy of Sciences
Martin Kabachnik, organic chemist; full member, USSR Academy of Sciences
Rakhil Freidlina, organic chemist, head, Lab. Institute of Elemental Organic Compounds, USSR Academy of Sciences
A. Solomonovich, department chief, Physics Institute, USSR Academy of Sciences
Alexandr Frumkin, physiochemist; professor and head, Chair of Electrochemistry, Moscow University; full member, USSR Academy of Sciences
Mikhail Strogovich, head, Institute of State and Law, USSR Academy of Sciences
S. L. Zivs, deputy director, Institute of State and Law, USSR Academy of Sciences
Alexandr Birman, economist; vice rector, Plekhanov Institute of National Economy
Grigoriy Byaly, philologist and literary specialist; professor, Chair of Russian Literature, Leningrad University
I. I. Gikham, department chief, Donetsk Computing Center, Ukrainian Academy of Sciences
S. A. Giller, director, Institute of Organic Synthesis, Academy of Sciences of the Latvian Republic
A. F. Blyuger, prorector, Riga Medical Institute
P. E. Zabludovsky, head, Department of the History of Medicine, Central Institute for Advanced Medical Studies*
Yevsey Katsman, head, Chair of Children's Diseases, Minsk Medical Institute
Iosif Kasirsky, internist and hematologist; full member, USSR Academy of Medical Sciences

Renowned artists, writers, and journalist:

Emil Gilels, pianist
Lev Ginsburg, pianist
Samuel Feinberg, pianist

---

*At the Central Institute for Advanced Medical Studies, seven other Departments are also headed by Jews.

David Oistrakh, violinist; professor, Moscow Conservatory
Igor Oistrakh, violinist; instructor, Moscow Conservatory
Leonid Kogan, violinist; instructor, Moscow Conservatory
Maya Plisetskaya, prima ballerina, Bolshoi Ballet
Mark Reisen, actor
Leonid Utyosov, actor
Arkady Raikin, actor
Ethel Kovenskaya, dramatic actress; singer
Natan Rakhlin, artistic director and chief conductor, Ukrainian Symphony Orchestra; professor, Kiev Conservatory
Moisei Vainbeng, composer
Sigizmund Kats, composer
Iosif Kheifetz, film director; script writer
Mikhail Romm, film director
Mark Donskoy, film director; script writer
Sergei Yutkevich, film director; professor, All Union Institute of Cinematography
Roman Karmen, film director; cameraman; script writer; journalist
Alexei Kapler, film director; actor; script writer
Lev Arnshtam, film director; script writer
Grigory Roshal, film director; script writer
Samuel Marshak, writer
Pavel Antakolsky, writer
Vera Inber, writer; poetess
Emmanuel Kazakevich, writer
Vassily Grossman, writer
Mikhail Svetlov, writer
Yevgeniy Dolmatovsky, poet; board member, RSFSR* Union of Writers
Boris Galin, writer; journalist; deputy first secretary, RSFSR Union of Writers
Alexandr Chakovsky, writer; editor in chief, Literaturnaya Gazeta, central organ of the Soviet Writers' Union (also listed above as deputy to the Supreme Soviet, USSR)
A. L. Vergelis, poet; editor in chief, Sovietish Heimland (Yiddish)
N. A. Korchminsky, editor in chief, Birobidzhaner Stern (Yiddish)

---

*Russian Republic, the largest of the 15 union republics in the USSR.

THE RIGHT TO EMIGRATE, ESPECIALLY TO ISRAEL

However fair and just the treatment of Soviet Jews or however much it may leave to be desired, the fact remains that there are Soviet Jews who do want to emigrate, the overwhelming majority apparently to Israel. And there is hardly an issue connected with Soviet Jewry that has, in recent years, stirred the emotions more or called forth more vigorous protests in the West than the alleged plight of these Soviet Jews and the means assertedly used by Soviet authorities to discourage or prevent their emigration.

The number of those eager to depart for a new home in the "promised land" is necessarily conjectural. In 1971, Western estimates of the number of Soviet Jews who had actually applied for exit permits for Israel ran from a typical estimate of 50,000 to as high as a quarter of a million;* and the estimated number of those who would have left if the gates had been opened runs as high as 500,000.†

---

*Henrick Smith thought that 50,000 was a "typical" Western estimate for 1971 (Smith, "1971 Has Seen Soviets Sharply Ease Curb on Emigration to Israel," New York _Times_, December 29, 1971). Louis Rosenblum, Union of Councils for Soviet Jews puts the number at "an estimated $\frac{1}{4}$ million" (_Soviet Jewry_, U.S., House of Representatives, Subcommittee on Europe of the Committee on Foreign Affairs, Hearings, 92d Cong., 1st sess. [Washington D.C.: Government Printing Office, 1972], p. 233); William Korey, director of the B'nai B'rith International Council, estimated that approximately 80,000 applications had been filed; but he asserted that so many of these were not individual applications but applications for entire families that they actually represented a quarter of a million Jews (_Soviet Jewry_ [Hearings], p. 145). But at the same congressional hearings at which Rosenblum and Korey testified, Joseph E. Karth, U.S. congressman from Minnesota, gave the figure as "over 80,000 Russian Jews" (p. 182). Other estimates, giving a figure of 80,000 applications as of the end of 1971, also seem to imply that this means 80,000 individuals. (For example, Anatole Shub, "From Russia with Chutzpah," _Harpers_, May 1972, p. 78.) And Richard Cohen, associate executive director of the American Jewish Congress, contends that "tens of thousands of Jews have applied for exit permits" (Cohen, ed., _Let My People Go_! [New York: Popular Library, 1971], p. 32). Note that all these estimates are for 1971.

†For instance, Anatole Shub ("From Russia with Chutzpah," _Harpers_, May 1972) and Congressman William S. Broomfield from Michigan (_Soviet Jewry_, U.S., House of Representatives, Subcommittee

Official Soviet sources have called estimates of would-be emigrés running into the hundreds of thousands "absurd" and "truly fantastic,"[105] and a Jewish Soviet professor, on the occasion of a visit to Israel in early 1972, gave 1 percent of Soviet Jewry, or somewhat in excess of 20,000, as what he regarded to be a more reasonable figure.[106] Actual emigration statistics for 1972 (discussed below) clearly prove that his estimate was too low; according to January 1973 Israeli sources, about 120,000 Soviet Jews had at that time pending applications for exit papers to go to Israel.[107]

Whatever the actual figures may be, there is no doubt that since the Arab-Israeli war of 1967, increasing numbers of Soviet Jews from all walks of life and from all parts of the USSR have applied for emigration permits. Prior to 1971, the Soviets denied most of these applications. But many of the would-be emigrants refused to be discouraged. They reapplied, they protested,[108] they wrote letters to Soviet, Israeli, and UN authorities, asking them to intervene in their behalf. These letters reflect the wide variety of motives that prompted the writers to want to give up all they had for a new life in Israel. In these letters, some of the applicants (especially some from Lithuania and the Ukraine) bring bitter charges of continuing anti-Semitism against the Soviets; but most of the others profess their loyalty and even their gratitude to the people of the USSR and to the land in which they were born and raised and where they have lived all of their lives. Yet, they explain, they feel compelled to leave, offering a variety of reasons for their decision. Some, unwilling to assimilate, feel frustrated in their endeavors to live a meaningful, religious, Jewish life in their native land; others have a nostalgic longing for "their own land—the land of their fathers"; yet others want to join members of their families in Israel. (For excerpts from selected letters, illustrative of the variety of motives for leaving, see pages 197-203.) However reluctantly, the Soviets have begun to heed their pleas, and increasing numbers of Soviet Jews have left for Israel since the beginning of the 1970s. But, quite often, the Soviets have not made their departure easy.

Would-be emigrants and their Western supporters point out that there are several UN resolutions—none of them opposed by the Soviet Union—that specifically guarantee the right of individuals to emigrate. The Universal Declaration of Human Rights, adopted by the

---

on Europe of the Committee on Foreign Affairs, Hearings, 92d Cong., 1st Sess. [Washington, D.C.: Government Printing Office, 1972], p. 160) estimated the number as 500,000; Henrick Smith ("1971 Has Seen Soviets Sharply Ease Curb on Emigration to Israel," New York Times, December 29, 1971) as from 200,000 to 300,000.

UN General Assembly without a dissenting vote on December 10, 1948, states, "Everyone has the right to leave any country, including his own, and to return to his country" (Article 13/2). In connection with UN declarations on colonialism, the Universal Declaration was re-affirmed by unanimous vote in the UN General Assembly in 1960, 1961, and 1962.* And almost identically worded guarantees can be found in the International Convention on the Elimination of all Forms of Racial Discrimination (Article 5/d[2]) and in the International Covenant on Civil and Political Rights (Article 12/2), both adopted unanimously by the General Assembly on December 21, 1965 and on December 16, 1966, respectively. The Soviet Union itself clarified its position by defining only three circumstances, widely accepted internationally, under which exit permits would be denied, namely, when the applicant (1) has been charged with an offense and judgment is still pending, (2) has been convicted of a violation of the law and is serving a sentence, or (3) still has to fulfill his legal obligations of service in the Soviet armed forces.[109] But while these were the only circumstances enumerated by the Soviets in the United Nations, official Soviet statements at other places and at other times dealing specifically with the right of Soviet Jews to emigrate to Israel have often been inconsistent. Soviet ambivalence on the issue is understandable. On the other hand, there are the above-mentioned commitments; and, in any case, a dissatisfied small minority, eager to leave, can be a disturbing factor in a nation's body politic so that from this point of view their departure should be welcome. But on the other hand, if large numbers of Jews were to leave, the world might believe "Zionist" charges of unbearable discrimination and might therefore question the validity of Soviet proclamations of the equality of all people under socialism; the USSR might lose invaluable scientists and technicians in whose education much has been invested (some of them might even have had access to classified information and thus pose a security problem); and Israel's armed forces might be greatly strengthened, to the detriment of the Soviet Union's Arab allies.

Recent official proclamations by Soviet leaders echo some of these fears and attest to the dilemma and to the complexity of the problem. Below are a few illustrative examples.

"Imperialist and Zionist propaganda in the West has recently been producing new fabrications about the departure of persons of

---

*The Soviet Union abstained from the 1948 vote but endorsed fully the 1960 Declaration on Colonialism, which required all states to abide "faithfully and strictly" by the Universal Declaration of Human Rights, and it also supported the 1961 and 1962 resolutions that re-affirmed it.

Jewish nationality from the USSR to Israel. Maoist propaganda has also had recourse to all kinds of slanderous inventions in this connection. . . .

"Small numbers of persons of Jewish nationality do apply to the appropriate Soviet organs requesting permission to leave for Israel. These persons may leave the USSR on the same grounds as other Soviet citizens, without distinction of nationality, ethnic group, sex or age.

"Requests concerning emigration are examined by organs of the USSR Ministry of the Interior according to rules established by law and are, generally, granted. . . .

"When applications to leave the USSR for Israel are examined, consideration is given, naturally, to the situation which has arisen in the Middle East. . . .

"It is for this reason that the competent organs introduce certain restrictions on the departure of some categories of Soviet citizens to Israel. The restrictions apply primarily to those who have had a certain degree of military training or are, by reason of their occupation, associated with work bearing on state interests. . . ." (April 1971)

Boris Shumilin, USSR deputy minister of the Interior[110]

"Jews who have families in Israel have the right to join them and Soviet authorities will raise no obstacle to the emigration of such Jews." (December 1971)

Izvestia[111]

"Whoever wants to emigrate to Israel has a *juridical* right to do so. As soon as peace has been restored to the region, the emigration procedure will be speeded up. . . .

"We do not want to see Russian Jews between 20 and 40 years of age going to swell the ranks of the Israeli Army." (February 1971)

(Jewish) Colonel General David Dragunsky, Soviet spokesman at the February 1971 World Conference of Jewish Communities on Soviet Jewry at Brussels [112]

As regards the emigration of Soviet Jews, "the preservation of the interest of the state and the so-called brain-drain will be taken into consideration." (1971)

Albert Ivanov, member, Central Committee, CPSU[113]

"As regards the reunion of families, if any families wish to come together or wish to leave the Soviet Union, for them the road is open and no problem exists here." (December 1966)

Alexei Kosygin, chairman, USSR Council of Ministers[114]

"There is no such thing as a Jewish question. . . . The Jewish people as well as all Soviet people are working hard and enthusiastically to build communism. . . .

"Perhaps it is true we restrict . . . those in whose education a great deal of money has been invested or those who could serve Israel as soldiers. . . .

"The pressure for Jewish emigration cannot be satisfied until the Middle East crisis is settled. . . ." (October 1971)

Alexei Kosygin, chairman, USSR Council of Ministers[115]

"The Soviet Union has no law restricting the emigration of its citizens if that departure is justified though it puts limits on certain categories of people connected with what is called national security." (June 1973)

Leonid Brezhnev, first secretary, CPSU[116]

But isn't it contrary to international law for a country to prevent its citizens from leaving? The Soviets argue that it is not, that Western contentions to the contrary notwithstanding, international law and UN pacts do give a state the right to restrict emigration. To wit:

"As for the standards of international law regulating human rights, it could be pointed out that a sovereign state is fully entitled, if it thinks it necessary, to restrict the emigration of its citizens. The right is recorded, for instance, in such an authoritative document as the International Pact [official title: Covenant] on Civil and Political Rights approved by the UN and signed by many states. Article 12, Paragraph 3 of the Pact says that the right to leave one's country can be restricted if this is stipulated by the law on the grounds of state security and in the interests of safeguarding law and order, the health or morals of the population, or the rights and freedoms of others."

Konstantin Gutsenko, deputy director, Research Institute of Soviet Legislation[117]

During the past few years, the Western world has been inundated with reports of harassment of Soviet Jews who apply for exit permits to Israel. University students have reportedly lost their fellowships and been expelled from school; wage-earners (whether factory workers, scientists, physicians, writers, or performing artists) have been dismissed from their jobs, often after collective trials by their peers;[118] and exorbitantly high fees have been charged, averaging 900 rubles for each adult emigré—about $1,000 before the devaluation of the dollar, the equivalent of almost half a year's wages for an average Soviet professional worker. Once a Soviet Jew has been notified that his application for an exit permit has been approved, he is given between

10 and 25 days to present documents attesting that he and all other members of his family going with him have resigned from their jobs, have returned their work books, their labor union books, and their military service books, have withdrawn their children from school, have left their apartment in good order or made necessary repairs, and have paid all required fees. There have been a few reports of families having done all this and also having sold their winter clothing, only to discover subsequently that their exit permits had been annulled, leaving them without job, home, or even suitable clothing.[119]

Since 1968-69, especially, there have been frequent reports of Jewish applicants for exit permits being arrested for a wide variety of alleged legal violations. Some have been charged with such relatively minor infringements as petty hooliganism or illegally importing Hebrew textbooks; others with more severe offenses such as attempting to bribe government officials, slandering "Soviet reality," or engaging in anti-Soviet activities; yet others with theft of government property or with "dangerous crimes against the state," such as treason. And sentences meted out have varied accordingly, from two-week jail terms to the maximum penalty under Soviet law other than the death penalty, namely 15 years in labor camps under "specially strict regime," plus confiscation of property.*

Some applicants for exit permits and their Western supporters have charged that these arrests and convictions were largely acts of repression intended to check the emigration movement. The Soviets disclaim any such intent, asserting that the accused were fairly tried,

---

*Death sentences in the Leningrad hijack trial of December 1970 were commuted to long prison terms. "Specially strict regime," usually meted out to "dangerous repeaters," is the most severe kind of imprisonment in the USSR. It entails solitary confinement, a bare cell except for a plank bed and a "slop tank" (no plumbing), one visitor per year, permission to send out but one letter a month, and a minimum caloric food intake. For greater detail and specific cases, see, for instance, "The Agony of Soviet Jews," Facts (New York: Anti-Defamation League of B'nai B'rith, n.d.), p. 6; Soviet Jewry, U.S., House of Representatives, Subcommittee on Europe of the Committee on Foreign Affairs, Hearings, 92d Cong., 1st sess. (Washington, D.C.: Government Printing Office, 1972), pp. 233-243, 257-261, 265-271, 280-294, and 300-301; Moshe Decter, ed., Redemption! Redemption! Redemption!: Jewish Freedom Letters from Russia (New York: American Jewish Conference on Soviet Jewry and Conference on the Status of Soviet Jews, 1970), pp. 18-19 and 76; and Richard Cohen, ed., Let My People Go! (New York: Popular Library, 1971), pp. 75-101 and 240-243.

judged, and found guilty of the crimes with which they had been charged. Undoubtedly, most if not all of the defendants had indeed violated Soviet law, as interpreted by the Soviet courts. However, such offenses as "hooliganism" or those covered in the RSFSR Criminal Code Statutes 70 (anti-Soviet propaganda) and 72 (anti-Soviet organization) are often defined vaguely enough to allow a wide spectrum of court interpretations. Add to this that charges have been brought against an unusually large number of hitherto loyal and respected Jewish citizens who had applied for exit visas; add furthermore that in many cases the sentences appear to have been unduly harsh; add finally the undeniable fact that the Soviets are less than happy at the prospect of a mass exodus of Soviet Jews and that there is evidence of other kinds of harassment (such as deprivation of jobs, as discussed above)—and some credence is lent to indictments of intended intimidation and attempted repression.

Perhaps because of the death penalties originally imposed (and later commuted), the case of the Leningrad hijacking attempt brought particularly strong reaction from the West. Some Western sources claimed that "the defendants were prosecuted solely for their desire to go to Israel."[120] Procedures were denounced bitterly for alleged entrapment (the pilot who offered to fly the Jews out of the Soviet Union was assertedly a planted informer), extorted confessions, prearranged convictions, partiality of judges and even of defense lawyers against the accused, and undue secrecy during the trial.* The Soviet News Agency Tass labeled the protests but another fit of "anti-Soviet hysteria," asserted that they were instigated by Israel for the purpose of diverting attention from the "sinister doings" of the defendants, and charged "Zionist circles in the U.S." with "interfering in Soviet judicial procedures."†

On August 3, 1972, the Presidium of the USSR Supreme Soviet enacted an enabling decree that provided that Soviet citizens leaving the country to take up residence in nonsocialist countries must "reimburse the state for expenditures for their education in institutions of higher education, graduate schools, medical internship, graduate studies at military colleges, and for academic degrees received for

---

*There was a second Leningrad trial in May 1971 in which eight out of nine defendants charged with organizing anti-Soviet activity were also accused of having been accomplices of the 12 hijackers convicted in December 1970 and were given prison sentences of between 1 and 10 years.

†Tass, December 26, 1970. Criticism of the death penalties originally imposed came also from the French and Belgian governments, and even from the French and British communist parties—facts not mentioned in the Tass dispatch.

such education."[121] This "education tax" was estimated to run anywhere from $5,400 for graduates from teacher's colleges to $26,000 for holders of the degree of "candidate" (approximately equivalent to the American Ph.D.)* and to over $37,000 for more advanced degrees[122] (and in the case of one prize-winning scientist was reported to have been set at $60,000);[123] it appeared that the tax might affect as many as one-third of those wanting to emigrate to Israel;[124] and the Israelis feared that it would cost $500 million "to secure the emigration of 65,000 Jewish professionals now awaiting exit visas."†

In the West, the new exit charges were regarded as yet another, novel form of harassment, another form of discrimination, against Jews desirous to leave for Israel. Coming shortly after President Richard M. Nixon's trip to Moscow, and at a time when U.S.-Soviet relations were to be "normalized" and trade was to be expanded, the August 1972 decree evoked extraordinarily bitter resentment, more bitter in some respects even than that which was kindled by the Leningrad trials. Rabbi Meir Kahane, leader of the radically militant Jewish Defense League, threatened that his group would kidnap Soviet diplomats if the education tax for emigrés was not rescinded within a month; over two-thirds of the U.S. Senate went on record opposing the extension of most-favored-nation status to the Soviet Union‡ as long as the exit taxes continued to be levied;[125] and the following spring, when the White House tried to persuade the Senate to abandon its position, Presidential Assistant Peter Flannigan was given the "blunt message" on Capitol Hill that "unless Moscow permits freer emigration of Soviet Jews to Israel, the White House has absolutely no chance of succeeding in its efforts to get 'most favored nation' trade treatment for Russia."[126]

---

*The doctor's degree in the Soviet Union is a degree higher than the U.S. Ph.D.

†United Press International report from Tel Aviv, August 22, 1972. The estimate of 65,000 Jewish professionals seems exceedingly high if compared, for instance, with the figure of 120,000 total applicants for exit permits to Israel (for Jewish Soviet men, women, and children from all walks of life) given by Israeli sources in early 1973. (See page 39 above.)

‡Granting "most-favored-nation" status to the Soviet Union means that the United States would extend to the Soviet Union any tariff reduction extended to any other, including the "most favored," nation—that is, import duties charged for the importation of any Soviet product would be no higher than those charged for the importation of that product if it emanated from the "most favored" nation with which the U.S. transacts business.

The Soviets, for their part, defended the new law. They explained that higher education required large investments, that in the USSR such investment expenditures were borne by the state, and that most Soviet students received state scholarships adequate to cover room and board as well as education-related expenses (for seniors such stipends are equal to minimum wages!). During the two or three years preceding the decree, the Soviets pointed out, one of the major UN agencies, UNESCO, had explicitly recognized that a country's progress could be seriously impaired by a "brain drain"; had, in a special resolution, urged UNESCO members to limit overtures to foreign scientists and specialists that would encourage them to leave their countries or not to return home; and had entertained proposals for effective steps to restrict the braindrain , among them a proposal to require compensation "for the losses caused by the drain of highly trained personnel."[127] In any case, the Soviets emphasized, the August 1972 decree was in no way discriminatory since it applied equally to all Soviet citizens. (While this was certainly true as far as the wording of the new law was concerned, the fact remains that in recent years applications for exit visas to nonsocialist countries have come principally from Soviet Jews.)

The law was on the books. But, apparently acceding somewhat to outside pressures, the Soviets lowered the reimbursement charges in December 1972. Moreover, the assessments were reduced by 25, 50, and 75 percent for men with a working record of 8, 15, and 25 years and for women with a record of 6, 12, and 20 years, respectively; men who had reached the age of 60, women who had reached the age of 55, and invalids were exempted altogether; and the authorities were also empowered to grant complete exemption to emigrés with inadequate financial resources.[128] After mid-October 1972, hundreds of working-age Jews with a higher education who were unable to pay the tax were actually given permission to leave without making restitution to the Soviet state;* and in April 1973 the law was rescinded.[129] The Soviet

---

*Such permission was, for instance, granted to 19 or 20 Jewish families from Moscow in October 1972, even before the new list of reduced payments was published (CBS News, October 18, 1972; also Associated Press report, October 19, 1972). Israeli sources report that out of a group of some thousand college graduates, about two out of every five did not have to pay the education taxes (Jerusalem Post, Weekly Overseas Edition, January 9, 1973). According to early 1973 Soviet sources, 530 emigrants were "recently" allowed to leave without refunding the costs of their education (B. T. Shumilin, "On the Departure of Soviet Citizens for Other Countries," Novosti Press Agency release distributed by the Soviet Embassy, Washington, D.C., n.d., received March 27, 1973).

Union's embittered Arab allies charged that the reported suspension of the emigration tax made Moscow an "instrument of Zionist aims."[130] "What is the use of Soviet friendship and assistance," asked one Arab leader, "if the Soviet Union continues to provide our enemy with human resources of various specialization?" And calling this action "a great conspiracy against the Arabs and the Palestinians," he demanded that it be stopped.[131] The Soviet Union's official counterargument that only 42,000 Jews had emigrated from the USSR to Israel in the past 42 years while more than 1.5 million had gone to Israel from the various Arab countries did not seem to convince the Arabs.[132] All in all there is no denying that over-all Soviet policy towards Jewish emigration eased up greatly during the early 1970s—and emigration figures prove it. In the early 1960s, no more than 200 Soviet Jews left the USSR annually to take up permanent residence in Israel;[133] in 1970, the figure stood at 1,000;[134] in 1971, it jumped to between 13,000 and 15,000;[135] in 1972, it reached an incredible 32,000,[136] 50 percent more in that one year than during the preceding quarter of a century;* and the Soviets assert that in 1972 permission to emigrate was granted to 95.5 percent of Jews who applied to go to Israel.[137] During the first half of 1973, emigration averaged more than 3,000 per month—an annual rate of 36,000-40,000.[138]

Among the reasons for the liberalization of Soviet policy, Westerners speculate, could be Soviet desires to rid their land of the most vociferous protesters, to flood Israel with immigrants (especially with the very young, the very old, and those for whose skills there is little use in Israel, such as unskilled workers and Soviet lawyers), and to implant in Israel a sizable Russian population (which could be a political asset in years to come when trials and tribulations are forgotten and "the good old days" remembered longingly). Or the Soviet leadership may simply have arrived at the conclusion that for the sake of domestic unity and tranquility and of good relations with the United States, it would be the better part of wisdom to reduce the curbs on the emigration of Soviet Jews.

Many Western supporters of would-be Jewish emigrés are not satisfied. Convinced of the inherent right of <u>every</u> Jew who so desires to leave the Soviet Union, they are unwilling to settle for anything less than complete freedom to depart without interference. Tying this demand to the previously mentioned prospective preferential trade

---

*From 1946 through 1971, 21,000 Soviet Jews are reported to have emigrated to Israel (<u>Keesing Contemporary Archives</u>, vol. 18 [London: Keesing Publishing, November 20-27, 1971], p. 24918). In 1972, Soviet Jews made up over half of that year's total immigration into Israel (Associated Press report from Jerusalem, May 7, 1973).

agreement with the Soviet Union, an amendment was proposed in the U.S. Senate that would require the president to certify that emigration was not being restricted before granting trade preferences to the USSR or to any other communist country. Sponsored by Senator Henry M. Jackson, the amendment had no fewer than 77 cosponsors in the U.S. Senate. When Leonid Brezhnev came to the United States in mid-June 1973 and discussed the issue of Soviet Jewry, senators commented that they "detected a willingness on the part of Mr. Brezhnev to compromise on the Jewish issue" and that they were hopeful that a way out of the impasse could be found; and Jacob Stein, chairman of the Conference of Presidents of Major American Jewish Organizations said that he "sensed a strong desire by the Soviet Union to arrive at an agreement."[139] But as this book goes to press, the issue is still unresolved: There has been no definite commitment on the part of the Soviets to permit free emigration of Jews and none of the U.S. senators who cosponsored the amendment appear to have changed their attitude on the matter.

Jews the world over, and particularly U.S. Jews, have been contributing generously to help defray the increasing expenses of resettling Soviet Jews in Israel;* and the U.S. Senate voted $85 million to assist in the project. Israel has gone out of its way to minister to the needs of Soviet Jews and to even give them special preferential treatment—for instance in housing, where one-quarter of all new apartments built in 1972 have been earmarked for them. Yet, for many, adjustments are difficult and the stark realities of life in Israel cannot match the overglorified image of their dreams back in the Soviet Union. There are the unaccustomed surroundings, a radically different climate, a new language—in all, a real "culture shock," especially hard on the older generation. And a religious Jew who had looked forward to a truly religious environment in Israel might find himself in a factory among nonreligious coworkers or in a housing development among nonreligious neighbors; a convinced atheist might feel totally lost on the sabbath, when virtually all activities cease; a professional man or woman or a skilled worker might have to adapt to totally strange and unfamiliar techniques and standards; a former Soviet lawyer, Communist Party secretary, or professor of Marxism-Leninism might find few employment opportunities for a person with his background and experience; a family settled in a new apartment might encounter the bitter resentment of some oriental Jews who had lived in slums for over two decades and of _sabras_ (native Israelis) returning

---

*The cost of absorbing an immigrant family in Israel is estimated at around $35,000 (Anatole Shub, "From Russia with Chutzpah," _Harpers_, May 1972, quoting Israeli sources.)

from military duty, ready to get married, only to find housing space hard to come by.[140]

There is no doubt that some of the emigrants who left the USSR for Israel are so unhappy that they wish to return to the Soviet Union—and some have indeed gone back. A 1972 English-language booklet, published by Novosti, Moscow,[141] contains excerpts from letters from such Soviet emigrés in Israel, addressed to Soviet Government institutions and to friends and relatives in the USSR. In these letters, writer after writer deplores his or her decision to emigrate to Israel as a "gross," a "terrible," a "catastrophic" mistake, and all beg for permission to return to the Soviet Union. Inquiries dispatched to seven of the letter-writers by this author brought three replies, all of which confirmed the authenticity and veracity of the statements reprinted in the Novosti booklet. (A second part of the booklet consists of letters to Soviet newspapers, of interviews, and of statements at press conferences by emigrants who had returned to the USSR.)

The Israelis do not deny Soviet reports of dissatisfied emigrants wanting to go back; but they dismiss their numbers as insignificant. Moshe Rivlin, secretary-general of the Jewish Agency, commenting on a report from Vienna that 93 Soviet Jews had cabled a personal appeal to Brezhnev, seeking permission to return, said recently that out of some 45,000 Soviet Jews who had arrived in Israel in 1971-72, only 86 had left again with the intention of going back to the Soviet Union.[142] At the other extreme, several of the emigré letter writers in the Novosti booklet referred to above assert that all the Soviet emigrants they know want to "go back home." But the claims of Soviet officials are much more modest; they say that by May 1972 they had received some 1,500 complaints from Soviet Jews in Israel about conditions there and that several hundred emigrés had asked permission to return to the USSR.[143]

The credibility of Soviet allegations of disenchantment of Soviet emigrés in Israel was greatly enhanced when in mid-July 1973 several thousand new immigrants from Soviet Georgia went on hunger strikes and rioted in the Israeli port city of Ashdod, demanding better jobs and living conditions. According to reports from Israel, enraged demonstrators seized most of the public buildings in Ashdod and beat up government officials; and one of their spokesman, Yehuda Yousef Schvili, shouted angrily that "we lived like kings in Georgia compared to this place," asserting that half of the Georgians in Israel (some 16,000 having arrived in 1971-72 alone) would return to the Soviet Union if they could.[144]

SUMMARY AND CONCLUSIONS

During the nineteenth and early twentieth centuries, the Russian Empire was a hotbed of violent anti-Semitism.* Restricted to live within the Pale of Settlement, despised and vilified, their professional opportunities greatly limited, their very lives frequently threatened and often at the mercy of crazed mobs, Russian Jews, by consciously designed Czarist policy, were made the underdogs, the scapegoats of prerevolutionary Russia.

Under Soviet rule, the professional orientation and the social and political fabric of the Jewish population have undergone fundamental changes. In prerevolutionary Russia, many Jews were self-employed merchants, tradesmen, and small shopkeepers; but with the exception of the brief NEP period (1921-28) there was no place for private enterprise in Soviet society. For those unwilling or unable to meet the exigencies of a socioeconomic system devoid of private business and private ownership of the means of production, life became hard—not because they were Jews but because they were remnants of the bourgeois past. But for other Russian Jews, opportunities were opened up such as had not existed for them before. They were given the right to a university education, to the pursuit of a career of their choice, and to integration into Russian society. From their ranks, from the sons and daughters of Jewish tailors, shopkeepers, and tradesmen, have come doctors, scientists, artists, authors, Lenin Prize winners, "heroes of labor," "heroes of the Soviet Union."

But there have been ups and downs for Soviet Jews—times when the future has seemed bright and they would henceforth be equals among equals, and times when their lot has looked precarious and the future foreboding. There were the exceptionally good years from 1917 to the beginning of the 1930s; then came Stalin's purges, which decimated the ranks of Lenin's Jewish associates and of old-time revolutionaries and loyal Party members in general, purges that inculcated understandable fear in the hearts of Soviet Jews; there followed the days of World War II when those Soviet Jews who did not fall under Nazi occupation again had reason to believe that whatever anti-Semitism might have existed in the USSR was a thing of the past; then, by 1948, new purges brought with them the liquidation or exile to Siberia of large numbers of leading Jewish artists, workers, musicians, and intellectuals who, Stalin feared, might encroach on his position as absolute ruler; and after Stalin's death, when the "thaw" of the

---

*One observer referred to it as "the locus of the world's most virulent anti-Semitism" (John A. Armstrong, "The Jewish Predicament in the Soviet Union," Midstream, January 1971, p. 27).

Khrushchev era began to melt the ice of Kremlin rigidity, Soviet Jews dared to hope once again; but once more they were disappointed; in a nation of citizens all presumably equal, they were in some respects made to feel less equal than others.

Since Khrushchev's demise, the dramatic changes in the lives of many Soviet Jews have not been the result of any new domestic policies. It was, rather, the Israeli victory in the six-day war of 1967 and the subsequent all-out backing of the Arabs by the Brezhnev-Kosygin regime that aroused in Soviet Jews deep-seated emotions and that led to a resurgence of national identification with Jewish people the world over. Consequently, a substantial minority of Soviet Jews, themselves not necessarily anti-Soviet or antisocialist, began nevertheless to look towards Israel as their true homeland.* The Soviets' reluctance to let all those who want to emigrate depart freely may be undesirable from the point of view of the would-be emigrés and of their friends and relatives abroad; it may be attacked as morally and legally questionable; but there is no reason to assume that in and of itself it is anti-Semitically motivated. However, the situation of many of the applicants for exit visas to Israel, and especially the situation of those among them who are highly educated and of working age, probably seems to them to be as shaky as that of a fiddler on the roof.

The Soviets are understandably sensitive when charges of anti-Semitism are brought against them. Discrimination of any kind against any nationality is contrary to everything Marx, Engels, and Lenin believed in; it is in violation of the Constitution of the USSR and of the Program of the Communist Party of the Soviet Union; it is inimical to all that socialism is supposed to stand for, to all that Soviet youth is taught, from nursery schools through universities, about the morality of Marxism-Leninism, about the final goal of communism, the brotherhood of all mankind, towards which all must work. In that "final stage" of humanity's social development, the nationality problem will have been solved, according to communist ideology, by the abolition of nations and the disappearance of nationality differences. Hence, the very Program of the Communist Party of the Soviet Union that contains assurances that under Soviet socialism (the "intermediate" stage on the road to communism) "nations flourish and their sovereignty grows stronger" talks about the "growing *rapprochement* of

---

*It certainly appears to be only a minority of Soviet Jews. Except for assertions by some extremists such as Kahane, even the very highest Western estimates do not claim that more than half a million Soviet Jews—fewer than one in four—would want to emigrate. And the number of those who have actually applied for exit visas is only a fraction of that.

their cultures" and calls for the eventual "obliteration of national distinctions, and especially of language distinctions."[145] Since the Soviets describe this general integration process as a natural, gradual, and voluntary development in Soviet society, they deny any attempts to curtail forcefully or eradicate Jewish cultural distinctiveness and portray state policy as but a logical supportive concomitant of the gradual voluntary assimilation of Soviet Jewry into Soviet society.* It is the "Zionists," "Imperialists," and "enemies of socialism and of the Soviet Union," the Soviets hold, who have blown all out of proportion steps taken by the Soviet leadership, who have labeled such steps as "anti-Semitic," who have presented them improperly and unjustly as attacks on the rights of Soviet Jews as individuals and as Soviet citizens, and who have invented alleged spheres of discrimination where none exist.

Whatever the motivations, there is hardly any doubt that from the very outset an all-out assault was launched on the Jewish heritage—first, with the full support of the revolution's top Jewish leaders, on the Jewish religion and on Zionism, and soon thereafter also on Jewish culture, customs, and traditions. At times, this assault has been relatively adamant, relentless, and uncompromising; at times it has been more forbearing, moderate, and subtle; at rare times (such as during part of the World War II era) it may even have been in temporary remission. Yet, it has been ever present as a distinctive feature of the Marxist-Leninist legacy, which prescribed and predicted that under socialism not merely anti-Semitism but also Judaism as such would in due course be eliminated and Jews would be absorbed into the mainstream of socialist society.† It would appear, however, that since

---

*The Party Program sees the obliteration of national and language distinctions as "a considerably longer process than the obliteration of class distinctions" (Programme of the Communist Party of the Soviet Union, adopted by the 22nd Congress of the CPSU, October 31, 1961 [Moscow: Foreign Languages Publishing House, 1961], p. 103), and Khrushchev once said that to overcome nationalism will be even harder and take longer than to overcome religion. In the meantime, the free development of nationalities, including the free development of languages and the right to speak, and educate one's children, in any language one chooses, is guaranteed in the Party Program (p. 104). "The way to the future merging of nations lies through a long period of development of the nations, their cultures and languages" is the manner in which one Soviet book explains it (Solomon Rabinovich, Jews in the USSR [Moscow: Novosti Press Agency Publishing House, n.d.], p. 61).

†It should be pointed out that notwithstanding the indescribably bad situation of Russia's Jews under the Czars, Hebrew and Yiddish

the death of Lenin the eradication of Judaism has often been a more vigorously pursued, more immediate target and the complete assimilation of Jews a somewhat more distant end.

In light of the general goals the Soviets have set for themselves, and in light of the over-all economic and social position of Soviet Jews, it would certainly be a gross exaggeration to label Soviet attempts to discourage Jewish religion and Jewish culture as "rampant anti-Semitism"—deplorable though some Western observers find such attempts from the vantage point of their own ideological and moral orientation. Those who would equate the treatment of Soviet Jews today with that of Jews under the Nazis* or even under the Czars are surely patently wrong. Soviet Jews are not being exterminated; they are not rounded up and thrown into concentration camps; there is not a single law directed against them as was the case under Hitler and under the Czars; they are not being dispersed; their freedom of movement, their rights to change jobs and take up residence wherever they desire are equal to those of other Soviet citizens; and theirs is certainly not a life of gross material deprivation. On the contrary, their average income is higher than it has even been before in that part of the world. Moreover, since disproportionately large numbers of Soviet Jews have a higher education, live in cities, and are artists, scientists, professionals, and white-collar workers, their per capita income today

---

were spoken within the Jewish settlements under Russian jurisdiction, the Jewish religion was practiced, Jewish customs were observed, and Jewish culture and tradition were passed on from generation to generation.

*This refers to such statements as the following: "The world regards [the USSR's] treatment of its Jewish citizens as sheer barbarism" (Philip Hoffman, president of the American Jewish Committee, in Richard Cohen, ed., Let My People Go! [New York: Popular Library, 1971], p. 134); "Those of us who remember the tragedy of the Warsaw ghetto uprising and the thousands of Jewish lives that were lost in that heroic encounter with the Nazis are fearful that history may repeat itself" (Rabbi Zev Sega, chairman of the Essex County Conference on Soviet Jewry and past president and honorary president of the Rabbinical Council of America, in Soviet Jewry, U.S., House of Representatives, Subcommittee on Europe of the Committee on Foreign Affairs, Hearings, 92d Cong., 1st sess. [Washington, D.C.: Government Printing Office, 1972], p. 76); or "Insofar as equating the holocaust in Germany with what is transpiring in the Soviet Union, insofar as Jews are concerned, there is no difference" (Bertram Zweibon, national vice chairman, Jewish Defense League, in Soviet Jewry [Hearings], p. 70).

is well above that of the population at large and is undoubtedly larger than that of any of the more than 100 nationalities that constitute the people of the USSR.

Does this mean, then, that the Soviets are right when they assert that Jews have been accorded and are now accorded treatment equal to that of other citizens of the USSR? Although many of the Soviet actions that have detrimentally affected some Soviet Jews may not necessarily have been discriminatory in nature, such an assertion goes too far to the other extreme and is not tenable either.

Opposition to Zionism dates back to the very beginnings of Soviet socialism. Lenin, as early as 1903, condemned it as a "completely false, reactionary concept";[146] yet, for reasons discussed earlier, Stalin backed the formation of the State of Israel in 1948. To understand the extremely bitter opposition to Zionism one must realize that to the Soviet mind the term means much more than merely favoring the existence of the State of Israel. As the Soviets perceive it, Zionism is an ideology aimed at creating a unity of Jews that transcends national boundaries; at dissuading Jews from assimilating into the cultural life-stream of other countries; at luring them to the "promised land"; at conveying the impression that Israel is not just the land of the Israelis but the Jewish state, the official and only true representative of Jews irrespective of their citizenship. And the idea that Soviet citizens, Jews or not, can regard a country other than the Soviet Union as their homeland is totally unacceptable. Since the 1950s the Soviets have depicted Zionists as U.S. allies in the Middle East, with Israel as a stronghold of "American imperialism"; and since the six-day war of 1967 they have branded Israel an "imperialist aggressor" nation in its own right.

Attacks on the Jewish religion may be partially explicable in terms of the official Soviet policy of promoting atheism: They may not be as vehement as those launched against some other religious groups (particularly sects with tenets that interfere with over-all Soviet policy, for instance by forbidding adherents to serve in the armed forces); but there appears to be evidence of discriminatory treatment, especially as compared with the major religious denominations.

The Soviet posture towards and curbs on Jewish culture certainly seem discriminatory. It is true that in the United States there are no publicly supported Yiddish-language schools either, and Yiddish-language theater performances are few and far between. But in the Soviet Union, the right to public education in one's native tongue is guaranteed to all nationalities in the Constitution and the Party Program; other nationalities do have schools and courses in their own languages while Soviet Jews do not, and these other nationals enjoy more cultural privileges and command more respect for their cultures than their Jewish fellow citizens. A Soviet citizen of Russian or Ukrainian nationality can hold the highest and most influential Party or government position and still adhere to and observe fully, openly, and proudly the traditions and customs of his ancestors, while the same would hardly hold true for a Soviet Jew. Finally, even if it were granted that campaigns launched under Stalin, Khrushchev, and Brezhnev and Kosygin against the Jewish religion, the Jewish heritage, and against Zionism have not been anti-Semitic in nature, they certainly appear to have often had the effect of stirring up age-old anti-Semitic sentiments among Soviet citizens who must have found it difficult to distinguish "regular" Jews from those who were stereotyped and reviled for their customs, their traditions, their religious and cultural practices, and their alleged attachment to Zionism.

In addition to attacks against various aspects of Judaism, there have been other actions, not directed against Jews alone, that, nevertheless, have involved relatively large numbers of Soviet Jews. There were, for instance, Stalin's purges of the Party and especially of the Party leadership in the 1930s that resulted in the liquidation of many Jews in high positions. One could argue that since Jews played leading roles during the revolution, and subsequently in the economic and political spheres of the new society, Stalin's purges necessarily involved many Jews. But the fact that those purged were generally not replaced by other Jews makes it difficult to discount charges that anti-Semitism played a role in the determination of who was and who was not to be eliminated. It is certainly true that the overwhelming majority of Soviet Jews were not affected by Stalin's purges, that many of them retained high positions, and that Jews were the recipients of state awards throughout the Stalin era; yet the fact that Stalin's post-World War II purges in the late 1940s involved such a disproportionately high percentage of Jewish intellectuals, artists, and doctors would seem to indicate that there is some truth to charges that Stalin became more and perhaps paranoically anti-Semitic during the last few years of his life. In a similar vein, Khrushchev's campaign against "economic crimes," with the special emphasis given to Jewish cases in the press, and the extraordinarily high percentage of Jews sentenced to death, would also appear to have had anti-Semitic overtones.

There have been charges of anti-Jewish discrimination in the field of higher education. It could well be that individual school administrators permit discriminatory practices to prevail. But the case for a general state policy of unequal treatment is inconclusive. The gradual decline in the percentage of Jews among Soviet university students is surely to a great extent due to increasing numbers of youths from formerly "backward," less developed parts of the USSR attending institutions of higher learning. And since there has been a continued <u>increase</u> of Jewish university students, both in absolute numbers and as a percentage of the total number of Soviet Jews, discrimination in higher education is not easy to prove. In the arts, the sciences, the professions—in the higher, well-paying positions in the Soviet economy in general—Jews are still represented in disproportionately large numbers. But there remains the obvious discrimination involved in Khrushchev's weeding out of Jews from the top echelons of the Party, the army, and the foreign service. The possible explanation (once advanced by Khrushchev) that the step was then pragmatically indicated to placate lingering popular (not official) anti-Semitism seems unacceptable. If this was the real reason, why, one wonders, have there been no all-out campaigns since the days of Lenin to combat anti-Semitism among the Soviet people? And if there is hardly any such anti-Semitism in the USSR any more, except in isolated cases of lingering remnants from the prerevolutionary era (as Soviet leaders assert), why has the Brezhnev-Kosygin regime failed to appoint Jews to positions from which Jews had been ousted under Khrushchev in numbers far exceeding their share in the Soviet population? There must be, and indeed there is, another compelling reason for making it so difficult for Soviet Jews to attain highly sensitive positions of political leadership, control, influence, and power.

Jews everywhere in the world belong to a people who, united by a common religion and a common culture, once lived in their own country. Although dispersed for two millennia in lands around the globe, Jews have never lost their bond of unity. In a sense, this common bond, this Jewishness, is anchored in Israel, a land that according to Jewish religion and tradition is the promised land, a potential homeland for Jews wherever they may dwell. And the overwhelming majority of Jews live in Israel and in the Western world, with the largest, wealthiest, and most influential community in the United States. All this makes Soviet Jews the only nationality suspect of having strong ties with leading "imperialist" countries. The resulting distrust and suspicion of Soviet Jews as Jews may well have been aggravated since the Israeli victory in 1967 by the number of formerly apparently loyal Soviet Jews who have begun to look to Israel as their true homeland. "We are not anti-Soviet but we no longer consider ourselves Soviets; we are Jewish," said a Jewish emigrant from the USSR in Israel.[147] "Of all nationalities in the Soviet Union, only we have our homeland," remarked another.[148] Comments such as these express the feelings of many of the Soviet Jews who want to leave for Israel; and in light of the Soviet Union's opposition to Zionism, of her alliance with the Arabs, and of her concept of Israel as a bulwark of anti-Soviet, Western imperialism, such comments also help to explain why the existence of that Jewish state has brought into question the basic loyalty of Soviet Jews. Jews who identify with the Jewish people, its history, its religion, its culture, its promised destiny are particularly suspect;

and a unified Soviet Jewry with at least some interests that transcend the borders of the USSR and of socialism, with at least some ideological and emotional links with countries deemed unfriendly towards the USSR, and even connected by friendship and family ties with Jews abroad, especially in Israel and in the United States, is unacceptable to the Soviet leadership (while other unified nationalities or religious denominations without similar ties may not be equally perturbing). Soviet Jews are therefore expected to disassociate themselves vigorously and unequivocally from Zionism and anything ideologically connected with it (which includes much of Jewish heritage and religion) and to identify themselves openly and vociferously with Soviet national interest as defined by the Party leadership. And from the days of Stalin to the present, Soviet leaders—apprehensive, suspicious, and mistrusting of Jews—have demanded without ever spelling it out or even admitting it that a Soviet Jew prove himself more than would be required of others before he could aspire to a sensitive position or to a position of political power. Yet it is probably true that, with the possible exception of the last few years of the Stalin regime, the Soviet Jews under Stalin and Khrushchev who were loyal to the regime, who were neither religious nor "Yiddish" nor "Zionist," who were willing to renounce their Jewish traditions and melt into Soviet society, and who did not have any sensitive or high-level political positions, had usually little more to fear than similarly situated non-Jewish citizens; and such Jews surely are in no way threatened under the current Brezhnev-Kosygin leadership, no matter what their position in society may happen to be.

In the final analysis, Soviet Jews have three choices. They can try to maintain their Jewish traditions and live as best they can a Jewish life in the USSR; they can attempt to leave the country; or they can abandon their Jewish heritage and in a sense their Jewish identity as well in an endeavor to blend into Soviet society. The first, to cling to the Jewish cultural, ethnic, and religious background and try to raise children in the Jewish tradition in the Soviet Union, is likely to prove increasingly frustrating; the second, emigration, primarily to Israel, is a path likely to be chosen by many, assuming that the situation in the Middle East does not deteriorate appreciably and that the Soviet leadership continues to relax its emigration policies; but the third, assimilation, can be expected to be the choice of the majority of Soviet Jews. As a matter of fact, the largest part of Soviet Jewry, and especially of Jewish youth, is apparently well on its way towards rapid assimilation. Intermarriage is very frequent, increasingly large numbers have renounced the Jewish faith in favor of state-endorsed atheism (in a recent survey of different religions in Byelorussia, an incredible 98.5 percent of Jews said they were atheists as compared with an average of 65.1 percent of 10 other faiths),* and the 1970 Soviet census showed an actual decline of the Jewish population, due to a considerable extent to assimilation.

There is, then, no rampant anti-Semitism in the Soviet Union today, but neither can one truly speak of complete equality in all respects. It has been shown that since Jews are considered generally poor security risks their chances of being appointed to high-level, sensitive political positions are small when compared to other groups; and Jews appear to be worse off than other ethnic minorities in regard to facilities to express their culture and live in the traditions of their forefathers. But there appears to have been no decline in opportunities open to Soviet Jews to attain well-paid positions of responsibility and respect in the Soviet economy; on the contrary, both in absolute and relative terms they rank remarkably high in education and economic status.

Barring unforeseen circumstances and assuming no material change in Soviet policy, whatever discrimination remains is likely to diminish and gradually fade away as more and more of those Jews who do not wish to surrender their Jewishness depart while the rest become increasingly assimilated into non-Jewish Soviet society and life.

NOTES

1. Bertram Zweibon, national vice chairman, Jewish Defense League, in Soviet Jewry, U.S., House of Representatives, Subcommittee on Europe of the Committee on Foreign Affairs, Hearings, 92d Cong., 1st sess., November 9 and 10, 1971 (Washington, D.C.: Government Printing Office, 1972), p. 70.

2. Quoted from the Young Worker, house organ of the Young Workers' Liberation League of the Communist Party of the United States, May 1971, in ibid., p. 275.

---

*Zvi Gitelman, "The Jewish Question," in Max Hayward and William C. Fletcher, eds., Religion and the Soviet State: A Dilemma of Power (New York: Praeger Publishers, 1969) p. 166. "Even allowing for the methodological shortcomings of the survey and the likelihood that Jews were more reluctant to declare themselves believers than others," Gitelman explains, "we cannot dismiss this figure entirely. Jews are very highly urbanized and concentrate in the larger cities, precisely where it is most difficult to practice religion and even where religion is weakest" (p. 167).

3. Richard T. Davies, then deputy assistant secretary for European Affairs, U.S. Department of State, in ibid., p. 295.

4. Gennady Terekhov in Solomon Rabinovich, Jews in the Soviet Union (Moscow: Novosti Press Agency Publishing House, 1967), p. 23.

5. Earl Raab, "The Deadly Innocences of American Jews," Commentary, December 1970, p. 39.

6. See, for example, Soviet Jews: Fact and Fiction (Moscow: Novosti Press Agency Publishing House, 1970), pp. 37-38.

7. Quoted by Deputy USSR Chief Prosecutor, Nikolai Zhogin, in Rabinovich, op. cit., p. 21.

8. New York Times, June 27, 1967.

9. See, for example, a September 5, 1965 editorial in Pravda.

10. Quoted from a 1966 Novy Mir article in Bernard D. Weinryb, "Antisemitism in Soviet Russia," in Lionel Kochan, ed., The Jews in Soviet Russia Since 1917 (London: Oxford University Press, 1970), p. 315.

11. Statement by Gennady Terekhov, reported in Rabinovich, op. cit., p. 21.

12. V. Bolshakov, Anti-Communism: The Main Line of Zionism (Moscow: Novosti Press Agency Publishing House, 1972) pp. 6-7. Sections of this booklet are reprinted on pages 172-187 below.

13. For example, Mezhdunarodnaia zhizn', June 1968.

14. See, for example, Komsomolskaya pravda, October 4, 1967. For similar, more recently published allegations, see pages 252-258 below.

15. Vladimir Katin, "Bankruptcy of Zionism," New Times (Moscow), no. 14, March 1971, p. 27.

16. Bolshakov, op. cit., p. 15.

17. J. Schrieder, "Zionism and the Swastika," New Times, no. 23, May 20, 1971, p. 25.

18. V. Bolshakov, Anti-Sovietism: Profession of Zionism (Moscow: Novosti Press Agency Publishing House, 1971), p. 11.

19. Krasnaya zvesda, March 10, 1970.

20. Pravda, March 6, 1970.

21. See, for example, Bolshakov, Anti-Communism: The Main Line of Zionism, op. cit., pp. 33-44. (In slightly abridged form, these pages are reprinted on pages 175-181 below.)

22. "The Agony of Soviet Jews," Facts (New York: Anti-Defamation League of B'nai B'rith, n.d. [1970?]), p. 2.

23. Hans J. Morgenthau, "The Jews and Soviet Foreign Policy," Perspectives on Soviet Jewry (New York: Academic Committee on Soviet Jewry and the Anti-Defamation League of B'nai B'rith, 1971), p. 87.

24. Paul Lendvai, "Jews Under Communism," Commentary, December 1971, p. 68.

25. La Stampa, November 18, 1972.

26. L'Express (Paris), April 2-8, 1973.

27. See, for example, Soviet Jews: Fact and Fiction, op. cit., p. 5.

28. I. Feldman in Kommunist Moldavii, June 1969.

29. See, for example, Vladimir Katin, "Zionist Crimes," New Times, no. 20, April 29, 1971, p. 11.

30. Col. General A. Tsirilin (Jewish), in Izvestia, February 27, 1970.

31. Pravda, March 6, 1970.

32. Soviet Jews: Fact and Fiction, op. cit., p. 6.

33. Herbert Gold, "The Soviet Jews Come Forward," Atlantic, May 1973, p. 100.

34. Trofim Kichko, Judaism and Zionism (Kiev: Tovarystvo "Znannia" of the Ukrainian SSR, 1968).

35. Ivan Shevtsov, In the Name of the Father and the Son (Moscow: State Publishing House Moskovskiy Rabochiy, 1970).

36. Richard Maas, chairman, American Jewish Conference on Soviet Jewry, "Fact Sheet on Soviet Jewry," in Soviet Jewry (Hearings), op. cit., p. 211. The "Fact Sheet" is reprinted on pages 89-98 below.

37. Shevtsov, op. cit.

38. Bolshakov, Anti-Communism: The Main Line of Zionism, op. cit., pp. 53-55. (In somewhat abridged form, these pages are reprinted on pages 182-184 below.)

39. Moscow Radio, March 6, 1969.

40. Kichko, op. cit.

41. Ivan Shevtsov, Love and Hate (Moscow: State Publishing House Moskovskiy Rabochiy, 1970).

42. See also page 44 above and note 68 below.

43. "The Agony of Soviet Jews," op. cit., p. 4.

44. See page 21 above.

45. Soviet Jewry (Hearings), op. cit., p. 114.

46. Schrieder, op. cit., p. 25.

47. "Fact Sheet on Anti-Jewish Discrimination in the Soviet Union" (translated from facts and figures compiled by the Bibliothèque Juive Contemporaine in Paris), in Richard Cohen, ed., Let My People Go! (New York: Popular Library, 1971), p. 145, gives a figure of "no more than forty" for 1971; Joshua Rothenberg, "Jewish Religion in the Soviet Union," in Kochan, op. cit., pp. 181-182, a figure of 62 for 1966.

48. JTA (Jewish Telegraph Agency), October 3, 1971.

49. Brandeis University Radio Station as reported by Associated Press, March 6, 1972.

50. "Fact Sheet," op. cit., p. 146 and Congressman Edward Koch of New York in Soviet Jewry (Hearings), op. cit., p. 114, both reported

only 3 functioning rabbis in the Soviet Union—and the chief rabbi of the Moscow Choral Synagogue, Yehuda Leib Levine, died November 17, 1971; JTA, October 3, 1971, gave the numbers as 6; Rothenberg, op. cit., p. 184 as "no higher than thirty-four to forty"; and Rabbi Mark H. Elovitz of Temple Beth El, Birmingham, Alabama, in Soviet Jewry (Hearings), op. cit., p. 12 as hardly "more than several times" the four rabbis in Birmingham.

51. Rothenberg, op. cit., p. 182.

52. 1973 Britannica Book of the Year (Chicago: Encyclopaedia Britannica, 1973) p. 597.

53. Rothenberg, op. cit., p. 185.

54. Alexander Werth, Russia: Hopes and Fears (New York: Simon and Schuster, 1969), p. 226.

55. See, for example, "The Agony of Soviet Jews," op. cit., p. 4, and "Fact Sheet," op. cit., p. 146.

56. Umberto Terracini, ed., Gli Ebrei nell' USSR (The Jews in the USSR) (Milan: Garzanti editor, 1966), Preface. Emphasis added.

57. For the report on the religious calendar, see Soviet Jews: Fact and Fiction, op. cit., p. 28; for a Western source on the rest, see, for example, "Fact Sheet," op. cit., p. 146.

58. William C. Fletcher's review of Joshua Rothenberg's The Jewish Religion in the Soviet Union (New York: Ktav Publishing House and Phillip W. Lown Graduate Center for Contemporary Jewish Studies, Brandeis University, 1971) in Slavic Review, September 1972, p. 700.

59. Chronicle of the Lithuanian Catholic Church, no. 1, 1972, samizdat (underground) publication as reported in "Recent Events Among Lithuanian Catholics," Radio Liberty Dispatch, February 15, 1973.

60. Peter Grose, "The Kremlin and the Jews," in Harrison E. Salisbury, ed., The Soviet Union: The Fifty Years (New York: Harcourt Brace and World, 1967), p. 423.

61. Moshe Decter, "Jewish National Consciousness in the Soviet Union," in Perspectives on Soviet Jewry, op. cit., p. 29; also, "Fact Sheet," op. cit., p. 45.

62. Boris Byalik, professor and doctor of Philological Sciences, in A Policy of Equality and Friendship (Moscow: Novosti Press Agency Publishing House, 1972) p. 30.

63. Soviet Jews: Fact and Fiction, op. cit., pp. 19, 25, and 26.

64. Solomon Rabinovich, Jews in the USSR (Moscow: Novosti Press Agency Publishing House, n.d. [1971?]), p. 65.

65. See, for example, Soviet News, May 17, 1966, p. 90 and Soviet Life, May 1972, pp. 28-29.

66. See, for instance, Hans Lamm, "Jews and Judaism in the Soviet Union," in William C. Fletcher and Anthony Strover, eds., Religions and the Search for New Ideas in the USSR (New York: Praeger Publishers, 1967), pp. 105-106.

67. Soviet Life, July 1971, p. 37.

68. For exact figures, see UNESCO Statistical Yearbooks, 1965-1970 (Paris, UNESCO), for 1965, pp. 373 and 378; for 1966, pp. 403 and 410; for 1967, pp. 434 and 441; for 1968, pp. 543 and 549; for 1969, pp. 647 and 653; and for 1970, pp. 708 and 715 in the respective yearbooks.

69. Soviet Jewry (Hearings), op. cit., p. 53.

70. William Korey, "The Legal Position of Soviet Jewry: A Historical Enquiry," in Kochan, op. cit., pp. 83-85; Ben Tzion, "The Jewish Question in the Soviet Union," New York Times Magazine, May 3, 1970; "The Agony of Soviet Jewry," op. cit., p. 4; "Profile of Soviet Jewry," in Cohen, op. cit., p. 173

71. Bernard D. Weinryb, "Anti-Semitism in Soviet Russia," in Kochan, op. cit., p. 317.

72. "Profile of Soviet Jewry," op. cit., p. 169, gives the figure as "an estimated 95 per cent"; Soviet Jews: Fact and Fiction, op. cit., p. 29, as 98 percent. As early as the end of the 1950s, the Soviet census showed 96 percent of Soviet Jews living in towns and cities (reported from the 1959 Soviet census in Rabinovich, Jews in the Soviet Union, op. cit., pp. 57-58).

73. Rabinovich, Jews in the USSR, op. cit., p. 65.

74. Boris Byalik in reply to a question posed by J. Poliakoff of the Jewish Telegraph Agency, as reported in A Policy of Equality and Friendship, op. cit., pp. 29-30.

75. Programme of the Communist Party of the Soviet Union, Adopted by the 22d Congress of the CPSU, October 31, 1961 (Moscow: Foreign Languages Publishing House, 1961), p. 104.

76. Decter, op. cit., p. 130.

77. Maurice Friedberg, "The State of Soviet Jewry," Commentary, January 1965, p. 41.

78. Rabinovich, The Jews in the Soviet Union, op. cit., pp. 78-79. The same paragraphs, mentioning the same courses and teachers (by name and rank), were included on p. 76 in the book's second edition, published three or four years later.

79. The New York Times, December 30, 1970.

80. Bolshakov, Anti-Communism: The Main Line of Zionism, op. cit., p. 74.

81. "Profile of Soviet Jewry," op. cit., p. 172.

82. Werth, op. cit., p. 226.

83. "Profile of Soviet Jewry," op. cit., p. 172.

84. Guy Vinatrel, "The Plight of Soviet Jewry," The American Zionist, December 1970, p. 33.

85. Religion in Communist Dominated Areas 6, May 15, 1967, p. 74.

86. Svetlana Alliluyeva, Only One Year (New York: Harper and Row, 1969), p. 148. Emphasis added.

87. William Korey, "The Origins and Development of Soviet Anti-Semitism," Slavic Review, March 1972, pp. 117-121, passim. Quote from p. 121.

88. "Fact Sheet," op. cit., p. 143.

89. Werth, op. cit., p. 227.

90. Narodnoe Khoziaistvo SSR, 1970 (Moscow: 1971), p. 651.

91. Pyotry Abrasimov (Soviet Ambassador to France), Soviet News, September 26, 1972.

92. This, for instance, is the reason given by Boris Byalik in A Policy of Equality and Friendship, op. cit., p. 29.

93. Soviet Jews: Fact and Fiction, op. cit., p. 23.

94. Mikhail Prokofyev, Soviet minister of Education, in Education in the USSR (Moscow: Novosti Press Agency Publishing House, 1968) p. 9.

95. Rabinovich, Jews in the USSR, op. cit., p. 55.

96. Boris Byalik in A Policy of Equality and Friendship, op. cit., p. 29.

97. Soyuz svobodnikh i ravnikh (Moscow: Novosti Press Agency Publishing House, 1972), p. 10.

98. Rabinovich, Jews in the USSR, op. cit., p. 55.

99. Werth, op. cit., pp. 225 and 227.

100. Alec Nove and J. A. Newth, "The Jewish Population: Demographic Trends and Occupational Patterns," in Kochan, op. cit., p. 154. (Alec Nove is professor of economics and director of the Institute of Soviet and East European Studies at the University of Glasgow and editor in chief of Soviet Studies; J. A. Newth is lecturer at Nove's Institute.)

101. Large Soviet Encyclopedia, 2d ed. (Moscow, 1950-1958), vol. 15 (1952).

102. Pravda, April 10, 1970.

103. "The Door Is Open Now, a Little," Newsweek, April 19, 1971, pp. 69-73.

104. Colonel General David Dragnusky, Soviet Life, July 1971, p. 36.

105. Statement by Boris T. Shumilin, Soviet deputy minister of the Interior, quoted in Theodore Shabad, "Moscow Defends Emigrant Policy," New York Times, March 28, 1972.

106. Professor Solomon Gilikov of Moscow University, quoted in New York Times, January 26, 1972.

107. Jerusalem Post, January 9, 1973.

108. For examples of mass protests, petitions, etc., see Cohen, op. cit., pp. 229-243 passim.

109. Conference Room Paper no. 85, February 7, 1963. For more details see William Korey, "Soviet Jewry's 'Right to Leave'—the Legal and Moral Issue", in Cohen, op. cit., pp. 200-212.

110. Soviet News, April 11, 1972, p. 111.
111. Izvestia, December 21, 1971.
112. Quoted in r.r.g., "Dragunsky Proclaims Juridical Right of Jews to Emigrate," RFE Research, USSR, February 24, 1971, pp. 1-2.
113. Facts on File, no. 11-17, 1971, p. 781.
114. Izvestia, December 5, 1966.
115. Associated Press report from Ottawa, Canada, October 21, 1971.
116. New York Times, June 15, 1973.
117. Soviet Life, January 1973, p. 42.
118. For specific cases, see, for instance, Cohen, op. cit., p. 129; Moshe Decter, ed., Redemption! Redemption! Redemption!: Jewish Freedom Letters from Russia (New York: American Jewish Conference on Soviet Jewry and Conference on the Status of Soviet Jews, 1970), pp. 19, 22, 47, and 57; Richard Krieger, executive director of the United Jewish Federation, after a visit to the USSR (Associated Press report, November 9, 1972); and statement by three American tourists who visited the Soviet Union and talked to Jews who had applied for exit visas for Israel, in Soviet Jewry (Hearings), op. cit., p. 201.
119. For a specific area, see for instance Decter, Redemption! Redemption! Redemption!, op. cit., 56.
120. Soviet Jewry (Hearings), op. cit., p. 265.
121. "Decree of the Presidium of the USSR Supreme Soviet: On the Reimbursement by Citizens of the USSR Who Are Leaving for Permanent Residence Abroad for State Expenditures for Their Education" (Vedomosti Verkhovnovo Soveta SSSR, No. 52 [1658], December 27, 1972, Item 519, p. 816).
122. New York Times, August 16 and September 22, 1972.
123. Gold, op. cit., p. 92.
124. New York Times, August 16, 1972.
125. Associated Press report, October 19, 1972.
126. U.S. News and World Report, March 26, 1973, p. 13.
127. For the above-mentioned resolution, see Acts of UNESCO General Conference, 16th session, Paris, October 12-November 14, 1970, vol. 1, Resolution 1, 243, p. 27. The proposal for compensation was brought up at the 89th session of the UNESCO executive committee, meeting in Paris on April 17, 1972. The Soviet position, as outlined here, was elaborated on by Konstantin Gutsenko, deputy director of the Research Institute on Soviet Legislation, in Soviet Life, January 1973, pp. 29 and 42.
128. B. T. Shumilin, USSR Deputy Minister of the Interior, "On the Departure of Soviet Citizens for Other Countries," Novosti Press Agency release distributed by the Soviet Embassy, Washington, n.d.; received March 27, 1973.

129. New York Times, April 19, 1973.

130. El Moudjahid (Algerian Government newspaper) March 23, 1973. Note that this was published three weeks before the emigration tax was officially rescinded.

131. From an address in early March 1973 by Libyan leader Muammar el-Qaddafi to a conference of Arab intellectuals in Benghazi, reported in Jean Riollot, "The Arabs and Jewish Emigration to Israel," Radio Liberty Dispatch, May 2, 1973, p. 1.

132. Statement by Igor Beliaev, prominent Pravda commentator and specialist in Middle Eastern and African affairs, at a seminar of the law faculty of Beirut University, reported in Al Nida (Beirut), March 20, 1973.

133. Lamm, op. cit., p. 108.

134. Fact Sheet on Immigration from the Soviet Union in 1972 and Cost of Absorption in Israel (Jewish Agency for Israel, February 1972) p. 1.

135. Ibid., gives the figure as 12,923; an Associated Press report from Moscow, dated March 13, 1972, as 13,905; and Henrick Smith ("1971 Has Seen Soviets Sharply Ease Curb on Emigration to Israel," New York Times, December 29, 1971) as 15,000.

136. Jerusalem Post, January 9, 1973.

137. Shumilin, op. cit.

138. Facts on File 33, 1702 (June 10-16, 1973): 503.

139. R. W. Apple, "Brezhnev Gets No Instant Results on Jews," New York Times, June 20, 1973.

140. For an interesting discussion of life for Soviet Jews in Israel, see Ernest Krausz, "Special Report: Israel's New Citizens," 1973 Britannica Book of the Year, op. cit., p. 387.

141. The Deceived Testify: Concerning the Plight of Immigrants in Israel, 2d ed. (Moscow: Novosti Press Agency Publishing House, 1972).

142. Jerusalem Post, January 9, 1973.

143. Reported in Anatole Shub, "From Russia With Chutzpah," Harpers, May 1972.

144. Terence Smith, "Angry Soviet Georgians in Israel Port City Await Improvements," reported from Ashdod, Israel, in New York Times, July 19, 1973.

145. Programme of the Communist Party of the Soviet Union, op. cit., pp. 103-104.

146. Shmuel Ettinger, "Russian-Jewish Relations Before and After the October Revolution," in Cohen, op. cit., p. 155.

147. Mendel Gordin, a 23-year-old biochemist, quoted in "The Door Is Open Now, a Little," op. cit.

148. Mrs. Rita Gluzman testifying before a U.S. congressional committee, in Soviet Jewry (Hearings), op. cit., p. 105.

PART II

READINGS

CHAPTER

3

SOVIET JEWRY: FACTS AND FIGURES

Several Zionist and Western non-Marxist organizations have released "fact sheets" on Soviet Jewry; the Soviet Union and Western Marxists have countered with "fact sheets" of their own. On some issues there is disagreement as to what the "facts" actually are (is there or isn't there a state policy that makes it more difficult for Soviet Jews than for non-Jewish Soviet citizens to attain positions of political power?); on others, the disagreement is not about facts but about causes (are there no Yiddish-language schools because Soviet Jews are discriminated against or because Jewish parents no longer want to send their children to Yiddish-language schools?); on yet others, the difference between Western non-Marxist and Soviet views is largely one of interpretation (when thousands of Jews sing and dance and make merry on the streets outside synagogues on Jewish holidays, is it a sign of national resurgence and open defiance of the Soviet Government or is it evidence that expressions of Jewish culture and traditions are permitted to flourish freely in the USSR?).

In the "fact sheets" in this section, opposing sides take divergent and often diametrically opposite positions on some of the most controversial issues concerning Soviet Jewry.

* * * * *

In the following selection, Richard Maass, chairman of the American Jewish Conference on Soviet Jewry, addresses himself to some of the most important issues connected with the position and treatment of Soviet Jews. Presenting his "fact sheet" in question and answer form, Maass expounds views generally reflective of those held by the majority of leaders and members of American

Jewish and Zionist organizations who concern themselves with what they believe to be "the plight of Soviet Jewry."

The Soviets would agree with some of the introductory statements, such as the fact that Jews rank eleventh in number among the more than 100 nationalities that constitute the peoples of the USSR, but they would challenge most of the answers to the questions posed as to factual accuracy, the correctness of causes attributed to phenomena or events discussed, or at least the significance of certain agreed-upon facts and the emphasis they merit.

FACT SHEET ON SOVIET JEWRY

Richard Maass

Q. How many Jews are there in the Soviet Union?

A. The 1970 official Soviet census recorded 2,151,000 Jews living in the Soviet Union. This signifies a marked decline from the official 1959 figure of 2,268,000. It is also significantly lower than a 1969 estimate of 3,000,000 made by NOVOSTI, the government press agency. However, some independent sources in East Europe, and in this country, place the estimate at close to 3,500,000.

The officially recorded decline may be due to the fact that many Jews, in these times of stress, prefer to be counted as members of non-Jewish nationalities—in most instances Russian. At the time of a census a Soviet citizen can claim any nationality, despite what is recorded on his internal documents.*

From Richard Maass, "Fact Sheet on Soviet Jewry," in Soviet Jewry, U.S. House of Representatives, Subcommittee on Europe of the Committee on Foreign Affairs, Hearings, 92d Cong., 1st sess., November 9-10, 1971 (Washington, D.C.: Government Printing Office, 1972), pp. 207-211. The answer to the fourth question, dealing with internal passports, has been inserted from "The Problem of Soviet Jewry," Answers and Questions, Pamphlet Number 7 (Jerusalem: Information Division of the Ministry of Foreign Affairs, December 1972), pp. 3-4. Reprinted by permission.

*According to official Israeli sources, "the figures of the latest Soviet population census, estimating the number of Jews at only a little over two million, are unreliable, because census-takers do not examine 'internal passports' (identity cards). Thus there is a distinction between 'census Jews' and 'passport Jews,' and there are about one million more of the second category" ("The Problem of Soviet Jewry," Answers and Questions, Pamphlet no. 7 (Jerusalem: Information Division of the Ministry of Foreign Affairs, December 1972), p. 3)—Editor.

Q. Where do they live?

A. According to the 1970 census, Jews are dispersed throughout the 15 Soviet republics. 36.6% of Soviet Jewry lives in the Russian Republic; 36% in the Ukrainian SSR, and 6.8% in Byelorussian SSR. It is estimated that well over 1,000,000 Jews live in Moscow, Leningrad, Kiev, and Odessa. There are also sizeable communities in Vilna, Kishinev, Minsk, Riga, and Tbilisi.

Q. What is the official status of the Jewish community?

A. In a formal sense, there is no Jewish "community" in the Soviet Union.

There is no Jewish religious community, although individual synagogues do have formal status in Soviet law. As distinguished from nationality, participation in the Jewish religion is a voluntary act.

Among the more than 100 nationalities in the USSR, Jews rank eleventh in number—and the numerical spread from seventh to eleventh place is less than three-quarters of a million.

Jews are identified both as a nationality group and as a religious faith. Jews ("Yevrei") have a fixed legal status as a nationality, a matter of strict juridical procedure.

Q. How are Soviet Jews identified as a nationality?

A. Apart from Israel, where circumstances and rationale are totally different, the USSR is the only State in the world which obliges every Jew (that is, the son or daughter of two Jewish parents) to register as a Jew under the rubric "nationality" (from the ethnic point of view) in his or her "internal passport" (identity card). The "internal passport" system of the days of the Czar was revived in 1932; under it, "nationality" must be registered, in the fifth rubric, and a holder's right to reside permanently in a given place, or to be employed, is always connected with the document. Registration by nationality has nothing to do with place of birth, mother-tongue, or culture. It has to do solely with ethnic origin, and affects over a hundred nationalities, from the large nations, such as Russians, Ukrainians, Uzbeks, and so on, to the small tribes in the east and in the far north, including the gypsies. Only a person with parents belonging to two different nationalities can, when first he gets an "internal passport" at the age of sixteen, choose between his mother's and his father's nationality, but not a third one. The USSR is a land of nationalities, and the most conspicuous recognition-mark of your identity there, at any rate if you are a non-Russian, is ethnic origin.

Q. What is Soviet policy on nationality groups?

A. Soviet ideology, law and practice actively encourage nationalities, whether territorially dispersed or concentrated, to perpetuate their group existence through cultural and educational institutions and activities in their own languages. (In the long run, however, gradual "Russification" may be the objective for most nationalities, especially non-Slavic.)

Q. How has policy been applied to Soviet Jewry?

A. In the first three decades of the Soviet regime, the state supported a wide network of cultural and educational institutions and activities for Jews in Yiddish, which was recognized as their official national language. For example, about 850 Yiddish language books were published in editions of several hundred thousand between 1932-39. Before World War II, there were ten permanent Yiddish theatres. As late as 1940, one hundred thousand youngsters were in Yiddish schools.

By 1948 Stalin had destroyed all Jewish communal-cultural institutions including publishing houses and printing presses which had issued a total of 110 publications in the previous three years. The remnants of the Jewish educational system were also dismantled. The famed Jewish State Theatre of Moscow was closed in 1949. Finally, many Yiddish actors, writers, and leaders were liquidated or imprisoned.

The essential elements of this policy were continued by Stalin's successors and for eleven years there were no books, publications, or theatres.

Q. What is the general situation today?

A. There is not a single Yiddish school or a single Yiddish class in the USSR, although Soviet law permits the organization of such classes at the request of ten parents. Intimidation, including the imprisonment of some active petitioners, has prevented such efforts.

There are no schools, classes, or courses in any language to enable Jews to learn Jewish history, culture or literature. The only place Hebrew is taught in the Soviet Union is in a Russian Orthodox seminary.

The Jews are even cut off from learning about their recent past. The heroism as well as the martyrdom of Soviet Jews during the Nazi holocaust has been constantly downgraded or ignored by Soviet authorities, including historians, local officials and the press. For example, at Babi Yar—the site of the Nazi slaughter of thousands of people, most of whom were Jewish—there stands a monument to the "citizens of Kiev." The authorities do not permit official memorial gatherings at the site, and they have tried to cover most of it with a new apartment development. In recent years Jews have come to Babi Yar on Tisha B'Av, and on the eve of the anniversary of the slaughter, as a symbol of protest against anti-Jewish policies.

Q. What about Jewish culture?

A. There is no Jewish publishing house or Jewish book distributing agency, and only token nods to Yiddish literature. Thus, few classic Yiddish writers, long dead and now part of general "Soviet history," have been published in small editions. On rare occasions the works of living writers have also been published. In 1964 some Yiddish publication was resumed, but only 15 Yiddish books were issued through 1969. In 1969, itself, there were 10 Yiddish books published; there were five published in 1970, and none in 1971.

Since 1961, a Yiddish literary magazine, Sovietish Heimland, has been published regularly. Much of its edition of 16,000—down from the original 25,000—is for export. In a few instances, contemporary Yiddish and Hebrew writers, especially pro-left Israelis, have been published in the journal. Most often the editor, Aron Vergelis, reflects official party and state views.

There is no longer any state Yiddish theater with a permanent base. However, there is a small amateur troupe in Vilna which has never been permitted to visit cities with large Jewish populations, such as Moscow. There are also about a dozen individual professional performers. In addition a few local amateur groups can be found in other smaller cities.

Q. How has Soviet policy been applied to other nationalities?

A. "A comparison with other Soviet nationalities exposes the basic injustices of their [Soviet Jews'] situation, for even the smallest nationality groups in the Soviet Union are given the opportunity to pursue a cultural, social and political life of their own denied to Soviet Jews." So wrote Bertrand Russell, February 27, 1966. This situation has not been radically altered.

We cite examples of nationality groups, smaller in population than Jews, which are provided educational and cultural facilities in their native tongue.

1. In the RSFSR (Russian Republic): Bashkirs, 1,181,000; Maris, 581,000; Buryats, 313,000. (Based on 1970 census.) In the Ukraine: Poles, 295,000 and Moldavians, 266,000 (1970 census); Hungarians, 149,000 (1959 estimate).

2. Case example: The 1,846,000 Soviet Germans dispersed and repressed by Stalin during and after World War II, were officially rehabilitated by his successors. Volga Germans have been encouraged to develop German language schools—publishing houses and book stores—libraries, radio and television broadcasts and stations—theaters—orchestras—and cultural associations.

Q. What is the official policy of the U.S.S.R. toward religion?

A. Ideologically it is committed to atheism, but formally it accords freedom of religious worship. According to official policy the Party, rather than the State, carries on anti-religious propaganda. By law the State asserts the principle of equality of religion.

Q. How has this policy been applied to Judaism?

A. The principle of equality has been observed in the breach insofar as Judaism is concerned. In Soviet society religious centers for various faiths are vital to meeting the needs of religious groups. Unlike other recognized religious bodies, Judaism is not permitted any central or coordinating structure; each congregation must function in isolation.

The late Rabbi Yehuda Leib Levin, of Moscow, who died on November 17, 1971, was one of three known ordained rabbis functioning in the European part of the Soviet Union. Increasingly in the past few years he was utilized as the authorized spokesman for religious Soviet Jews, and, in 1968 and in 1969, he was allowed to visit the United States and Hungary, respectively, the first such actions in decades. While he participated in a few meetings of religious leaders of various faiths and denominations from the several Soviet Republics, Rabbi Levin was the only Rabbi in Moscow and did not represent any official group of religious Jewish communities.

Q. How does Judaism compare to other, recognized religions, or "cults"?

A. Judaism, unlike other faiths

- Cannot publish periodicals and devotional literature including journals, prayer books and Bibles. After years of world protest, 10,000 prayer books were permitted in 1968 but only several hundreds were known to have been distributed;
- Cannot produce essential devotional articles such as "Talethim" (prayer shawls) or "Tfilin" (phylacteries);
- Cannot have regular and official contacts with coreligionists abroad as contrasted to the experience of Protestant, Catholic and Moslem faiths;
- Cannot publish (except in isolated instances, especially the "showpiece" Central Synagogue in Moscow) religious calendars, indispensible guides to religious holidays and observances.

Q. Have there been other official pressures applied to Judaism?

A. Yes. In contrast to other recognized religions, there are no Yeshivot, rabbinical schools or seminaries functioning because of bureaucratic maneuvers, such as a denial of housing permits to students. Thus, there are no rabbinic replacements.

The Soviet government allows theological students of many other faiths to study in their own institutions, as well as in foreign seminaries or religious educational institutions. Judaism is the only significant exception.

Synagogues have been closed in almost systematic fashion as a result of both direct and indirect government action. In 1956, there were 450 synagogues in the Soviet Union and in April of 1963, there were under 100. Today, according to non-Soviet sources, there are about 60 official synagogues, in addition to private prayer meetings. However, few of the former function all the time.

By 1962, restrictions on the public baking and selling of "matzoh," indispensable to the observance of Passover, had blanketed the country. Only a few years ago the ban was eased in the large Jewish population centers, after widespread protests from outside the country.

Q. What is the U.S.S.R. policy on anti-Semitism?

A. Soviet ideology condemns anti-Semitism and there are laws against incitement of hatred on religious, national and social groups dating from the Bolshevik Revolution. In recent years there have been a few public pronouncements, such as Premier Kosygin's in July, 1966, assailing anti-Semitism. In 1969, Pravda and Izvestia responded to criticism by simply denying the existence of anti-Semitism in the Soviet Union. This has been the formula in the last two years.

But there have also been manifestations of anti-Semitism, even in the post-Stalin years, such as the so-called "economic" trials in the late 50's and the early 60's.

In the guise of anti-religious propaganda, attacks on Judaism have been anti-Semitic and racist. While Soviet officials criticized the notorious Judaism Without Embellishment by Trofim Kichko, after world-wide public protest, other equally vicious material has been printed by government and Party publishing houses and newspapers, and broadcast on State radio.

In general, since the June 1967 Six-Day War in the Middle East, Kichko in Judaism and Zionism (1968), Yuri Ivanov in Beware Zionism (1969), Ivan Shevtsov in Fathers and Sons (1970), and other Soviet propagandists have intensified their efforts to debase Jews and Judaism, and to revive medieval anti-Jewish concepts, such as the canard of a world-wide Jewish "conspiracy."

This campaign reached a peak in 1970 when mass meetings were organized and prominent Jews, under pressure, publicly denounced Judaism, Zionism and any affinity to Israel. In defiance of official displeasure, however, other Soviet Jews countered with petitions to the Soviet government.

More recently and with increasing frequency, articles under such titles as "Zionism—a Racist Ideology" and "Zionism and the Swastika" have appeared denouncing Israel and those Jews in the Soviet Union whose sole desire is to move to Israel.

Q. Is there discrimination against Jews?

A. Apparently there is none in housing, nor in various aspects of social life. It also appears that employment opportunities in most fields are generally open, although advancement to highest ranks is almost impossible.

However, discrimination against Jews does exist in vital, decision-making sectors of Soviet society, particularly government, political life and in fields involving foreign contact.

The number* of Jews in the scientific field has also been declining sharply. In 1958, over 10% of Soviet scientific workers were Jewish; in 1966 the figure had dropped to 8%.

The quota system at universities, the key to advancement in Soviet society, operates, according to one study, "to the particularly severe disadvantage of the Jewish population." In 1935, Jews represented 13% of all university students, but by 1970 they comprised only 2.5%.

Q. How have Jews reacted to this policy?

A. Despite hostile pressures, there are ever-increasing expressions of courageous Jewish identification.

In 1969, Jews from all over the USSR began to assert their self-expression by petitioning leading governmental and Communist authorities, as well as the United Nations. They demanded freedom to go to Israel where they can live as Jews.

Tens of thousands of young Soviet Jews, who know little Yiddish or Hebrew, have gathered to sing and to dance outside synagogues in various cities. Initially held on Simchat Torah, this practice has spread to other festivals including the Sabbath.

In the western areas, under Soviet control only since World War II, the determination of those with traces of Jewish backgrounds to remain Jewish is clearly evident. Hebrew is being taught; informal study groups are being conducted; Jewish and Hebrew texts are circulated and/or reproduced by hand.

According to the 1970 census, nearly 380,700 Soviet Jews officially regard Yiddish as their "mother tongue." Thousands of others consider it a "second language," not listed on census tracts. The Soviet authorities speak of the lack of interest in Yiddish, but despite this, thousands of Soviet Jews have jammed the halls for the rare Yiddish concert occasionally permitted.

In the earlier protest period, individual Jews, such as Boris Kochubiyevsky, have publicly protested, usually on pain of imprisonment. Since then many thousands of Jews have publicly demanded to

---

*Should read "percentage" instead of "number"—Editor.

be allowed to emigrate, despite harassment and pressures at school and at places of work.

Groups of Jews, from many Republics, have staged sit-ins at local Party Headquarters, and have even demanded to be received by the Central Committee in Moscow in order to have their demands heard, notably the right to live as Jews in Israel.

Q. What has been the Soviet response to Jewish activism?

A. Not only was a major propaganda effort launched in the USSR and in the West, but the Soviets have tried to crack down, while avoiding the most extreme of Stalinist practices. In 1970 and through mid-1971 trials were staged in Riga, Kishinev and Leningrad at which the incriminating evidence included collections of Bialik's poems, Hebrew literature, and similar "illegal" material.

In December, 1970, the Soviet government brought nine Jews and two non-Jews to trial for allegedly plotting to hijack a plane in order to flee the country. Hoping to break the back of the Leningrad activist group, and to exploit the world-wide anti-hijacking sentiment existing at that time, the authorities imposed death sentences—which were later commuted—on some of the "conspirators." Today these and other "political/religious" prisoners of conscience are languishing in "strict regime" prison camps, where they are required to do hard labor on semi-starvation rations.

Q. Can anything be done to change Soviet policy?

A. The voices of concern have been growing. Thousands of human rights advocates throughout the world, including eminent Soviet scientists, have protested, despite Soviet denials of anti-Semitism.

Major Communist and Socialist parties, including those in France, Holland, Austria, Britain, the United States and Australia, have publicly reflected their concern as has the Council of Europe, the United States Government and the Socialist International. The American Jewish community and others have demonstrated a determination to continue to expose the pattern of discrimination against Soviet Jewry until Soviet policy is reversed.

In 1964, the American Jewish Conference on Soviet Jewry was organized. Other groups interested in advancing the cause of human rights for Soviet Jews have been formed in the United States, Europe, Israel, and Latin America. In February, 1971, many groups met in Brussels, at the World Conference of Jewish Communities on Soviet Jewry, where the delegates declared:

> Profoundly concerned for their fate and future, we denounce the policy pursued by the government of the Soviet Union of suppressing the historic Jewish cultural and

religious heritage. This constitutes a flagrant violation of human rights which the Soviet Constitution pledges to uphold. . . . To cut them off from the rest of the Jewish people, as the Soviet authorities are attempting to do, is a crime against humanity.*

Q. Have protests and interventions been helpful?

A. There is evidence to indicate that the Soviet officials are increasingly concerned about the unfavorable impressions circulating abroad. For example, they sent representatives to Brussels to hold a "counter-conference" and in 1971 various apologists, including Colonel General David Dragunsky, went to the United States and to South America.

When public protests became world-wide, the Soviet government launched a major public relations campaign and made new promises and minor concessions. (A major concession was the commuting of the death sentences for those convicted in the first Leningrad trial, in December 1970.) After the Brussels conference, the Soviet government also quietly increased the number of Jews allowed to emigrate to Israel.

Articles on Soviet Jewry by NOVOSTI Press Agency and in publications such as Soviet Life, aimed almost exclusively for foreign consumption, appear more frequently. Other examples are:

Official condemnation in 1964 of Kichko's book; and in 1970 of Shevtsov's books;

A lifting of the ban on matzoh;

A few Jewish books in Yiddish or in Russian;

An easing of some emigration restrictions;

An end to the "economic crimes" trials;

The printing of 10,000 prayer books;

The publication of the Yiddish literary journal, Sovietish Heimland.

This tokenism however still fails to provide the basic cultural and religious instrumentalities essential for Jewish survival, nor does it answer the demands of those Jews who no longer believe that Jewish life in the Soviet Union is possible and wish to emigrate to Israel. However, it does give hope that ultimately the Soviet government will act on the demands of a world-wide enlightened and outraged public opinion.

* * * * *

---

*For the full text of the Brussels Declaration and for the Soviet evaluation of the Brussels Conference, see pp. 190-192 and pp. 209-212, respectively—Editor.

In the following brief selection, official Israeli sources ask some pungent questions. All of them are based on the implied or alleged existence of highly unfavorable and discriminatory conditions for Jews in the USSR; all of them undoubtedly appear to the Soviets similar in nature to the well-known question: "Have you stopped beating your wife?"

SOME UNANSWERED QUESTIONS

If Jewishness is a nationality recorded in identity cards yet Jews are denied the "national" life which is enjoyed by other nationalities in the USSR—what can be the object of this form of registration, if not to make things easier for the authorities in discriminating against Jews?

Is there any other minority in the world which is barred from studying its own history, literature and ancient tongue; from celebrating its festivals as tradition bids; from writing about its experiences; from keeping in touch with its fellow-nationals in other lands?

For years, anti-Semitism, implanted so long and so deeply among the peoples of Eastern Europe, has been officially encouraged and propagated by the Soviet authorities. We may well ask, on the basis of our historical experience, what might happen to the flesh and blood objects of this sponsored hatred if Soviet society were to undergo a calamitous upheaval or a desperate crisis?

If a State robs a minority of its right to uphold a national and cultural identity, can that minority be prevented from fighting to regain its identity and the right of repatriation to its free, historic, Homeland?

Is not Soviet Jewry's struggle for its identity and for the right to go to Israel evidence that Zionism is a national liberation movement?

Are not the Jews of the Soviet Union, as Jews, entitled to the right of self-determination, exactly as are Ukrainians and Uzbeks, or even the Germans dispersed in the several Soviet Republics, who enjoy cultural and educational rights and exercise them in their native language? If so, why do the Soviet authorities withhold these prerogatives from the Jews alone?

If the Soviet Union will not grant the Jews parity with the Russians, the Ukrainians, the Uzbeks and the Germans, does that not

---

*From "The Problem of Soviet Jewry," Answers and Questions, Pamphlet no. 7 (Jerusalem: Information Division of the Ministry for Foreign Affairs, December 1972), pp. 19-20. Reprinted by permission.

signify that it is seeking to coerce them into what is, from the cultural and the human points of view, a status of inferiority?

If the citizens of a State must live with feelings of deprivation and discrimination, are they not at least entitled to the human right that is enshrined in the Universal Declaration on Human Rights—the right to depart?

* * * * *

Put together from a number of Soviet and Western Marxist sources, the following selection is intended to familiarize the reader with the official Soviet and Western pro-Soviet position on the situation of Soviet Jewry.

SOVIET JEWS: FACTS NOT FICTION

Some Zionist organizations have stated that Jews are oppressed in the Soviet Union. Is this true? What are the facts?

Q. Is there anti-Semitism in the Soviet Union?

A. Any manifestation of national intolerance, including anti-Semitism, is incompatible with the Soviet mode of life and severely punished by law.

The Declaration of Rights of the People of Russia was signed by Lenin on November 16, 1917, just after the victory of the Great October Revolution. It gave the same right to all peoples, including the Jews.

When the draft of this document was ready, Lenin added in his own hand: "The Council of People's Commissars orders all Soviets of Deputies to take drastic measures to eradicate the anti-Semitic movement. . . ."

The USSR Constitution and the penal codes of all the union republics provide for severe punishment (imprisonment from six months to three years or exile from two to five years) for any direct or indirect restriction of the rights of, or, conversely, the establishment of any direct or indirect privileges for, citizens on account of their

---

From Soviet Jews: Fact and Fiction (Moscow: Novosti Press Agency Publishing House, 1970) passim; "Soviet Jews: Facts and Figures," Soviet Life, July 1971, pp. 38-40; Mike Zagarell, "True Facts on Soviet Jews," Young Worker, November 1971, pp. 14-15; and Hyman Lumer, "The Truth About the Lies at Brussels," Daily World, magazine section, March 20, 1971, pp. M5 and M10. Reprinted by permission.

race or nationality, as well as any advocacy of racial or national exclusiveness or hatred and contempt.

In the USSR publication of anti-semitic literature is illegal and anyone who violates this is subject to a prison sentence. In the U.S. there is no such law, and as a result the U.S. is the number one world publisher of anti-semitic literature.

However, in the Soviet Union there still are isolated instances of anti-Semitism and prejudices towards an "alien" nation. As a rule it is people who are culturally backward, mainly older people, who still have such prejudices. National intolerance is manifested in disrespect for people of other nationalities, in insulting remarks, in attempts by certain parents to prevent "mixed" marriages of their children. In other words, these are isolated cases, survivals of the past which never turn into social conflicts and run counter to the nationality policy of the Soviet state and the Communist Party.

In the Soviet Union, it is hard to believe that there are restrictions on Jews visiting certain golf clubs in Britain or staying at certain hotels in the United States.

What is the reason for the still surviving manifestations of national intolerance in Soviet socialist society?

For centuries Russian tsarism fostered national discord and hatred between the nations of the Russian empire. In this way the aristocratic-landlord oligarchy and, subsequently, the bourgeoisie sought to keep the mass of working people in subjugation and to divert their discontent with the prevailing social system into national hatred and chauvinism. Widespread anti-Semitism was one of the manifestations of such a policy.

The Socialist Revolution of October 1917 eliminated the social and economic basis for national intolerance and discord.

Complete equality, rising material standards, encouragement and promotion of national cultures helped mold a closely-knit community of Soviet people of different nationalities. The inviolable friendship uniting the Soviet peoples was vividly demonstrated during the grim years of the war against fascism. Joint efforts of all Soviet nations in building a communist society helps eradicate the survivals of national intolerance, including anti-Semitism.

Q. What is the purpose for the introduction in the Soviet Union of the Domestic Passports indicating nationality?

A. The passport in the USSR is the main document certifying that the bearer is a Soviet citizen. It is issued to all citizens residing in the Soviet Union, irrespective of nationality, on reaching the age of 16.

The passport contains the photo of the bearer, indicates his surname, first name, and patronimic, the date and place of birth, nationality (not only Jewish but any other, too), domicile, registration of marriage, the number of children. Distinguishing marks of the bearer are not indicated.

The passports are necessary to enable Soviet citizens to exercise their rights guaranteed by the Constitution and to enjoy the benefits they are entitled to. These include the right to elect and be elected, the right to work, to free medical aid, to free education, free use of libraries, to maintenance in case of sickness and disability, the right of mothers of large families to obtain a grant, the right to hotel accommodation at reduced cost (Soviet citizens pay only about one-third of the amount paid by foreigners for hotel accommodation), etc.

The Soviet Union is a federative state incorporating over a hundred nationalities who are all Soviet citizens. This makes it necessary to specify in the Soviet passport the nationality of the bearer.

At the time when the Soviet passport system was introduced there were proposals to specify only the Russian or a few of the most numerous nationalities, or to denote nationality according to the place of birth or domicile. These proposals were turned down since they objectively could be construed as disregard for other nationalities or as an attempt at forced assimilation.

For that reason the bearer's nationality is determined by the nationality of his parents regardless of the place of birth or domicile (be it Russia, the Ukraine, Uzbekistan, Georgia, Latvia or any other republic). The bearer of the passport is free to choose the nationality of either parent.

Thus, the Soviet passport is an important means of national identification. Specifying nationality betokens respect for the nation of its bearer.

Q. What is the Soviet Union's attitude towards the Jewish religion?

A. The Soviet Union has nearly one hundred synagogues located in Moscow, Leningrad, Kiev, Vilnius, Riga, Kishinev, Tbilisi, Kutaisi, Tashkent, Odessa and many other cities. Besides, there are more than 300 minians in various places, large and small, where religious Jews live. (A minian is a group of at least ten Jewish male worshippers).

In the Soviet Union the Church is separated from the State. Therefore the number of churches, synagogues, mosques and houses of worship depends on the requirements and financial resources of the communities and parishioners and not on the state.

It should be mentioned that the majority of the Soviet people long ago became atheists, by no means as a result of state coercion. The overwhelming majority have a materialistic world outlook, and Jews are no exception.

There is no official record of the number of believers in the USSR. But selective sociological studies have shown that 3-6 percent of the Jews in the Russian Federation and the Ukraine are religious. In the Baltic republics—Lithuania, Latvia and Estonia—the figure is 5-9 percent, in Georgia, the Northern Caucasus and Bukhara—7-12 percent. Mostly they are aged people. In the Soviet Union, as all over the world, progress and science are winning the debate over religion.

However, during big religious festivals—Simhath Torah, Rosh Hashana, Passover—many non-worshipping Jews in keeping with national traditions gather near the synagogues to make merry, sing and dance. Jewish national dishes are frequently served in Jewish families on traditional holidays when relatives, friends and colleagues gather together.

In the Soviet Union believers are absolutely free to profess any religion and to perform their religious ceremonies and rituals. This is specifically stated in the Constitution.

Soviet Jews who wish to do so are also perfectly free to practice their religion. Any group of 20 or more may establish a synagogue, and any group of 10 or more may form a minian, conducting religious services in members' homes or other places.

The late Rabbi Yehuda Leib Levin, Chief Rabbi of Moscow, in an address delivered during his visit to the United States in 1968, reported:

"The doors of our Moscow Great Synagogue, from the time of the Revolution to the present day, have been open to all worshippers and for all visitors . . . and prayers are conducted there throughout the day, the Talmud is studied there, and the Mishnah, the Shulchan Aruch, and the Chumosh. There is available a slaughterhouse for poultry, a ritual bath, and those who perform circumcisions. The Community Council provides Jews with matzoh, not only for Moscow Jews but also for Jews of other places."

Two Georgian correspondents of Soviet Weekly report (March 21, 1970) that in the city of Kutaisi, where there are three synagogues, "there are kosher slaughterhouses, and both the Great and Small synagogues have their own bakeries for matzoh. There are eight butchers selling kosher meat, a Jewish bath-house and a Jewish cemetery."

A religious calendar is published every year by the Moscow Central Synagogue, and in 1968 a new prayer book edited by Rabbi Levin was issued in 10,000 copies.

The libraries of synagogues have thousands of religious books. The Moscow Central Synagogue has a theological school—the Yeshiva—training rabbis, shohets,* etc.

---

*Religious slaughterers—Editor.

Q. Why are there no Jewish schools in the Soviet Union?

A. We can speak here only of secular schools since the Church in this country is separated from the State, and the School is separated from the Church.

During the first years of Soviet government general and vocational schools, with teaching conducted in Yiddish, were established in localities with compact Jewish populations. However, they did not last long for several reasons.

Firstly, in tsarist Russia the most cherished dream of every Jewish family was to educate the children in a Russian secondary school. Very often they failed to do so (just recall Sholem Aleichem's stories). Therefore, after the establishment of Soviet power many Jewish families preferred to send their children to Russian schools since they regarded this opportunity as a manifestation of their equality.

Secondly, many Jews realised that on graduation from a Russian school their children would be better equipped for continuing their education in the country's higher learning establishments and choosing their career.

Thirdly, the abolition of the Jewish pale* promoted massive Jewish migration from settlements into big towns all over the country. This led to the gradual closing down of Yiddish-language schools in settlements which once had compact Jewish population.

Of course, there still are some Jewish families who would like their children to learn Yiddish. How do they manage this?

Soviet Jews are not prohibited from studying Yiddish. Any group which wishes to organize classes is not only free to do so but can secure official assistance. Thus, Soviet news sources reported [in early 1970] that in Leningrad special courses in Yiddish had been organized by a group of parents. The authorities had aided them in getting teachers and classrooms, for which they paid a nominal fee. In addition the Yiddish literary monthly, Sovietish Heimland, has for some time been presenting lessons in Yiddish in its pages.

Q. What about Jewish culture in the Soviet Union?

A. In the Soviet Union the Jewish people have the right to both develop their distinct culture and become part of Soviet society as a whole.

Jewish writers, poets and people in the arts have been contributing greatly to the Soviet culture. The following writers have won general recognition among the Soviet people: Samuel Marshak, Ilya Ehrenburg, Pavel Antakolsky, Vera Inber, Emmanuel Kazakevich, Vasily Grossman, Isaak Babel, Mikhail Svetlov and many others.

---

*See page 4 above—Editor.

Violinists David Oistrakh and Leonid Kogan, ballerina Maya Plisetskaya, film directors Mikhail Romm, Mark Donskoi, Grigory Roshal, Sergey Yutkevitch, Roman Karmen, singer Mark Reizen, actors Leonid Utyosov, Arkady Raikin, conductor Natan Rakhlin, composer Moisei Vainberg are well known and admired both at home and abroad.

Books by Jewish authors are printed in large editions in this country. They are published in Yiddish and in the languages of the other peoples of the USSR.

During the past few years Sholem Aleichem's works have appeared in a six-volume Russian edition and four-volume Ukrainian edition. Millions of copies of his works have been printed. Altogether over 300 books by Jewish authors have been translated from Yiddish into Russian and other languages of the Soviet peoples in the last few years, totalling more than 40 million copies.

Books in Yiddish are published regularly. In 1968 and 1969 books by David Vendrov, David Gofshtein, Mendel Lifshitz, Ilya Gordon, Zinovy Telesin, Grigory Dobin, Avraam Gontar, Iosif Rabin, Girsh Osherovich, and Sammuil Gordon were printed. Books by Aron Vergelis, Isaak Borukhovich, Itsik Kipnis, Girsch Polyanker and others will soon appear.

An important event in Soviet literary life was the publication of an anthology in Yiddish of modern Jewish prose including the works of over 50 writers.

A Jewish literary monthly—Sovietish Heimland—has been published in Moscow since 1961. It has a monthly circulation of 25,000 copies. The works of over one hundred Jewish writers living in various parts of the country—Moscow, Kiev, Minsk, Vilnius, Riga, Birobidjan, Odessa, Kharkov, Chernovtsy, Kazan, etc.—appear regularly in the magazine.

Dozens of novels and hundreds of short stories have been published by the magazine. The contributors include David Vendrov, Elli Shekhtman, Natan Lurie, Iosif Rabin, Itsik Kipnis, Sammuil Gordon, Grigory Polyanker, Ikhil Falikman, Ikhil Shraibman, Natan Zabara, Moisei Altman, Boris Miller, Riva Rubina, Grigory Dobin, Mikhail Lev, Khaim Melamud and many others.

Poems by Girsh Osherovich, Moisei Teif, Yakov Shternberg, Aron Vergelis, Shloime Roitman, Zinovy Telesin, Isaak Borukhovish, Khanan Vainerman, Avraam Gontar, Matvei Grubian, Yevsei Driz, Khaim Maltinsky, Matvei Saktsier, Riva Balyasnaya, Dora Khaikina, Matvei Saktsier, Riva Balyasnaya, Dora Khaikina, Matvei Talalaevsky, Meyer Kharats, Iosif Lerner, Mendel Lifshitz, Shifra Kholodenko and David Bromberg appear frequently.

Aside from Jewish authors, Russian, Ukrainian, Byelorussian, Moldavian, Lithuanian and Chuvash writers contribute to the magazine. Sovietish Heimland also prints material by Jewish writers living in the United States, France, Israel, Poland, Argentina and other countries.

The Jewish drama company in Moscow directed by Veniamin Shvartser, Merited Artiste of the Russian Federation, is very popular. There are some 20 actors in the company whose repertoire includes "Two Hundred Thousand" and "Tevye the Milkman" by Sholem Aleichem, "Spaniards" by Lermontov and "Witch" by Golfaden. The company gives performances in different towns and communities of the country.

"Wondering Stars" presented by Anna Guzik's group has been a hit with the public for a number of years now.

Sidi Tahl's group from Chernovtsy presents musical skits and sketches mainly in the Ukraine and Moldavia.

The Leningrad Jewish drama company directed by Esther Roitman often gives guest performances in other cities. Its repertoire consists mainly of Sholem Aleichem's stories.

Recitations by Emmanuil Kaminka, Iosif Kolin and Sofia Saitan are enjoyed by lovers of Jewish literature. Concerts of Jewish songs by Klementina Shermel, Dina Potanovskaya, Mikhail Magid and Mikhail Alexandrovich are well attended.

Jewish amateur art groups are also very popular. The Vilnius, Birobidjan and Kishinev amateur companies have been classed as people's theatres for their high standard of acting and production. These people's theatres give performances of works by Sholem Aleichem and modern authors.

At least half a million people a year attend the Jewish professional and amateur drama companies.

The complaint is made that there are no Yiddish state theaters in the Soviet Union but only some "wandering troupes." But how many Yiddish theatrical companies, stationary or travelling, are there which produce serious drama in the United States—or for that matter in Israel? The Polish actress Ida Kaminska who hoped to find greener pastures, finds herself instead without a theater and with the prospects of only occasional productions in the United States.

In the Soviet Union, Yiddish is spoken by a small group of people and it is mostly the older generation who read literature in Yiddish.

But Yiddish is undoubtedly alive. It can be heard in Deribasovskaya Street in Odessa, on Kreshchatik in Kiev, in the streets of Vilnius and Chernovtsy, in Moscow concert halls, over the radio and TV. Contemporary Jewish writers and poets write poems, stories, novels and essays in Yiddish.

It is ironic that in Israel, to which some Soviet Jews wish to migrate in order "to live as Jews," Yiddish is discouraged more than in any other country. One such emigrant, in a letter to the progressive (U.S.) Yiddish weekly Der Veg, says: "My disappointment stems, among other things, from the discrimination and abuse to which our mother tongue—Yiddish—is being subjected. It is noteworthy that at the same time the Soviet Union is being attacked for allegedly discriminating against Yiddish. The attackers completely forget what they are doing to Yiddish in their own country—Israel."

Q. What kind of work do Soviet Jews engage in?

A. Jews work in all sectors of the Soviet economy. The so-called Jewish occupations have long since become a thing of the past. Apart from doctors and lawyers, shoemakers and tailors, Jews are also engaged in the building trades and the iron and steel industry. They are fitters, lathe-operators, mechanics, locomotive and truck drivers, miners, pilots, teachers, office workers, artists, actors, architects, Party functionaries, geologists, seamen, army officers, writers and journalists, professors and academicians.

The personal success of any individual, his social standing and career depend on his skill, abilities, diligence, his patriotism and attitude to people. Nationality or race is not taken into account.

About eight thousand Jews are deputies to the USSR Supreme Soviet, the Supreme Soviets of the Republics and local Soviets. . . .

From amongst the people, from amongst those who cast aside the isolated and restricted way of life within the Jewish pale when the revolution began, came such noted soldiers as . . . [A list of Jewish generals in the Red Army follows here—Editor].

Among those holding high posts in the Soviet Union are . . . [A long list of high Jewish officials in the Soviet government follows here—Editor.]*

Jews comprise the third greatest number of research workers (after Russians and Ukrainians) though they account for only 1.2 percent of the country's population.

Twenty Jews are members and corresponding members of the USSR Academy of Medical Sciences.

Five hundred thousand Jews in the country have a higher or specialized secondary education.

3.15% of the Jewish population are students whereas the ratio of students to the total population is 1.82%.†

Q. Are meritorious Soviet Jews held in proper esteem?

A. The Soviet press often prints decrees by the USSR Supreme Soviet conferring Soviet orders and medals on people for outstanding

---

*Most of the names of Jewish generals and high government officials in the USSR contained in this Soviet publication can be found on pages 55 and 56 above—Editor.

†These figures and percentages are for 1969—Editor.

contributions to the national economy, culture and art. The recipients of these awards include Jews.

The title of Hero of Socialist Labour has been conferred upon 55 Jews, four have received the title twice, and three have become thrice Hero of Socialist Labour.

Out of 844 persons who have won Lenin Prizes, 564 are Russians, 96 are Jews and 184 are of other nationalities.

It has long been a tradition in the Soviet Union to name streets and squares after people who are greatly esteemed. Very often this is done at the request of residents themselves. This tradition is a way of honouring famous countrymen—scientists, writers, revolutionaries, generals, war and labour heroes.

Sverdlovsk, a large administrative and industrial centre in the Urals, dozens of factories, collective farms, educational establishments, a central district and a central square in Moscow have been named after Yakov Sverdlov, first President of the Soviet Union.

During the last 10-15 years alone, dozens of streets have been named after Jewish celebrities, including Sholem Aleichem Street in Kiev; Sammuil Galkin (a Jewish poet) Street in Rogachov; Nakhimson (a revolutionary) Street in Yaroslavl. In Kronstadt there is a street named after Grigory Feigin, a Civil War hero; in Berdichev—a street is named after the Slomnitsky sisters who were revolutionaries. A street in Vilnius is named after Itskhak Vitenberg, an anti-fascist resistance hero; a street in Sverdlovsk bears the name of Yakov Shenkman, a hero of the Civil War. Dnepropetrovsk has a street named after Grigory Chudnovsky, a revolutionary. In Moscow there is a street named after Hero of the Soviet Union Lazar Papernik. Two streets in Gomel were named after Heroes of the Soviet Union Katunin and Shandalov. A street in Novosibirsk bears the name of Hero of the Soviet Union Boris Kugel; Vitebsk has a street named after Hero of the Soviet Union Iosif Bumagin. In Pinsk there is a street bearing the name of Alexander Bekovich, a partisan; in Gdov (Pskov Region) one of the streets is named after Tevye Pechatnikov, a Second World War Hero, etc.

A number of Soviet sea and river boats are also named after distinguished Jews.

The facts and data about Soviet Jewry, cited here, show how far from reality is the gloomy picture of Soviet Jews usually painted by bourgeois propagandists in the West. Soviet Jews actively contribute to all aspects of socialist society of which they are full-fledged members. Like the other nationalities they enjoy all rights, privileges and advantages granted to the Soviet people by the state and the Constitution irrespective of nationality, race or religion.

To those who still doubt all this we would like to repeat what Yehuda Leib Levin, Chief Rabbi of Moscow, said from the rostrum of New York's Hunter College in 1968:

"Come to us and see things for yourselves!"

CHAPTER

4

LET MY PEOPLE GO!

Efforts of Western Jewish organizations on behalf of Soviet Jewry focus on one particular goal above all others: to bring world pressure to bear on the Soviet leadership to let Jews emigrate freely. In this struggle the well-founded assumption that most of those who would leave would opt for Israel as their new abode is a major factor involved, on the one hand because many would-be emigrants, aided by their Western supporters, emphasize the right of Soviet Jews to live a Jewish life in their "own land," and on the other hand because the Soviets' reluctance to permit their departure is at least in part accounted for by an unwillingness to strengthen Israel at a time of conflict with the Soviet Union's Arab allies.

A small minority of individuals, such as the members of the militant Jewish Defense League, advocate disruption of cultural events involving Soviet artists and physical attacks on Soviet personnel and visitors in the West as proper tactics in support of Soviet Jewry. Most Western Jewish organizations oppose the use of force and violence as morally wrong and counterproductive but are united, firm, and uncompromising in their demands to "Let My People Go!" and in their determination to keep up the pressure until the Soviets acquiesce. The Soviets on their part condemn all such activities as part of the anti-Soviet Zionist conspiracy.

* * * * *

Rabbi Meir Kahane, founder and leader of the controversial Jewish Defense League, represents the militant anti-Soviet position. If Jews want to survive in the Soviet Union, or for that matter anywhere else in the world, he maintains, they must not only regain their dignity and pride as Jews, they must also be ready to fight and to train to become efficient fighters. NEVER AGAIN! A Program for Survival is the title of his book from which the selection below has been reprinted. NEVER AGAIN! he proclaims, alluding to the Nazi era, must Jews submit to persecution without fighting back. NEVER AGAIN! must Jews fail to be prepared to use force if necessary in their defense and in the defense of their brothers.

Kahane's book is not devoted primarily to Soviet Jewry. He sees anti-Semitism, whether overt or covert, prevailing everywhere in the world, and especially in the United States. "The white establishment hates the Jew," he roundly asserts (p. 106), pleading with his fellow-Jews to realize that "anti-Jewishness is a permanent part of human society" (p. 209) and that "people in America today do not like Jews" (p. 110). Assimilation offers no solution, so far as he is concerned, for it is but a "subtly soft disease that is raging throughout the American and Western Jewish body and which threatens it with oblivion" (p. 115).

Interesting though his analysis of anti-Semitism in the West and of Western Jewry's reaction to it (trying to "melt" into non-Jewish society) may be, the fame (or perhaps the notoriety) of Rabbi Kahane and of his Jewish Defense League (JDL) rest primarily on his advocacy of violence as the proper tactic to be used for the "rescue of Soviet Jewry." Violence in defense of fellow-Jews is often necessary, Kahane explains in his NEVER AGAIN!; and if a Jew says that the Bible commands turning the other cheek, "let him know that he has been reading the wrong Bible" (p. 147). "If one comes to slay you—slay him first," he quotes from Jewish scriptures (p. 149), and "Thou shalt not stand idly by your brother's blood" (p. 150). Soviet Jews will not be saved, Kahane is convinced, by "petitions, sermons, or tepid twice-a-year protests" (p. 230). The plight of Soviet Jews calls for the "escalation of the war of the Jewish people against their Soviet oppressors through the use of physical force and violence" (p. 146). Proclaiming that "violence is not necessarily unthinking hooliganism [but] can be a well thought out, responsible, political weapon" (p. 266), Kahane asks Western Jews to engage in "militant and violent protest" (p. 268) in furtherance of the cause of their bretheren in the USSR.

Allegedly on behalf of Soviet Jewry, numerous acts of violence were indeed perpetrated against Soviet citizens and Soviet property in the United States during the early 1970s. Performances by Soviet artists were interrupted; Soviet housewives were spat upon in New York streets; rifle shots were fired into the living quarters of Soviet diplomats; bombs exploded in the buildings of Aeroflot and Intourist in New York and of the information and trade departments of the Soviet Embassy in Washington; incendiary devices were set off at the New York office of impresario Sol Hurok (causing two deaths and injuries to five others) and of Columbia Artists Management Corporation, a block away—both booking agents for Soviet artists—and so on. The Jewish Defense League may not have officially confessed to any individual bombings, but it frequently has applauded the use of violence,* and its leader, Rabbi Kahane, openly credits it with a principal role in the perpetration of violent acts. Arguing that recent progress in the "deliverance" of Soviet Jews has been the direct result of mounting pressure brought to bear on the Soviet Union by increased world attention, Kahane wrote,

> Like it or not, the attention of the world was finally focused on the problem by means of the violence unleashed by militant Jews, primarily of the Jewish Defense League. It was their "outrageous" actions which forced a world that would have rather slept to pay attention, that forced the Soviets to retreat in the face of world opinion . . . (NEVER AGAIN, p. 266).

Acts of violence, endorsed as basically correct tactics by Kahane and his Jewish Defense League, have met with the strongest disapproval of the overwhelming majority of Jews and of Jewish organizations throughout the world. Among those who have officially repudiated such lawless acts as "reprehensible" and "self-defeating," are Premier Golda Meir of Israel, the American Jewish Conference on Soviet Jewry, B'nai B'rith, the Union of Orthodox Jewish Congregations of America, the American Jewish Committee, the American Jewish Congress, the Jewish War Veterans, and the Synagogue Council of America. But perhaps the most emphatic and strongly worded condemnation of acts of violence and of the men who perpetrated them with the declared intention of furthering the cause of Soviet Jewry has come from three American Jewish leaders. Said Max Fisher, president of the Council of Jewish Federations and Welfare Funds; Rabbi Herschel Schacter, chairman of the American Jewish Conference on Soviet Jewry; and Dr. William

---

*Bertram Zweibon, national vice chairman of the Jewish Defense League, stated unequivocally before a congressional committee that violence perpetrated in New York in support of Jewish hijackers to be tried at Leningrad was "applauded by the League" (Soviet Jewry, U.S., House of Representatives, Subcommittee on Europe of the Committee on Foreign Affairs, Hearings, 92d Cong., 1st sess. [Washington, D.C.: Government Printing Office, 1972], p. 72).

A. Wexler, chairman of the Conference of Major American Jewish Organizations in a joint statement:*

> The handful of reckless and dangerous men guilty of attacking Soviet installations in this country stand condemned as imperiling the cause of Soviet Jewry. Their outrageous, cowardly acts do malicious harm to the courage and dignity of Soviet Jews who are speaking out for their human rights. Such desperate and criminal tactics win sympathy for the Soviet Union by the use of a mindless violence that all decent men abhor. . . . In the name of the Jewish community of America, we denounce this strategy of terror and the men who are guilty of it.

Rabbi Kahane's militant Jewish Defense League may represent only a small minority of Western Jewry; it may be confronted by the opposition of virtually all other Jewish associations; yet as an apparently well-organized, well-disciplined, and strongly motivated group, it constitutes a movement that may have to be reckoned with in years to come. Therefore, anyone interested in Soviet Jewry should be aware of the JDL's philosophy and activities. This chapter focuses on actions taken, intended, or recommended on behalf of Soviet Jewry; but it is also concerned with the main theme of this book, namely, the position and treatment of Jews in the USSR as perceived by individuals of various persuasions.

In the following selection, Kahane expresses his views on what he considers to be a very dangerous situation for Soviet Jewry; and he strongly rebukes the West, and especially the Jewish leadership in the West, for having missed opportunity after opportunity to force the Soviets to let the Jews depart and for failing, even today, to exert enough pressure to achieve that goal.

---

*Soviet Jewry, U.S., House of Representatives, Subcommittee on Europe of the Committee on Foreign Affairs, Hearings, 92d Cong., 1st sess. (Washington, D.C.: Government Printing Office, 1972) p. 47. Statements by Golda Meir and by the organizations mentioned can be found in Soviet Jewry (Hearings) pp. 46-47.

NEVER AGAIN!

Rabbi Meir Kahane

In 1917, the Bolshevik revolution came to Russia and the curtain came down on one of the great sagas of Jewish history. The Russian Jew would never be the same again. The Russian Jewish community, warm and throbbing, the cream of world Jewry, was irrevocably changed.

The land that brought forth such fertile Jewish minds as Rabbi Elijah of Vilna and Rabbi Yitzhak Elchanan; the land in which sprang up the Torah centers of Volozhin and Slobodka; the country where the spirit of Zionism flowed to give life to the bones of Herzl's dream and which saw such burning Jewish leaders as Jabotinsky, Usishkin, and Pinsker; the land of the so very warm and beautiful Jewish masses who were oppressed by poverty but uplifted by their faith, who dreamed their Jewish dreams, lived their Jewish dreams, lived their Jewish lives, and died in a Jewish embrace; the Russia of the cheder (school) and the pripichek (fireplace) where young little Jews learned their Aleph Bet in preparation for taking upon their little backs the yoke of the Kingdom of Heaven; the place where Jews in their poverty never turned away a Jew who was poorer than they and whose prayers were so poignant as to reach as high as the Throne of Glory and pierce the curtain of iron that separated the Almighty from His suffering children. This was the Russia that was irrevocably destroyed in 1917. In its place there arose the Kingdom of Marx and the Fiefdom of Lenin. Communism had come to Russia and all Jews would soon understand its full impact.

From the beginning it was clear that Judaism, as all other religions, would be hunted down and eradicated. Communism was a jealous mistress and could tolerate no rivals for the love and the soul of the one she desired to master. And so, with a zeal that would have done justice to the Church, the high and the low priests of the new faith searched out Judaism. Their finest tool proved to be the Yevesekzia—the Jewish wing of the Communist Party. It is not a new thing. There is no great anti-Semite than the Jewish one, and none hates the Jewish people more than the Jewish traitor and apostate. No traditional Jew ever searched for leaven on the eve of Passover as the Communists sought out the tools of Judaism.

Rabbis and teachers were arrested and sent to Siberia. The schools were closed and synagogues shut down to be converted to youth clubs. No religious books were permitted to be printed, and the great works of the Bible, the Talmud, and the Jewish commentaries were banned from the Russian presses. Those who had prayer books watched over them as over precious stones, and, in the absence of religious calendars, Jews had to find some other means of learning when their holidays occurred.

With no religious schools and with private teaching of Judaism forbidden by law, the greatness that had been Russian Judaism began to wither and die. The rabbis grew grey and the elders, older still. State schools mocked and scorned Judaism, and Jewish history was distorted. Moral wedges were driven between parents and children, and religious tradition and practice were cruelly derided and hunted down.

The holidays were attacked as tools of bourgeois nationalism, intended to instill a separatist spirit into the Jew. They were condemned as hindering production plans and violating work discipline since the Jew did not labor on those days. The Passover was singled out for special assault since it oriented Jews to thinking of their nationalism and of next year in Jerusalem.

Circumcision, central to Judaism, was attacked as a barbaric rite and the Bar Mitzvah as an attempt to spiritually disfigure the young boy. Those who attended synagogue were barred from any meaningful advance in Soviet society and were subjected to harassment and taunts. . . .

In the decades that stretched from 1917, there were so many golden opportunities to force the Soviets to yield and to let our people go—when the Soviets needed engineers and technicians in the 1920s, when Stalin sought recognition from Roosevelt in the 1930s, and when, in desperate need of a second front, they sent their Jewish Anti-Fascist Committee here to propagandize for support in the 1940s. Does anyone recall our grasping these opportunities to demand the Moscow's wants be withheld until they paid a Soviet Jewish price?

Can anyone remember street protests for Soviet Jews in all the decades from 1917 to 1963? Let the awesome truth be known. For nearly half a century, there was not one single, solitary mass street protest for Soviet Jewry by the Jewish community of the United States.

And we knew all that was happening. We knew that it was not only the Jewish faith that was being plowed under, but the Jewish national concept too. Other peoples were oppressed within the U.S.S.R., but at least they were able to live in their own land. At least they were able to study in their national languages; at least they were able to study their individual Latvian or Ukrainian or Lithuanian cultures; at least they could delve into their own national history. The Jew was not granted even that. What every other minority was given the Jew was denied.

For Lenin had decreed that Jews were not a nationality. They had no territory in the U.S.S.R., they had no language or a rooted peasant class. Lacking these absolute prerequisites, they failed to qualify as a separate national entity and would have to assimilate. Thus decreed Lenin; and Stalin, his heir, underscored the judgment by calling the Jews a "nation on paper only." Forgotten was their common history and suffering. Over looked was their common culture and common Hebrew and Yiddish language. The Jew was not a nation, and he would be assimilated. As a nation he did not exist, and as a religion he would not exist. There was only one other choice for the new Soviet Jew: Disappear.

We knew all this and watched all this and were silent. Already our sin is greater than we can bear. If by our silence with Hitler we allowed millions to lose their Jewish lives, by our failure to protest against the Soviet Union we have permitted millions to lose their Jewish souls.

There is little doubt that if they opened the gates of the Soviet Union tomorrow and allowed all Jews to leave, the majority might very well stay. If so, each and every Jew . . . who chooses to stay and cut his ties with his people, is on our conscience. We created them all. By our silence for half-a-century we gave the Soviet Union fifty years to assimilate, integrate, amalgamate, and dissolve these Jews.

American Jewish leaders in the past would tell the community that they were conducting all manner of secret negotiations. Perhaps this was true; butthey lacked the sense of urgency needed to succeed, and they were conducted with the kind of respectability that is doomed to fail. Messages to the State Department and infrequent visits to the White House were the weapons of the Jewish Establishment. From the outset they were tepid and grotesque failures that had no chance of success and whose obvious impotence brought forth no other, more desperate, reaction by these leaders.

Indeed, when rebel-types and young people demanded that more be done, they were silenced with the eternal warning: You will only make things worse. And in the end, whatever protests first began and whatever street demonstrations were first started were the products, not of the Jewish Establishment, but of young Jews and mavericks who broke with the policy of silence. They were immediately condemned by the major Jewish organizations before they proved that their way was the only one to shake a world. . . .

Today, the danger to Soviet Jewry grows with every passing hour. For almost a score of years we have had a golden opportunity to do the militant and outrageous things needed to shake the world and the Soviets. From the death of Stalin in 1953, the U.S.S.R. was governed by men and institutions that were weak and incapable of the authoritarian measures practiced by the Georgian dictator. These were years of rare opportunities, and we let so many of them go. And who knows what tomorrow can bring.?

We forget so easily, we whose world is encompassed by our own little problems which assume, for us, such awesome proportions. We forget so easily the final years of Stalin, the final nightmarish years of horror. The years when Stalin gathered together the last of the Jewish intellectuals, writers, and poets and shot them. The years when he threw hundreds of Jews into prisons because they were "cosmopolitans." The insane and deadly "Doctors Plot" in which the dictator accused Jewish doctors of plotting to kill him and other Soviet leaders.

Those were the years when Stalin drew up lists of hundreds of thousands of Jews to be sent to Siberian camps for his own version of the Final Solution. They were the years when Jews dared not travel too far from their homes for fear that the secret police might come in their absence and take away their families. They were the years when Jews kept suitcases packed, filled with necessities, and waited for the knock on the door.

G-d was good to Soviet Jewry, and Stalin died. But what of tomorrow? Who, but the eternally trusting and eternally proven-wrong lemming-pacifist can vouch for the end of Stalinism? A time of increased Western isolationism and growing indications of a Free World's unwillingness to fight, is a time for adventurism and brazenness. A time of lessened need of world public opinion is a time of growing totalitarianism. And for the Soviet Jew, there is something else. For him there is a growing, logical probability of physical punishment and assault.

There is a miracle today within the Soviet Union, and we have observed it with our own eyes. Twenty-five centuries ago the Prophet Ezekiel was shown a field filled with dry, Jewish bones and was asked: Can these bones live? We have seen the answer. They can and do. The dry and sterile and dead bones of the young Soviet Jews have come to life, defying all logic and rationality in their defiance of the Kremlin.

Denied an opportunity to study their Jewish religion and heritage, they go to the Moscow synagogue to dance on Simchat Torah—the holiday of the Rejoicing with the Law. Most do not know what they sing; they only know that it is Jewish and thus beautiful. That is enough for them. Having been robbed of any chance to learn their history and their national culture, they now demand to go to the land that the Kremlin calls fascist, racist, and aggressor. Having been tyrannized and subjected to national-cultural genocide, they stand and shout to their oppressors: Up against the wall, Mother Russia!

And what does the Kremlin see as it watches tens of thousands of young Jews dance their Jewish dances and shout "Long Live Israel"? It sees Soviet citizens shouting their praise of a "fascist" state whose pilots shoot down Soviet pilots (because Jewish pilots are better than the Russians). And it cannot long stand for such a thing.

And what does the Soviet dictatorship see when a young Soviet Jew enters the Ministry of Interior's OVIR office that distributes exit visas for Israel? It sees a young Jew applying to go to Israel because he has an aunt in Haifa and cannot live without seeing her. But it knows full well that he has other aunts in Moscow, and what he really yearns for is to be free in his land, to be a Jew with his own people. And it cannot long abide this.

And is it, therefore, so improbable that the angry and violent Russians, whose basic Jew-hatred has been held back only by weakness and need for the support of world-wide public opinion, will in some future date explode in a physical assault on Soviet Jews? Is there one whose soul is so at peace with himself that he can assure us that this is not a distinct possibility?

Indeed it is. And because it is, we have no time. We have not the luxury of time to call international conferences and fly hundreds of Jewish leaders thousands of miles at the cost of hundreds of thousands of dollars in Jewish money, merely to sit for three days and emerge with a resolution declaring solidarity with Soviet Jewry. We have no time for such nonsense and precious little future opportunities that we can fritter away on foolishness.

There is a need for feeling the pain of the Soviet Jew. There is a need for feeling the essence of Ahavat Yisroel. There is an obligation to do outrageous things, and there is a hallowed duty for Jewish leaders to do today the things they did not do in the past for Soviet Jews and the things they failed to do for the Six Million.

There is a need because there is no time, and we cannot repeat this too many times. On the contrary, it is incumbent upon us to shout it from the rooftops and to din it into the ears of all who would hear—or not hear. There is no time! Another holocaust could well approach! And we are pitifully silent, woefully inept.

* * * * *

In the selection below, Bertram Zweibon, national vice chairman of the Jewish Defense League, presents to a congressional committee the extreme position of his organization on the alleged plight of Soviet Jewry. Some of his charges (such as the charge that Soviet Jews are still denied matzoth) would not be backed by other Jewish and Zionist organizations; some of his requests for action to be taken by the U.S. Government in support of Soviet Jewry (for instance the proposal that all disarmament talks be suspended until the Soviet Government permits Jews to emigrate freely) would find little support in the West. But for readers who want to familiarize themselves with the entire spectrum of divergent views on the issue of Soviet Jewry, Zweibon's exposition will be a valuable supplement to Kahane's militant position presented in the preceding selection.

54 YEARS OF AGONY
Bertram Zweibon

Prior to the Communist take-over in 1917, Russia was the heartland of the Jewish faith, with flourishing seminaries and synagogues. This, despite the anti-semitism of the Czarist government. The Soviet campaign to arrive at a "final solution" to the "Jewish problem" has proceeded in three descending stages.

The first stage was to divert the attention of the Jewish population from the real purpose of the regime, which was the destruction of the Jew. This was done by the creation of a Jewish Communist section,* called the Yeveseksia. It established media in Yiddish, the basic language of Russian Jewry. The purpose was to make the Jew feel grateful, and to use this media for the purpose of propaganda and indoctrination in Communism.

These new institutions were not Jewish institutions but rather institutions for Jews. Under the smoke screen of the media for Jews, the truly Jewish institutions, like Yeshivas,† were abolished, and no Jewish child was thereafter permitted to study his faith. In a decade, the greatness of the Russian Jewish community was destroyed.

Phase two was the elimination of even the institutions for Jews. By 1936, the Communists believed that an indoctrination vehicle was no longer necessary. Jewish intellectuals and leaders were liquidated. This phase was stalled when Hitler attacked the Soviet Union. The Commissars created a puppet Jewish anti-Fascist Committee to create support for the Soviet Union in its battle with Hitler (second front campaign, etc.). The members of this committee were liquidated soon after the war came to an end.

The third phase—physical liquidation of Jews—was launched by the blatantly anti-Semitic "Doctors plot." In so far as Jews are

---

From "Statement by Bertram Zweibon, National Vice Chairman, Jewish Defense League, Inc." in Soviet Jewry, U.S. House of Representatives, Subcommittee on Europe of the Committee on Foreign Affairs, Hearings, 92d Cong. 1st sess., November 9-10, 1971 (Washington, D.C.: Government Printing Office, 1972), pp. 73-74.

---

*In the Communist Party of the Soviet Union—Editor.

†Derived from the Hebrew word yashab, "to sit," a Yeshiva is a school of advanced Jewish learning—Editor.

concerned, the differences between Fascism and Communist declined sharply.

The death of Stalin has caused a pause in phase 3, but the oppression has not ceased.

There are no schools to teach Judaism, while other faiths are allowed seminaries to train priests and ministers. The Jewish seminary opened by Khrushchev has been closed.

Ritual circumcision, a most vital part of Judaism, is banned. The circumcisions now are however performed in cemeteries, or similar places to avoid detection, most often upon adults, which is very painful.

Synagogues continue to be closed.

Jews are not permitted to enter a federation of the synagogues that are open, so as to have contact in different cities, while other faiths are so permitted.

Jewish Bibles are not allowed to be printed, while the printing of the Bibles of other faiths are permitted.

Other faiths are permitted to send representatives of their faith to world conferences, Jews are not.

During Passover, the matzoh is denied the Jew. The matzoh, which signifies liberty, is considered a threat to the Soviet State.

No Talis, prayer shawl, has ever been made in the Soviet Union,

In the last 48 years, no Jewish calendar has been printed.

There are no Jewish theaters, while other ethnic groups have such theaters.

In Moscow, with 2 1/2 million Jews,* there is no Jewish cemetery.

The foregoing is but a sketch of 54 years of the agony of Soviet Jewry. Despite it all, Soviet Jewry lives and breathes. It wishes to go home, to that ancestral place of their fathers, to that place—Israel—where they will be able to live as Jews.

The 54 years of Soviet oppression has not succeeded. As news of Israel's victories in 1956 and 1967 became known in Russia, a miracle occurred. An explosion of Jewish identity erupted, bursting the myth of the success of Soviet indoctrination.

The 3 1/2 million Jews of the Soviet Union are embattled in their fight for the right to go home.

The greatness of America does not lie in the wheat fields of Kansas or in the steel mills of Pittsburgh. Our greatness has always been our response to the oppressed of the world, our search for justice and ethics, our sense of morality. These have been our distinguishing

---

*Undoubtedly a printing error, this should probably read 1/2 million—Editor.

features. We come to our government on behalf of an oppressed people, asking justice and appeal to ethical and moral standards.

The Soviet Union desires detente with the United States. It does so for its own purposes, and has been building bridges for the past 6 or 7 years. Its reason is possibly the problem created by Red China. The Russians are maintaining large numbers of troops on the Chinese border. There is increasing speculation of a Russian surgical strike against China's nuclear capability. Russia must know or at least be assured of the position of the U.S.A. in the event of a Sino-Russian confrontation.

We have a right to ask our government to demand as a condition of detente, the granting of permission to Soviet Jewry to repatriate.

To impress the Soviet Government with our determination to honor our heritage, we ask:

1. That there be a suspension of all disarmament, trade and space talks with the Soviet Union until the right to leave is honored.

2. That there be a cessation of all cultural programs with the Soviet Union until the Soviets act humanely to minority groups.

3. That the Congress use its influence to bar the Soviet Union from the Olympic games. If South Africa is barred due to apartheid, the Soviet Union should be barred for genocide.

4. The Congress should go on record as being in favor of exchanging those in our prisons, who so desire it, with Jews imprisoned in the Soviet Union.

The ability to save millions from extermination does not come often to small groups of men. History will record the conduct of this Congress, this government, this country, at this time. Let it be said that the land made up of the oppressed and driven of the world has not forgotten how it feels to be oppressed.

* * * * *

The World Conference of Jewish Communities on Soviet Jewry met on February 23-25, 1971 in Brussels, Belgium. The conference was attended by 760 delegates of Jewish organizations from 38 countries and was addressed by prominent Jewish figures from the arts, sciences, professions, and public life. Rabbi Kahane's application for delegate status and his request to address the conference was turned down

because the Jewish Defense League was not a member of either the American Jewish Conference on Soviet Jewry or the Conference of Presidents of Major American Jewish Organizations—the two American sponsors of the Brussels Conference whose representatives made up the U.S.

delegation—and because the tactic of violence committed or condoned by Rabbi Kahane and the Jewish Defense League had been publicly repudiated by every constituent member of the American delegation, by Prime Minister Golda Meir on behalf of the Government of Israel, and by Soviet Jewry groups not only in the U.S. but around the world.*

The conference was intended to affirm the "commitment of the world Jewish community to the urgent demand 'Let my people go' "; to let the Jews in the Soviet Union know that they had not been forgotten and that world Jewry would support them "in their struggle to be free" and to provide a "framework for mapping out a coordinated global strategy in behalf of Soviet Jewry in the months and years to come."†

The text of the Brussels Declaration by the World Conference of Jewish Communities on Soviet Jewry, adopted at the closing of the conference on February 25, 1971 is reprinted below.

THE BRUSSELS DECLARATION

We, the delegates of this Conference, coming from Jewish communities throughout the world, solemnly declare our solidarity with our Jewish brothers in the Soviet Union.

We want them to know—and they will take encouragement from this knowledge—that we are at one with them, totally identified with their heroic struggle for the safeguarding of their national identity and for their natural and inalienable right to return to their historic homeland, the land of Israel.

Profoundly concerned for their fate and future, we denounce the policy pursued by the government of the Soviet Union of suppressing the historic Jewish cultural and religious heritage. This constitutes a flagrant violation of human rights which the Soviet Constitution pledges to uphold and which is enshrined in the Universal Declaration of Human Rights. To cut them off from the rest of the Jewish people,

---

*Richard Cohen, ed., Let My People Go! (New York: Popular Library, 1971), p. 132.

†Ibid., p. 120

From Richard Cohen, ed., Let My People Go! (New York: Popular Library, 1971, pp. 141-142. Reprinted by permission.

as the Soviet authorities are attempting to do, is a crime against humanity.

Soviet spokesmen claim that there is no need for Jewish culture and education, that there is no Jewish problem in the Soviet Union and that there is no anti-Semitism. These assertions have been proven false by the Soviet Jews themselves. The entire world has heard their protest.

Tens of thousands of Jews have petitioned the Soviet authorities for the right to settle in Israel and raise their children in the Jewish tradition and culture. Letters, messages and petitions, sent at the signatories' peril from the Soviet Union to individuals, to governments, to the United Nations and other international organizations, all demand recognition of these rights.

The reaction of the Soviet authorities to this Jewish awakening has been to mount a campaign of harassment, arrests and virulent anti-Jewish propaganda. The Leningrad trial, shocking to the world, was but one manifestation of such persecution. Far from being crushed by such intimidation, Soviet Jews today demand their rights with ever greater courage and determination.

This Conference urgently calls upon the civilized world to join with us and with the Jews of the USSR in urging the Soviet authorities

- TO RECOGNIZE the right of Jews who so desire to return to their historic homeland in Israel, and to ensure the unhindered exercise of this right.
- TO ENABLE the Jews in the USSR to exercise fully their right to live in accord with the Jewish cultural and religious heritage and freely to raise their children in this heritage.
- TO PUT AN END to the defamation of the Jewish people and of Zionism, reminiscent of the evil anti-Semitism which has caused so much suffering to the Jewish people and to the world.

We assembled in this Conference to commit ourselves, by unceasing effort, to ensure that the plight of Soviet Jewry is kept before the conscience of the world until the justice of their cause prevails.

We will continue to mobilize the energies of all Jewish communities. We will work through the parliaments and governments of our countries, through the United Nations and other international bodies and through every agency of public opinion.

We will not rest until the Jews of the Soviet Union are free to choose their own destiny.

LET MY PEOPLE GO!

* * * * *

A large number of prominent Jewish speakers addressed the World Conference of Jewish Communities on Soviet Jewry, held in Brussels in February 1971. Among them was Arthur J. Goldberg, former U.S. Supreme Court Justice, secretary of Labor under President John F. Kennedy, and U.S. ambassador to the United Nations under President Lyndon Johnson. Goldberg emphasized that the delegates assembled held no animosity towards any country and had not met to malign the Soviet Union; but he was nevertheless firm in his charges of discrimination against Jews in the USSR and in his demands that the Soviet leaders "pay a decent respect to the opinions of mankind" and open the door for all Jews who so desire to depart.

Goldberg's address to the conference is reprinted below.

UNTIL JUSTICE IS DONE

Arthur J. Goldberg

We meet out of a common concern for human rights and dignity, and not out of animosity toward any country or people.

We are citizens of many nations and deeply attached and loyal to our respective countries. And we are Jews proud of our spiritual heritage. We feel a common and uniting bond with our fellow Jews who have settled in the ancestral home, Israel, and a similar bond with our fellow Jews in the Soviet Union and elsewhere throughout the world. We believe that these attachments and loyalties are completely consonant and compatible.

I do not claim that my country has a perfect record of safeguarding basic human rights. But there is a governmental commitment to the still unrealized goal of equal rights for all our citizens, and our independent judiciary is vigorously seeking to enforce this great constitutional guaranty.

On a matter of particular relevance to this Conference, I recall a decision which I wrote on behalf of the Supreme Court during my service as Justice. In it, we upheld the right of two leading Communists to hold passports, to travel from the United States to countries of their choice, including the Soviet Union, and to return without penalty. The two individuals involved were Elizabeth Gurley Flynn, chairman of the American Communist Party, and Professor Herbert Aptheker, its leading theoretician. I do not have to say that my colleagues and I shared none of their ideology. But we did understand that, under our Constitution, basic rights of liberty include the freedom to travel We quoted the principles of an earlier Court decision that:

From Richard Cohen, ed., Let My People Go! (New York: Popular Library, 1971), pp. 175-181.

> The right to travel is a part of the "Liberty" of which the citizen cannot be deprived without due process of law under the Fifth Amendment. . . . Freedom of movement across frontiers in either direction, and inside frontiers as well, was a part of our heritage. Travel abroad, like travel within the country, may be as close to the heart of the individual as the choice of what he eats, or wears, or reads. Freedom of movement is basic in our scheme of values.

In reaching this decision, I will add, we were faithful not only to our Constitution but also to the Universal Declaration of Human Rights, which clearly states: "Everyone has a right to leave any country, including his own, and to return to his country."

We are aware of the unwarranted attacks against us in the Soviet government-controlled press. But the concerns we express here today are of the deepest and noblest sentiments of our common humanity. They occur in the spirit of the most fundamental of the commands of moral and international law. They express our duty not to condone by silence further assaults of basic human rights. We have learned the price of silence in the face of oppression from the bitterly tragic experience of the Holocaust. And we are determined that we now will not be silent.

In exercise of this sacred duty, we meet not to malign the Soviet Union but rather in sorrow and concern to speak the truth about the repression of Soviet Jews. The Soviet Union is a great power and a proud nation, and it is precisely because of this that we appeal to her today, in the interests of humanity and in her own self-interest, to grant to her Jewish citizens their human rights.

I do not believe that the Soviet Union can, in good conscience, deny the existence of widespread discrimination against her Jewish citizens. The testimony is in from too many sources, too many journalists, too many Soviet publications, too many emigrés to permit serious dispute over the nature and magnitude of this discrimination.

Just a year and a half ago I visited the Soviet Union, where I was warmly and hospitably received. While traveling to the birthplace of my parents in the Ukraine, I visited the capital of this great Soviet Republic. Ukrainian is freely spoken and taught, there are numerous books and publications and television broadcasts in Ukrainian. But the synagogue in Kiev, this city of more than 150,000 Jews, was "closed down for repair."

It is true that the Soviet Union is a materialistic country which does not believe in religion. Its repression of all religious groups is to be condemned. But it is also true that no other religious groups are treated as harshly as Jews.

The Soviet Union is a land of many nationalities. With one exception, each is permitted its own schools, books, language and culture. The one exception: Russia's Jews. Yet they are required always to have on their person the internal passport that gives their nationality: Ivrei—Jew. Thus the Jews of the Soviet Union are set apart but not allowed to live as Jews. This is indeed a cruel dilemma.

Soviet authorities contend there is no substantial demand for Jewish religious and cultural facilities. But if this is true, there would be no need for the barriers to free religious and cultural expression. If there is really no demand, then let it be tested through free and unpenalized opportunities for religious worship and cultural expression. By refusing to grant this opportunity, the Soviet Union is violating its very own Constitution which guarantees the free exercise of religion.

The Jews of the Soviet Union since Stalin's death do not face physical annihilation. But it cannot be seriously denied that they face the reality of spiritual annihilation. Nor, sadly, is the religious and cultural repression the whole of the matter. There is more. Official reprisals against individual Jews have increased, and Jews with a "Jewish consciousness" today risk loss of jobs and sometimes arrest. They, and even Jews who are so fully assimilated that no Jewish self-consciousness remains, endure a hate campaign under the cloak of anti-Zionism. Cartoons depict Jews in an unsavory light. Israel is infamously compared with Nazi Germany. Pseudo-scientific studies and even "literary works" published with government sanction portray Jews as swindlers, usurers, corrupters of Soviet morals and base agents of "foreign capitalists." Anti-religious tracts condemn Judaism as preaching "the bloody extermination of people of other faiths."

There is also increasing evidence of discrimination against Jews in employment and areas of public service. Of course there are Jews who are permitted to rise in the Soviet hierarchy. But the prerequisite for their doing so is abandonment of their Jewish religion and culture. And not so long ago an undue proportion of Jews were being prosecuted for alleged economic crimes.

Even more ominously, Pravda recently warned Soviet Jews that anyone espousing Zionist beliefs would "automatically become an agent of international Zionism and an enemy of the Soviet people." What a hideous and fantastical libel this is! How reminiscent of the frightening anti-Semitic Stalinist attacks! Not all Jews are Zionists, but Zionism is the supreme expression of the Messianic expectation—the belief in the Old Testament prophecy that God selected Eretz Israel to be the Holy Land and set it aside for the people of Israel.

Indeed, the Pravda article highlights what is perhaps the essence of Soviet disregard for the rights of its Jewish citizens—its callous refusal to permit all Soviet Jews who wish to leave to depart and seek a life of dignity elsewhere. To be sure, there has been a trickle of emigration, authorized professedly to unite families. But for the many who might wish to leave—and the estimates suggest that hundreds of thousands would depart if permitted—there is truly no escape. A request for permission entails long delays, harassment, personal abuse, loss of jobs and property, and great expense. And even then permission is granted or denied on a completely arbitrary basis, often fragmenting families.

The requirements of the Universal Declaration of Human Rights, to which the Soviet Union is a signatory, are in the process ignored. We are told by Soviet authorities and apologists that all Jews are happy and few wish to go. Again, I say if this is true, let its truth be tested by opening the doors.

Discrimination against Russian Jews is best grasped from the perspective of history. I will not belabor this Conference with a history of Czarist repression and pogroms. Nor will I repeat the infamous details of the "Doctors' Plot" and of Stalin's anti-Semitism. Instead, I wish to advert briefly to the lessons of these and other events. Can it be denied that Czarist repression of Jews was part and parcel of the very reaction Soviet Communism professed to end? Can it be ignored that Stalin's anti-Semitism was part and parcel of his arbitrary and dictatorial rule? Can it be denied that some of the victims of anti-Semitism, be they the physicians of the "Doctors' Plot" or the defendants in the Slansky trial, have been exonerated and rehabilitated? Can it be refuted that the lesson of history is that anti-Semitism may begin by claiming Jews as its victims, but ends in a wave of repression of all enlightened opinion?

Yes, it is clear that repression of Jews is incendiary stuff. It burns all, Jew and non-Jew alike. It may start as an exercise in narrow and controlled discrimination. But it invariably ends by reviving the rule of terror, recrimination and mistrust. Nor is this really a mystery to the Communist world. It is why many Western Communist parties have objected to anti-Jewish policies by the Soviet Union and why they have understood that anti-Zionism can readily be a spark for the illimitable ravages of anti-Semitism.

It is a profound anomaly that the Soviet Union, which in 1948 was prominent in supporting the establishment of Israel, now launches a campaign of hatred and vituperation against this democratic state. The explanation can only be in terms of Russia's Middle East political objectives, but repression of Soviet Jewry cannot be condoned on this basis. Whatever one's views about the Middle East, Soviet Jewry has not affected the course of events in this area.

But there is even more to it than this. There is also the fact that we live in a world where all of us dedicated to peace wish to lessen international tensions and achieve détente among the superpowers. Speaking for myself, I am not a cold warrior. I have worked earnestly, officially and privately to improve relations between my country and the Soviet Union. I labored hard and successfully for the treaties controlling weapons in space, and I hope that we may soon achieve agreements on East-West trade and on strategic arms limitation. I know what is at stake here in terms of human survival.

But I would be less than candid if I did not say that these tentative steps toward détente may all too easily become steps of retreat if Soviet repression of Jews persists. For repression of any group is an expression of disregard for the opinion of mankind and there is nothing so quick to erode mutual trust on which international understanding depends.

And so I say to the Soviet leaders: Do not turn your back on the civilized world. Pay a decent respect to the opinions of mankind. Do not jeopardize the cause of peace and the progress of your land for so unfounded and inexcusable a prejudice. Understand that today all of us are in truth our brother's keeper, with a duty to speak out and act against the denial of human rights whenever and wherever they occur, in the Soviet Union or in our own lands.

In matters of conscience, there can be no missing voices. This is why we raise our voices here today. This is why we shall persevere in this cause until justice is done.

* * * * *

The selection below represents the official Israeli view on the "national resurgence," of Soviet Jewry that allegedly followed the six-day Arab-Israeli war of 1967 and on the Soviet reaction to the "tide of Jewish applicants for exit visas" that has reportedly "swollen" since the spring 1971 Brussels Conference. The solution of the problem of Soviet Jewry, the Israelis submit, is the lifting of all restrictions on emigration of Jews who wish to leave. A revision of Soviet policies along these lines, the Israelis hold, would be in the interest of the USSR itself; and there are indications that, under the impact of mounting pressures, such a revision may not be too far off.

LET OUR PEOPLE GO!

For many a long year the Government of Israel and the Jewish public in general have been concerned with the problem of Soviet Jewry. Recently, it has become a subject which troubles men and women throughout the world, it is discussed in international forums, it is on the agenda of contacts between the Soviet Union and other States. The overall issue is comprised of the following principal factors:

From "The Problem of Soviet Jewry," Answers and Questions, Pamphlet no. 7 (Jerusalem: Information Division of the Ministry of Foreign Affairs, December 1972), pp. 2 and 9-15. Reprinted by permission.

The Beginning of World Protest

After the death of Stalin, and particularly after the Twentieth Congress of the Communist Party (1956), facts about the persecution of Jews in the USSR began to penetrate the outside world. Then, too, the putting to death of Yiddish authors in 1952 became widely known, shocking the Jewish and the non-Jewish world, so that even Western Communists demanded reform. The response of the Soviet authorities at the end of the 1950's and the start of the 1960's was two-fold—total denial of the existence of a Jewish problem, and fabricated "token" proofs of the existence of "Jewish culture," such as a Yiddish monthly, a few Yiddish books, Yiddish folklore evenings, amateur Yiddish theatricals here and there, the sending of Jewish "spokesmen" to the West, not excepting a general, a "Hero of the Soviet Union," and a Moscow rabbi. The strategy failed utterly. Awareness of a Jewish problem in the USSR proliferated in the non-Soviet world and among Communist and pro-Soviet circles in the West. Prolonged, systematic and tenacious efforts by Israeli representatives at the UN and in other international forums, as well as the activities of Jewish bodies, intellectual leaders in many countries, parliaments and Cabinets, the European Council, the Socialist International and many another worldwide organization, drove the USSR into a defensive moral position. But no Soviet representative—whether an official or a "Jewish" spokesman—could vindicate what was happening. . . .

The Jewish Revival in Russia Vis-à-vis Israeli Achievements

The unusual tension and the great relief which were felt by Soviet Jews after Israel's victory in the Six-Day War coincided with the first appearance of non-Jewish protests in the USSR, for human rights and more "national" rights for minorities, and with the accentuation of formal legalism and the easing of centralized control. In the meantime, the Soviet Union has signed the Universal Declaration of Human Rights and ratified an international convention establishing, among other things, that "every man has the right to leave every country, including his own . . ." It was in this "change of wind"—if not a "change of heart"—that thousands of Soviet Jews, particularly of the rising generation, began courageously to put forward their claims to the right to depart to Israel, either under "family reunion" arrangements, as in the past, or in outright "repatriation" to the historical national homeland of the Jewish people.

There are many aspects of this national resurgence. Defying the vehement opposition of the authorities, Soviet Jews keep trying—

and the enumeration that follows is not exhaustive—to correspond with Israel; to study and teach the Hebrew language, its literature and poetry; to learn Jewish history, even if, for that purpose, they must "bribe" the staff of public libraries to be allowed to read, for example, the books of Graetz or Dubnow; and to celebrate, "congregationally," Jewish and Israeli festivals.

What—in all this—calls for the greatest fortitude is to apply for an exit visa, which is tantamount to lopping off the branch of the tree on which a Jew, as Soviet citizen, is precariously perched. Once he submits the application—and submission, too, is the same as saying that he no longer recognizes the Soviet Union as his homeland—the Jew endangers his place in society, his job and his income. The more resolute, the more daring and open the decision to emigrate to Israel, the graver the risks involved. It is this readiness to pay whatever price, fearing neither imprisonment nor exile, that gives the new Zionist movement in the USSR its revolutionary complexion.

The knowledge that Israel and world Jewry—together with many non-Jewish intellectuals and statesmen—are behind them inspires Soviet Jews to finer mettle.

There are signs that Soviet leadership is growing more and more aware of the influence of the Jewish factor on world opinion. This is evidenced negatively, by the intensified campaign against "international Zionism," and positively, by a readier response to the demands of outstanding Soviet Jews whose cry is heard throughout the world. It is in this light that the nervous diplomatic and propagandistic retort of the Soviet Government to the Brussels Conference of February 1971 should be viewed.

Since the spring of 1971, that is, after that Conference, the tide of Jewish applicants for exit visas has swollen. Official reaction pursues two very disparate courses: acceptance of thousands of applications, particularly from the Western border regions annexed to the Union after 1940, but also from Georgia; and, in the opposite direction, stratagems to deter Jews from applying at all, by inflicting economic and administrative sanctions, to say nothing of the trials staged in Leningard, Riga, Kischinev and elsewhere, in which scores of young Zionists were sentenced to long terms of jail and penal servitude.

The Left in the West and the Problem of Soviet Jewry

Leftist circles in the world know that there is overwhelming testimony that condemnation of Soviet policy towards the Jews is not "an anti-Soviet plot," as Soviet propaganda tries to argue. Communists and Communist newspapers in Italy, Switzerland, Sweden, Austria, Britain, USA, Canada, Australia and other countries, as well as such personalities are Bertrand Russell, Jean-Paul Sartre, Linus Pauling and many more, known as friends of the Soviet Union and as all-out opponents of the anti-Soviet Cold War, would not have joined in the global denunciation if it were not based on proved and convincing facts.

For all the difference between the problem of Soviet Jewry and that of American negroes, there are certain similarities:

- In both cases, there is a gulf between formal equal rights and their gross violation in daily life.
- In both cases, the focus is in the large cities, where the ethnic minority which is the object of discrimination constitutes an anomaly in the eyes of the majority, and, not a little also, in the eyes of the authorities responsible for law and order.
- In both cases, the first indications may be discerned of a real move towards a positive solution, by a combination of the rebellion of the victims and the indignant protestations and moral support of world opinion.

How to Solve the Problem

The problem can be solved positively by breaking the impasse which has come about by opening up options to Soviet Jews:

These three prerequisites were affirmed in 1971 in the Brussels Conference in a programme agreed upon by representatives of world Jewry—Zionist and non-Zionist. They must also be the basis for a wider plan, calling for action to solve the problem on the part of the non-Jewish public, Communists and pro-Soviet circles included.

It is becoming evident that, even in the Soviet leadership, there are individuals who understand that the problem has become an added irritant in the discord between the USSR and the rest of the world, and that easing it will make for a slackening of global tension, including those Middle Eastern manifestations of it that are calculated to endanger world peace. The fact that some of the States of the Soviet bloc have solved, or are solving, their particular Jewish problem, in part or whole, on the basis of the Conference programme, proves the absence of any "ideological" chasm which cannot be pragmatically bridged.

Yugoslavia and Bulgaria, on the very morrow of the Second World War, Poland, Romania and the rest suffered no harm either in their internal regimes or in their international positions and relations, when they permitted their Jews to emigrate to Israel and allowed those who stayed behind to set up their own communal and religious organizations, their own secular educational and cultural institutions.

There is evidence enough that public pressure of this kind—Jewish and international—can avail. It stopped the closure of synagogues and the staging of "economic trials" in the middle of the 1960's. Publication of anti-Semitic literature was shelved for a time, although renewed in the guise of "anti-Zionism" after the Six-Day War. A quota of "family reunions" was countenanced. There was a slight, symbolic, relaxation in the realm of culture in Yiddish medium.

Recently, with pressure exerted by dauntless Jews within the bounds of the Union itself, it is becoming plainer and plainer that there is some yielding in official quarters to an insistence that thunders all over the world: the swift remission of the sentences passed in Leningrad, the grant of thousands of exit visas. The clear inference is that, as pressures mount, so will prospects brighten of a basic revision in Soviet policy on the Jewish question.

* * * * *

The reader of this volume has become familiar with Soviet and Western Marxist disavowals of the existence of Soviet state policies of anti-Semitism or even of discriminatory treatment of Soviet Jews; and he has also seen the Soviets' uncompromising condemnation of Zionism.

The selection below is not merely an elaboration on these issues. Instead, it represents more specifically the official Soviet position on Rabbi Kahane (the "would-be Jewish Mussolini"), his Jewish Defense League (a "rabid, pro-fascist, Zionist organization"), its members ("Kahane's stormtroopers"), the Brussels Conference (a "Zionist witches' sabbath"), and the American Jewish Conference on Soviet Jewry, which is depicted as an extremely powerful, wealthy, and smoothly functioning machine whose influence must not be underestimated. The author is a prominent Soviet journalist who specializes in questions of ideology.

THE "JEWISH MUSSOLINI" AND THE "ZIONIST WITCHES' SABBATH"

Vladimir V. Bolshakov, USSR

During the preparations for, and after, the June 1967 war against the Arab countries, international Zionism intensified anti-communist activity. During 1966-68, the Zionists switched to a policy of outright interference in the affairs of the socialist countries, firstly

---

From V. Bolshakov, Anti-Communism: The Main Line of Zionism (Moscow: Novosti Agency Publishing House, 1972), pp. 59-72. Reprinted by permission.

Czechoslovakia and Poland. In early 1969, when all hopes of successful counter-revolution in Czechoslovakia had been completely dashed, the international Zionist corporation decided to declare a "psychological war" against the USSR; This was started under the repeatedly discredited pretext of "defending Soviet Jews."

In early 1970, international Zionism announced through the Israeli Premier, Golda Meir, a "total campaign" against the USSR. All the Zionist organisations active in the capitalist countries were mobilised for it. . . . Special attention was given to work among young people of Jewish descent. Such "psychological tactics" as "protest" demonstrations outside Soviet embassies and trade missions, provocations against Soviet diplomats and all Soviet delegations visiting capitalist countries and the boycotting of Soviet concert performers on tour and of exhibitions and shows dealing with life in the USSR were worked out in detail. It was advised that extensive use be made of former Soviet citizens of Jewish descent—who had emigrated to Israel or to the USA—for purposes of "visual propaganda" and the fanning of anti-Soviet hysteria. Millions of dollars are allocated from the coffers of the World Zionist Organisation to carry on this odious campaign and to publish anti-Soviet material containing fabrications about "anti-Semitism" in the USSR and other socialist countries.

In order to expose the instigators of this campaign and to show how the campaign is being conducted, it is necessary to say something about one of the most rabid, pro-fascist, Zionist organisations—the Jewish Defence League. Over recent years this organization has been given much publicity for its criminal provocations against Soviet people visiting the USA. . . .

The League was founded in the summer of 1968 by the Orthodox rabbi, Meir Kahane,[1] a Zionist extremist from boyhood. While still at the Heder (school) he joined the Betor Youth movement, a kind of a youth section of the frankly pro-fascist Israeli Herut party.[2] . . .

In 1947, Zionist hoodlums staged a clamorous and disorderly anti-Soviet demonstration outside the UN building, and a number of them were taken to the police station. Among them was the then sixteen-year-old Meir Kahane, already a master of Zionist Jabotinsky-type terrorism. . . .

His ambition to become the "Jewish Mussolini" gave him no rest. As he pored over the Torah, Kahane at the same time studied Karate, dynamiting and other terrorist "disciplines," which would seem to have nothing whatever to do with an Orthodox rabbis' calling. However, he soon changed the yarmulke* for a beret. He nurtured his "congregation" not only on biblical sermons about the "exclusiveness

---

*Traditional skull cap worn by religious Jews—Editor.

of God's chosen people" but also on the frankly fascist concepts of modern Zionism. . . . The New York Times gave the information that in the 1960's his services were employed more than once by government offices such as the notorious House Un-American Activities Committee, for which Kahane was a "consultant."[3]

As the American journalist, Newberry, said: "Witnesses are not called before the Committee to secure information, but to secure confessions. A witness subpoenaed by the HUAC is presumed guilty, either on the basis of previous testimony by an informer or Committee 'expert,' or by reason of his dossier in the filing system."[4] It is easy to understand what kind of "consultations" Kahane could have given this Committee. "Kahane," the Daily World wrote in this connection, "helped finger progressive people as a pay-roller for the House Un-Americans."

The "consultants" and "interrogators" of this Committee have always been connected with ultra-right organisations in the USA. It need only be recalled that a former Committee interrogator, John Matthews, upon retirement became very active with the John Birch Society, to which he presented his personal file of "subversives." It is not surprising that Kahane has close contacts with ultra-right organisations, including the John Birch Society, the American Legion and the National Gun Alliance which in turn is connected with the Minutemen and other neo-fascist terrorist groups in the USA. And it is only recently that the führer of the USA's Nazis proposed "pooling efforts." . . .

In 1965, when country-wide protests against the Vietnam war gathered momentum, the CIA and FBI frantically strove to "rally public support" for it. And it was just at that time that Meir Kahane, who then called himself Michael King, together with a man called Joseph Churba, announced the formation of his so-called July Fourth Movement, branches of which were soon set up at six US universities. In an advertisement published in the New York Herald-Tribune on June 29, 1965, and signed by Churba and King, the objective of this "movement" was clearly stated: unreserved support for the war in Vietnam. . . .

In the summer of 1967, Churba and Kahane started their Crossroads Publishing firm, which among other things published their ultra-Zionist, anti-Soviet The Jewish Stake in Vietnam.

In those days Kahane usually hid behind a penname to publish his trash but now he has come out into the open. In a "Metromedia" programme on US television on January 24, 1971, he declared his support for US aggression in Indo-China, emphasising that this war "prevented Soviet-American agreement at the expense of the Jews." The leaders of the USA's ultra-right neofascist organisations, incidentally, employ exactly the same kind of "logic," only the word "Jews" they substitute with "patriotic Americans." There is no doubt whatever about their ideological affinity with Kahane. . . .

The links are quite clear. Together with Ku-Klux-Klan thugs, Kahane's fascist riffraff have smashed up premises of the Negro Civil Rights Movement. Following in the footsteps of the Minutemen, these "blue-shirts" have been trained in terror tactics at the League's special military camp in the Catskill mountains near New York, where they were also indoctrinated in a spirit of rabid chauvinism and anti-Sovietism.

But let us return to the Jewish Defence League. It was founded in 1968, a noteworthy year. "The anti-Soviet Zionist propaganda," says the Israeli Communist Party resolution "About the Jewish Question and Zionism in Our Days," "intensified after the June war (of 1967) but its successes diminished.". . .[5]

In this situation the International Zionist Centre adopted new tactics of wide-scale, unveiled provocation against the USSR and other socialist countries. The Zionists sought to divert world attention from the criminal actions with which the Israeli rulers have soiled their hands in occupied Arab territory by means of their long-tested method of screaming about "the persecution of Jews" in the USSR. . . .

The pogrom-instigators of the Jewish Defence League have declared a real war against Soviet citizens working in the USA. "From now on," Meir Kahane declared at one of his many news conferences, "no Russian is safe in New York."[6]

The "blue shirts" have more than once obstructed concerts of Soviet performers, ransacked the offices of Amtorg, Aeroflot and Intourist and have exploded bombs in houses in which Soviet diplomats and journalists live and work. Moreover they do not hide the fact that this is their handiwork. After each act of terror somebody has called a wire service or newspaper office to say that he was from the Jewish Defence League and announce the latest bomb explosion at one Soviet office or another in the USA. . . .

One certainly cannot deny the candour of this would-be "Jewish Mussolini"! As the Daily World has emphasised, the USA's many Zionist organisations, have long adopted an anti-Soviet stand. It is they who have incited the League to its crimes.[7] These activities are in complete accord with the aims of the Zionists, who have declared a war on socialism throughout the world, not just in New York. Zionist leaders are obviously not averse to giving Kahane the chance to extend his activities. With outright admiration for these blue-shirted fascists, the Anti-Defamation League has said that now the Zionists have "a force they never had before." Kahane had already professed intentions of organising a World Jewish Defence League with its centre in Jerusalem. Fans of this Zionist Mussolini have appeared in Israel, Britain, West Germany, Australia, Belgium, Holland and the other capitalist countries, where Kahane is opening "branches." Aping their New York counterparts, and in league with the neo-Nazi thugs, they commit outrages outside Soviet embassies, terrorise Soviet people, and toss bombs into the buildings of Soviet diplomatic legations. The tattered banners of anti-communism now also sport—with the help of storm troopers like Kahane—the Zionist symbol of the Star of David. . . .

The Jewish Defence League is by no means the only arm of the international Zionist cartel which has been pump-priming anti-Soviet hysteria over the past 18 to 24 months. The plan was to climax this campaign by the so-called "World Conference of Jewish Communities on Soviet Jewry" in Brussels on February 23-25, 1971. This Zionist witches' sabbath was attended by some 750 prominent Zionists from nearly forty countries, including also representatives from such international Zionist organizations as the World Zionist Organisation, the World Jewish Congress, B'nai B'rith and the World Union of Jewish Students.[8] To play safe, they disowned the Jewish Defence League and its odious führer whom the Brussels authorities expelled from the country soon after his arrival. Kahane was not granted the honour of taking a seat on the platform with such members of the Zionist elite as Ben Gurion, Arthur Goldberg, Paddy Chayefsky, Otto Preminger and Hans Morgenthau. Only Begin and a few others closely associated with the Herut party proposed that he be allowed in. However if not there physically, he was there in the spirit. The sponsors of the conference borrowed from the Jewish Defence League arsenal all that could possibly be used for "respectable" anti-Sovietism, meanwhile assiduously trying to avoid action bordering on crime. However, basically, their subversive activity is identical with that of Kahane's storm troopers. The difference between the "respectable" and the hooligan anti-Soviet Zionists lies only in the methods used. To realise this one must examine the "luggage" that the Zionist leaders took along with them to their Brussels conclave and note the dubious activities they so proudly boasted about.

I have before me a folder containing the reports of regional and local Zionist organisations, which have clubbed together in one common anti-Soviet front.

As was to be expected the wordiest was the report from international Zionism's American centre. In Brussels, 200 delegates represented the American Jewish Conference on Soviet Jewry, which, founded in 1964, today incorporates twenty-eight leading Zionist national and international organisations. Even their simple enumeration gives an idea of the way Zionist organisations sporting diverse shingles, join hands in anti-Sovietism.

What are these organisations? The American Jewish Congress, one of the USA's biggest Jewish unions with a membership of thirty thousand, whose leadership is now fully Zionist (similar take-overs occurred in most Jewish organisations in the USA during, and especially after, the Second World War).[9] B'nai B'rith, one of the biggest organisations, founded in 1843, has a membership of about half a million in over five thousand lodges in forty-two countries. Its members are mostly representatives of financial, political, scientific and literary circles—Zionism's "intellectual élite." The Anti-Defamation League of B'nai B'rith, an organisation whose aim is to propagate Zionist views and publish Zionist, particularly anti-communist, literature. The B'nai B'rith Women with a membership of 137,000, an active anti-Soviet organisation and a branch of B'nai B'rith.[10]

The Jewish Trade Union Committee, a federation of Right-wing Social Democrats of Jewish origin, with a membership of about half a million, which enjoys considerable influence among Jewish workers in the USA and Canada.[11] Affiliated with this organisation are several Bundist-oriented Zionist groups and "parties" representing so-called "socialist Zionism.". . . Among these are the American Trade Union Council for Histadrut and other Zionist trade unions, including the Pioneer Women, with a membership of 45,000, and the Workmen's Circle.[12] The Hadassah, a big women's Zionist organisation, which in the USA alone has 1,380 local branches with a total membership of 318,000, and publishes, in a circulation of 320,000 copies, the magazine _Hadassah_ which is notorious for its anti-communist and anti-Soviet material.[13] The National Council of Jewish Women, another women's Zionist organisation, which specialises in work among non-Jewish Americans, in order to rally support from Negro organisations, women's organisations, etc., takes an active hand in organising anti-Soviet rallies, demonstrations and picketing, and carries on propaganda among Congressmen. The Mizrachi Women's Organisation of America, the national branch of an international Zionist organisation of this name which has 50,000 members united in numerous local branches. The Zionist Organisation of America, which, founded in 1897, has a membership of 180,000, sponsored the American Jewish Conference on Soviet Jewry, and, carrying on energetic anti-Soviet propaganda, features in its several publications (and circulates) slanders galore about the supposed "persecution" of Jews in the USSR.[14] The American Zionist Federation, founded in May 1970, has branches in forty-seven states. A number of religious organisations also actively contributed to the work of the American Jewish Conference on Soviet Jewry. Among these were the Union of Orthodox Jewish Congregations of America uniting 3,100 synagogues,[15] and the National Women's League of United Synagogues of America with its membership of 200,000,[16] as well as the Conference of Presidents of Major American Jewish Organisations led by William Wexler and the Council of Jewish Federations and Welfare Funds led by Max Fisher. The steering bodies of the American Jewish Conference on Soviet Jewry have been staffed by the National Jewish Community Relations Advisory Council, which, with offices in eighty-seven cities and contacts with Jewish community centres in another 150 cities, has been fully responsible for co-ordinating Conference activities.[17]

This detailing of the structure of the American Jewish Conference on Soviet Jewry has not been done out of a whim. Looking at this collection of Zionist organisations, it is easier to grasp the scope of the activity of the USA's most influential lobby for international Zionism, and particularly for Israel. It has a smoothly functioning machine for mobilising public opinion, and fantastic connections with leading American political and public figures, and can bring pressure to bear, not only on individual Congressmen and cabinet members, but even on the leadership of both political parties, including the man in the White House. It has thousands of millions of dollars at its disposal and controls four-fifths of the US and international wire services catering for periodicals over practically the entire capitalist world. As the Jewish Chronicle has smugly admitted, the Zionists control half the periodicals published in the USA, half the radio stations, and three-fourths of the foreign bureaus of American periodicals and news agencies.[18] The most active propagandist of Zionism, of course, is the Jewish Telegraphic Agency, the mouthpiece of the World Zionist Organisation, to finance which 135 "social welfare funds," controlled by the American Jewish Federation, have been set up in the USA. Another publicity agent is The New York Times, which, owned by Zionist capital, has an information service that caters for another seventy-two papers in the USA, Canada and Europe. "Magazines and newspapers, news stories and editorial columns, television and radio were almost exclusively presenting the Jewish nationalist point of view," Lilienthal writes in his book, The Other Side of the Coin.[19]

The influence of this powerful machine on public opinion in the USA and on the people who make American foreign policy, cannot be underestimated.

References

1. Newsweek, 25.1.1971.
2. The New York Times, 13.1.1971.
3. Ibid.
4. Mike Newberry, The Yahoos, New York, 1964, p. 110.
5. IB CPI, 3/4-69, p. 201 (Information Bulletin, Communist Party, Israel).
6. Time, 18.1.1971.
7. Daily World, 12.1.1971.

8. *Daily World Magazine*, 20.3.71.

9. *Encyclopaedia of Associations*, Vol. 1, National Organisations of the United States, Detroit, 1964, p. 732.

10. Ibid., p. 735.

11. Ibid., p. 740.

12. Ibid., p. 746.

13. Ibid., p. 738.

14. Ibid., p. 742.

15. Ibid., p. 748.

16. Ibid., p. 746.

17. *Documents. Conference Mondiale des Communautés Juives Pour les Juifs d'U.R.S.S.*, Bruxelles, 23-25 fevrier 1971, *American Jewish Conference on Soviet Jewry, a Summary Report on Activity During 1970*, p. 1.

18. *Jewish Chronicle*, 5.1.1968.

19. Alfred Lilienthal, *The Other Side of the Coin*, New York, 1965, p. 112.

CHAPTER

5

ANTI-ZIONISM OR DISGUISED ANTI-SEMITISM?

Most of the Western observers who have accused the Soviets of pursuing anti-Semitic policies will readily acknowledge that discrimination against any national minority is contrary to Marxist-Leninist ideology. Therefore, such Western observers hold, Soviet leaders have never openly admitted their anti-Semitism; instead, they have draped it in the garment of anti-Zionism (and also occasionally in campaigns against "cosmopolitanism," "economic crimes," and the Jewish religion). In other words, they use anti-Zionism to disparage and discredit Jews, and in the process they are rekindling in non-Jewish citizens the dormant flames of age-old distrust and hatred not just of Zionists but of Jews per se.

The Soviets do not deny their bitter opposition to Zionism and all it stands for. But they emphasize that anti-Zionism is not equivalent to anti-Semitism; that there is no Soviet policy in theory or in practice intended to reduce Soviet Jews to second-rate citizens; that on the contrary Soviet Jews are fully the equals of other Soviet citizens; that it is the Zionists who would have everyone believe that all their opponents are anti-Semites; and that the "problem of Soviet Jewry" is a fraud, a concoction carefully brewed by the world Zionist movement to foster anti-communism, to discredit the USSR, and to lure Soviet Jews to Israel.

* * * * *

In the selection below, Paul Lendvai, Austrian political journalist and author of Anti-Semitism Without Jews: Communist Eastern Europe (Garden City, N.Y.: Doubleday, 1971) who left his native Hungary in the mid-1950s, describes Soviet attacks against Zionism as much more than a mere exercise in propaganda, much more even than an assault against Israel, Western "imperialism," or Soviet Zionists. He sees the "tissue of ludicrous fantasies and half-truths," spun with particular vehemence since the Israeli victory in 1967, as nothing less than the "greatest program of organized anti-Semitism since Hitler."*

JEWS UNDER SOVIET COMMUNISM

Paul Lendvai

Since 1967, an "anti-Zionist" campaign of almost unprecedented dimensions has been waged by the Communist propaganda apparatus in the Soviet Union and in several countries of Eastern Europe. Although no serious observer would go so far as to equate the present situation with that which obtained at the turn of the century in Czarist Russia, or in Eastern Europe between the two World Wars, it would be equally misguided to overlook the plain fact that in areas of both domestic and of foreign policy the Soviet Union has in the past few years displayed an increasingly hostile attitude to Jews as Jews. . . .

In the vast array of Soviet . . . literature devoted to the theme, one age-old motif predominates: the motif of a global Jewish conspiracy. Again and again in recent years Soviet ideologists have come forward with new theoretical formulations designed to adapt this most essential component of "classical" anti-Semitic and Nazi propaganda to "Marxist-Leninist" ends. As Norman Cohn has written in *Warrant for Genocide*, the myth of the Jewish world-conspiracy posits the existence of "a secret Jewish government which, through a worldwide network of camouflaged agencies and organizations, controls political parties and governments, the press and public opinion, banks and economic development. The secret government is supposed to be doing this in pursuance of an age-old plan and with the single aim of achieving Jewish dominion over the entire world; and it is also supposed to be perilously near to achieving this aim." The prime literary embodiment of this doctrine is of course that turn-of-the-century forgery, the *Protocols of the Elders of Zion*, an updated version of which served as the "theoretical" basis for Stalin's last great anti-Semitic

---

From Paul Lendvai, "Jews Under Communism," *Commentary*, December 1971, pp. 67-74. Reprinted from *Commentary* by permission; Copyright (C) 1971 by the American Jewish Committee. Most of the parts of the article dealing with Eastern Europe have been omitted.

---

*Lendvai quoted this phrase in his article from Earl Raab's "The Deadly Innocences of American Jews," *Commentary*, December 1970, p. 39.

witch-hunts: the 1952 trial of Rudolf Slansky, the Secretary General of the Czechoslovak Communist party and of his mainly Jewish colleagues (eleven of the fourteen defendants and eight of the eleven executed victims were "Zionists, cosmopolitans, Jewish bourgeois nationalists"); and the 1953 "Doctors' Plot" in Moscow.

The death of Stalin ended the nightmare to which "Zionists" and "cosmopolitans" from Moscow to East Berlin, from Prague to Budapest, had been exposed in the "Black Years" of 1948-52. One of the first moves of the new regime was to denounce the "Doctors' Plot" as a "fabrication" perpetrated by "despicable adventurers." On the other hand, the official repudiation of the Slansky trial as an invention from start to finish did not come until 1963, and it was not until 1968 that the truth (or at least part of the truth) became known about the degree of direct Soviet responsibility for this, the most horrendous show trial ever staged in an East European country.

It is against this background that we must view the recent reemergence, on a broader scale, of the "Zionist" conspiracy myth. To begin with, some of the fantasies from Stalin's time have been revived, blended with new absurdities, and integrated into a refurbished mythology. Back on the scene are the chief villains of Stalin's last script, the Joint Distribution Committee in particular and international Zionism in general—both described as instruments of espionage in the service of American intelligence. Communist experts on Judaism and Zionism now repeat almost verbatim the source-material prepared for the Slansky trial and the "Doctors' Plot"—a fact that became painfully evident in the vicious attacks leveled by the Soviet press against Professor Eduard Goldstuecker, the noted Czech literary historian who was president of the Czechoslovak Writers' Union during the Prague Spring of 1968.* Five weeks after the Soviet invasion, Literaturnaya Gazeta, the Moscow literary weekly, singled out Goldstuecker as a "particularly dangerous Zionist." A pre-war Jewish Communist, Goldstuecker had been among those tortured and compelled to testify in the Slansky trial, and had been sentenced to life imprisonment. Now the Soviet paper charged instead that Goldstuecker had in fact turned witness for the prosecution in order to save his life. Rarely if ever before in Communist history has the victim of a frame-up been accused a second time of the same crime—and by a spokesman of the same power that nearly succeeded in murdering him fifteen years earlier.

Thus, more than fifteen years after the revelation that the "Doctors' Plot" was a "fabrication," a strikingly similar campaign has

---

*Goldstuecker is at present in voluntary exile in the West—Editor.

focused attention on the alleged espionage activities and political and ideological subversion engineered by "Zionism" against " the socialist countries." The erstwhile "murderers in white aprons" have been shown to be innocent doctors, Slansky and his co-defendants have been exonerated, but the rope with which they were hanged is once again being dangled before the Jews of Eastern Europe. In the wake of the Soviet-sponsored "normalization" in Czechoslovakia, Colonel B. Molnar, a leading secret-police official in Prague, took the occasion of an interview to trace the "Zionist excesses" in 1967-68 back to World War II when Goldstuecker and Eugen Loebl (former deputy Foreign Trade Minister, also sentenced to life imprisonment at the Slansky trial) set up "Zionist cells" in London. In all, the web of inventions concocted at the time of Stalin's last plots has been taken over, in spirit and method, in the recent spate of Soviet allegations concerning the "omnipotent international Zionist corporation," the "invisible but huge and mighty empire of financiers and industrialists" created by the blackest forces of world reaction and acting as a "driving force" of imperialist efforts at world domination.

None of this is to say that the millions of Soviet and East European Jews are faced today with wholesale persecution and imprisonment. There is still a world of difference between not being able to get a particular job or an exit visa on the one hand, and deportation to Siberia, or worse, on the other. Nevertheless, the massive and incessant "anti-Zionist" propaganda campaign in recent years has provided a theoretical groundwork that is in some ways potentially more dangerous—because more coherent—than even the pathological fabrications of the Stalin era. The most cursory glance at a few selected quotations from the veritable avalanche of anti-Israel, anti-Jewish, and anti-Zionist literature will suffice to indicate the ominous implications of this latest variant of the myth of the Jewish world conspiracy. What we have here is not, as was the case in the years after Stalin's death, the occasional indictment of an Orthodox believer or a shady speculator with a Jewish-sounding name, or even the indictment of Judaism itself as a "reactionary political force" or Israel as "an aggressive outpost of imperialism." Nor can the current propaganda offensive be seen as merely an attempt to justify an unpopular and costly foreign policy at home and placate Arab clients abroad. What we have here, rather, is an apparently definitive, officially approved, theoretical doctrine, one that provides "new" historical evidence for the old stereotype of the Jews as agents of a conspiracy for world control, and therefore "new" justification for a policy of active discrimination and harassment.

Of course, the ostensible targets of the new campaign are not "Jews" but "Zionists" and "world Zionism." But as Vilem Hejl, a Czech novelist, aptly put it at the time of the "anti-Zionist" campaign after the invasion of Czechoslovakia: "Jews can be set apart and defined more easily than, for instance, the intellectuals, the opposition, or the deviationists. Neither a janitor nor a mailman can be 100 percent certain that an attack on the intellectuals is not also in some way aimed at him. The terms 'opposition' or 'extremist forces' are even more oblique and flexible. But every Aryan knows quite definitely that he is not a Zionist." The average Soviet, Polish, or Czech reader of the by now daily diet of "anti-Zionist" literature would have to make an almost superhuman effort to remember that the stereotypes apply only to the nebulous Zionists and the far-away Israelis, not to the Jew who may happen to live next door.

The potential impact of the campaign may be gauged by the citation of a few characteristic passages from two of the most authoritative works linking Judaism with Israel's "Nazi-like bestiality and racism" and the international Zionist conspiracy. Trofim Kichko, the Ukrainian author already known for his Judaism Without Embellishment (1963), states as follows in his latest work, Judaism and Zionism (published in 1968 in Kiev with a first printing of 60,000 copies):

> What was there that so attracted the Zionists in the Torah and the Talmud and in the ideology of Judaism? First and foremost the chauvinistic idea of the God-chosenness of the Jewish people, the propaganda of messianism and the idea of ruling over the peoples of the world. . . . Such ideas of Judaism were inculcated into the Jews first by their priests and later by the Rabbis for centuries and are inculcated today by the Zionists, educating the Jews in the spirit of contempt and hatred toward other people. . . . The ideologists of Judaism through the Holy Scriptures teach the observant Jews to hate people of another faith and even destroy them. . . . Having proclaimed as their task the creation of a Jewish State, the Zionists state that Israel should not only revive a Jewish State, but also establish an empire from sea to sea, which should rule the entire world. . . .

Whereas Kichko's writings are couched in what may be called a more "traditional" vein and are primarily distributed in the Ukraine, Yuri Ivanov's Beware: Zionism! has become an all-Union bestseller and the main focus of the anti-Semitic campaign since 1969. Published in 1969 in a first edition of 75,000 copies—a second, enlarged edition of 200,000 copies came out a year later—the book was immediately and very favorably reviewed, obviously on orders from above, in all major newspapers and was extensively serialized in mass-circulation magazines. It officially introduced the new motif of an internationalist

Zionist conspiracy linked to Jews everywhere and carrying on subversion against the Soviet bloc. In a key passage, by now frequently quoted as an official definition of Zionism, Ivanov states:

> Modern Zionism is the ideology, the complex system of organizations, and the political practice of the big Jewish bourgeoisie which has merged with the monopolistic circles of the United States and other imperialist powers. The main substance of Zionism is militant chauvinism and anti-Communism. Coming out against the socialist camp, the international Communist and workers' movement, Zionism also fights against the national-liberation movement of the people. . . . The ruling circles of Israel entered the international Zionist concern as Junior partners (this was precisely one of the most important conditions of their existence as ruling circles). The Zionist concern itself . . . represents simultaneously one of the largest alliances between capital and a self-styled "Ministry" on a global scale concerned with the affairs of "Jews the world over" as well as a very large international intelligence center and a well-organized service for misinformation and propaganda on an international scale. The main aim of the concern's "departments," all acting under a single management, is profit and enrichment, safeguarding, within the framework of the capitalist system, its power and parasitic prosperity.

What are the distinguishing and, to my mind, most disturbing features of the new Communist "general line"? They are essentially four in number.

First, Israeli and Jewish leaders are no longer described simply as the collaborators of Nazis in the past and of the "ruling circles" of present-day Western Germany. They are now identified as Nazis, and Zionism is now equated with fascism.

Second, and as a kind of corollary of proposition one, it is regularly held that the victims of Nazi persecution in the past were themselves responsible for the persecution they suffered. According to this argument, it was the Jewish officeholders and "the agency of the international Zionist concern" who were the principal accomplices of the program of genocide, whereas all Poles, Russians, and Ukrainians did their best to save the Jews. . . . According to an authoritative two-part article in Pravda (February 18-19, 1971), Zionists had allegedly collaborated in the carrying out of programs as long ago as the 1918-21 Civil War, when they had worked closely with Petlyura and Denikin in order to further their plan of stimulating emigration to Palestine. Then came the "dirty alliance of the Hitlerites and the agents of the Zionist concern"; during the war the Soviet army saved the lives of millions of Jews, "yet, paradoxical as it may seem at first glance, it is this the Zionists cannot forgive."

Perhaps even more repugnant than statements like these is the spectacle of Jews themselves publicly assenting to them. In a widely-publicized declaration issued by fifty-one prominent Ukrainian Jews, "Zionists" were made to share the blame for the massacre at Babi Yar: "The tragedy of Babi Yar will forever remain not only a symbol of the cannibalism of the Nazis but also an indelible disgrace to their accomplices and followers—the Zionists." This charge, not the least fantastic aspect of which is the obvious cynicism with which it was advanced, has lately been cited as "authentic evidence" of Zionist criminality in a pamphlet now circulating in, of all places, East Germany.

International Zionism—and this is the third feature of the new doctrine, though perhaps the least novel—"represents one of the greatest concentrations of financial capital and one of the greatest international centers of espionage as well as of misinformation and slander." The "cosmopolitan capital" which ranges from the French Lazard bank to the Rockefellers, from the Morgans to Kuhn, Loeb, from West German and Israeli bankers to the Rothschilds, is said to be involved in financing Zionist activities not only against the Arabs, but also against the Soviet Union and "other socialist countries." Enormous quantities of propaganda material have been put out along these lines by the Soviet and Polish, and lately also by the Czech and East German mass media. Variations in style and tone aside, all such articles purport to show that the "Zionists," by exercising control over press, radio, and publishing firms "in almost all capitalist countries," are able to manipulate the policy of the great powers of the West. In their more virulent formulations these writings are almost indistinguishable from those put out in pre-war Germany by Nazi ideologists like Alfred Rosenberg.

Fourth, and finally, by far the most dangerous new motif is the frequent assertion that the plots and subversive activities of the "international Zionist corporation" and Israel are directed not only against the Arab states but also, and increasingly, against the Soviet bloc itself. Thus it is now officially claimed that "the Zionist center" played a key role in seeking to overthrow socialism in Czechoslovakia in 1968. "Zionist elements" were also allegedly involved in the 1956 and 1968 upheavals in Poland. And in connection with the Jewish protest movement in the Soviet Union, *Pravda* repeatedly warned this year that "anyone espousing Zionist beliefs automatically becomes an agent of the international Zionist concern and hence an enemy of the Soviet people." Three months later another authoritative article in the same paper, coinciding with the opening of the second Leningrad trial, was wholly devoted to the theme of how international Zionism seeks to gain ideological and political control over "citizens of Jewish origin in the socialist countries" and to induce them to commit crimes against their own countries. The implications are obvious: all Jews (and only they) are actually or potentially involved; the corporate Jew is a twin symbol of external danger and internal treason.

It would be a mistake to conclude that this tissue of ludicrous fantasies and half-truths is merely an exercise in propaganda, designed perhaps to intimidate but not really to coerce. On the contrary, it has furnished theoretical justification for wave upon wave of what Communist spokesmen like to call "administrative measures," ranging from selective arrests, to group trials like the three that have so far opened in Leningrad and Riga, with more to come, to mass persecution. The simple fact is that the Communist-ruled countries have become the center, as Earl Raab has remarked, . . . of "the greatest program of organized anti-Semitism since Hitler."* What the final consequences of this program will be it is hard to foretell, but it might be helpful, in attempting to assess its full significance, to trace some of its roots in the history of 20th-century Communism. For although anti-Semitism of the Communist variety, as we have seen, has much in common with traditional Jew-hatred of every stripe, it is also in some respects a unique phenomenon. In a very real sense it springs from what may be called an imminent and inevitable conflict between a unique minority group and the operative logic of a single-party system structured along strict ideological lines.

In saying this I do not mean to underestimate the enormous power of popular hostility to Jews, the centuries-old prejudice and hatred inculcated in the minds of Russians and Ukrainians, Lithuanians and Poles, Hungarians and Rumanians alike. The long history of this hostility, which culminated in the profound indifference displayed by the majority of Russians and East Europeans to Hitler's "Final Solution," not to speak of the active assistance given to that program by a minority, is not in need of elaboration here. Nor is it necessary to stress that the persistence of anti-Jewish prejudices in society as a whole has provided, and continues to provide, a basis for the successful perpetration of various forms of governmental anti-Semitism. The main point, however, is that under a totalitarian system there is not necessarily a direct relationship between folk (or emotional) anti-Semitism and the growth of political anti-Semitism. Under the conditions of a single-party system, with a single dogma

---

*"The Deadly Innocences of American Jews," Commentary, December 1970, p. 39.

preached by the party and state, official anti-Semitism or institutional racial discrimination does not arise from the grass-roots level and therefore needs no mass movement in order to succeed.

Thus, it seems to me of secondary importance to ask whether the incidence of political anti-Semitism in Moscow, at a particular time is tied to the personal anti-Semitism of individual Communist leaders. There is of course ample evidence that Stalin harbored crude racial prejudices and that Khrushchev himself was hardly free of "normal" anti-Jewish attitudes. Yet it would be a mistake to assume that the personal sentiments of the dictator or of members of the "collective leadership" govern policy toward the Jews, when in fact they merely color it. Even Stalin's last anti-Jewish campaign, the "Doctors' Plot," sprang less from anti-Semitism in the strict traditional sense than from considerations of policy, as a means to an end: the last great purge, as Khrushchev revealed in his secret speech in 1956, of the old members of the Soviet Politburo. While personal or emotional impulses are of some significance (and under Stalin often spelled the difference between life and death for many individuals!), we should keep in mind the old truism that one need not be an anti-Semite in the conventional sense to engage in or to support anti-Semitic behavior. The question is not whether Stalin or Khrushchev or Brezhnev disliked Jews, but whether they allowed or encouraged or instigated anti-Semitic policies. The troubled history of the Jews under Communism must be viewed in the wider context of general politics, for the fact is that any improvement or deterioration in the status of Jews as citizens has been, and remains, closely tied with the progress or decline of society as a whole, with the rising or ebbing tide of political reforms, even within the framework of the single-party system.

Going back, then, to the origins of forces that are still at least partially operative in the Communist world, we find one peculiar circumstance: no matter how ambiguous may have been the attitude of many socialists and radicals in Western Europe, and particularly in Russia, toward anti-Semitism in the hundred years following the French Revolution, by the turn of the 20th century both Russian and West European socialists had become implacably hostile, both in theory and in political practice, to what August Bebel once called "the socialism of fools." Of course, the special "Jewish angle" was already important in the early days of Russian Social Democracy because of the very strength of the Jewish Bund, the first mass workers' party in Russia on the eve of the first revolution. . . . Lenin himself was certainly free of anti-Semitic attitudes. The point is that on the issue of Zionism, as well as on the issue of Jewish separateness in general, all the Jewish revolutionaries, from Martov to Trotsky, from Rosa Luxemburg to Belá Kun, were of one mind, and not only in 1903, but all along: they all opted for assimilation as against Jewish separateness, for universalism as against any kind of particularism. As anti-Semitism was held to be a mere by-product of capitalism, the coming socialist revolution would, in overthrowing the bourgeois system, also uproot anti-Semitism for good. For the Jewish revolutionary—and not only in Russia—the Jewish Question was not an independent issue; Jewish emancipation was inseparable from the universal emancipation of alienated man from the bourgeois order.

This brings us to the much debated issue of the disproportionate Jewish participation in revolutionary movements in general and to the potent myth of the "Judeo-Communist" conspiracy in particular. The fact is that wherever they had a choice, most Jews favored liberal or moderate Social Democratic parties over the Communists. I do not mean to deny the clear-cut susceptibility of "certain segments of the Jewish intelligentsia," in Walter Laqueur's words, "to the party of revolution." But here two distinctions must be made. In reality, the Jews were much more heavily represented among the Mensheviks than among the Bolsheviks—a fact which was duly noted by the young Stalin at the Fifth Congress in 1907. In the underground paper he then edited at Baku, Stalin wrote, "Somebody among the Bolsheviks (I believe Comrade Alexinski) remarked jokingly that since the Mensheviks were a faction of the Jews, and the Bolsheviks of the native Russians, it would be a good thing to have a pogrom in the party." (Even more instructively, this anti-Semitic joke was republished by Stalin in his collected works forty years later!) But on the other hand, as a look at the number of Georgians, Poles, and Latvians in key positions in the early history of Soviet Russia will reveal, Jews were only one of the "Communist-producing social and ethnic groups" in Eastern Europe.*

Yet the fact remains that at an early date Jews were prominent in leadership positions in Soviet Russia and their prominence left an indelible mark on world opinion, and especially on the populations of Eastern Europe. . . .

In view of their role not only in Russia but in every East European Communist party except the Yugoslav, the Bulgarian, and the Albanian, the Jews came to be regarded throughout the entire area as the group that profited most from revolutionary upheavals. Coming from an urban group and boasting a higher level of education, Jewish revolutionaries were often able to get to the top faster than their non-Jewish comrades. . . .

But if from one point of view the October Revolution appeared in the early days to be the product of a "Judeo-Communist" conspiracy,

---

*See R. V. Burks, The Dynamics of Communism in Eastern Europe (Princeton, 1961), pp. 188-190.

from another point of view the Revolution seemed to embody the first real breakthrough in the struggle against ethnic discrimination. The presence of Jews (in the sense of persons of Jewish descent) in top positions could be seen, and could be represented, as evidence that the Revolution was in some way particularly favorable to the Jews as a group. (Did not Jews, Trotsky, Zinoviev, Kamenev, at one point even constitute a majority in the ruling Politburo?) As a sign of full Jewish emancipation, great numbers entered the ranks of the state and party bureaucracy at all levels. As late as 1927, Jews occupied over 10 per cent of the civil-service posts in Moscow, a fifth of the offices in the Ukraine, and no fewer than 30 per cent of the posts in Byelorussia. These percentages, about four times greater than the respective Jewish proportions of the total population in these areas, clearly show the absence of any discriminatory quota regulations. Thus the Revolution not only freed Jews from the danger of pogroms (at any rate after the unspeakable sufferings during the Civil War) but also provided them with a ticket of entry to political power.*

It was, however, in this same period that anti-Semitism began to be used as a calculated political device, and by none other than Stalin himself, who in 1925-26 relied on it as a weapon for attacking the inner-party opposition. Cynically and deliberately he exploited the circumstance that the most prominent opponents of the ideal of "Socialism in One Country" were old Bolsheviks of Jewish descent (who incidentally had never felt or displayed the slightest sympathy toward religious or "particularistic" Jews). As Isaac Deutscher tells it, it was then that Trotsky, first in a letter to Bukharin and then a fortnight later at a Politburo meeting, asked the "astonished and indignant" question: ". . . is it true, is it possible that in our party, anti-Semitic agitation should be carried on with impunity?" Despite the continued presence of some prominent Jews, above all his loyal henchman Kaganovich, in Stalin's entourage, the pattern of surreptitiously abetting anti-Semitic sentiments was set, and soon became a corollary of the "revolution from above" that came to be increasingly infused with the spirit of Great Russian nationalism.

---

*It is nevertheless important to remember that even in the 1920's the majority of Soviet Jews found themselves trapped in what Isaac Deutscher called a "tragic impasse." "Simpleminded Communists often looked upon the Jews as the last surviving element of urban capitalism, while the anti-Communists saw them as influential members of the ruling hierarchy." Social and economic upheavals wiped out the "unproductive" elements among the Jews: middlemen, shopkeepers, peddlers. In the campaign aimed at the destruction of religious and communal life, Jewish functionaries were second to none in their zeal.

The strains and tensions of an isolated, poor, and primitive society, staggering under Stalin's brutal collectivization and industrialization campaigns and shaken by successive waves of bloody purges, hit the various segments of Jewry more sharply and more cruelly than any other ethnic or national group in the country. The departure from the traditions of internationalism and the reassertion of crude national arrogance, with a concomitant xenophobia that reached a climax during and after World War II, coincided with the "proletarianization" of the party and state apparatus and the emergence of a new generation of bureaucrats. (It is usually forgotten that the current generation of Soviet officials, who attained positions of power in the 1950's and 1960's, was trained at the height of the Stalin era, in an atmosphere of intense paranoia, suspicion, and chauvinism.) In one of his last interviews Trotsky referred to the technique of scapegoats developed to perfection during this period: "Since 1925, and particularly since 1936, an anti-Semitic demagogy, well camouflaged, unassailable, goes hand in hand with the token trials against inveterate pogromists. An important part of the Jewish petit-bourgeoisie has been absorbed by the powerful apparatus of the state, industry, commerce, cooperatives, etc., primarily in the lower and middle echelons. This fact engenders an anti-Semitic mood and the leadership cunningly attempts to canalize and to direct the discontent with bureaucracy particularly against Jews." . . .

If we examine the fundamentals of Soviet policy toward the Jews since Stalin's death, we see only differences of degree, not of substance. True, his last great purge was stopped before it could envelop the entire Jewish community, but no explicit condemnation of Stalin's "errors" with specific regard to the Jews has ever appeared. Apart from minor concessions to public opinion abroad, and in contrast to all other countries of the Soviet bloc (even including Poland), the Soviet Union has consistently suppressed Jewish cultural and educational institutions. Even during the more liberal Khrushchev era there was no real let-up in the imposition of restrictive quotas in higher education and the virtually total exclusion of Jews from the party apparatus, diplomatic service, and other "sensitive" posts. The very prominence of Jews in the artistic, literary, and scientific worlds, so often cited by Soviet spokesmen, dramatically points up their almost total absence from leadership positions. In 1939 Jews constituted almost 11 per cent of the party's Central Committee; in 1952 this figure had dropped to 3 per cent and in 1961 to a mere 0.3 per cent. Among the 241 full and 155 candidate members of the current Central Committee, only one person is a Jew, V. E. Dymshitz; Dymshitz is also one of the nine Deputy Premiers and is therefore often displayed at press conferences as evidence for the absence of anti-Jewish discrimination. In fact, however, the top political leadership is now judenrein.*

The thrust of discriminatory practices directed against Jews in the Soviet Union is basically twofold. The regime attempts to suppress Jews as a group (by refusing to sanction the establishment or maintenance of cultural facilities allowed to all other nationalities, including even such non-territorial groups as the Germans) while at the same time it discriminates against them as individuals (official insistence on Jewish identity through the device of the internal passport, restrictive quotas, etc.). There is a fundamental contradiction in Soviet policy toward the Jews as a nationality, part of the unresolved dualism of Soviet nationality policy in general, which claims to be promoting individual national cultures but also to be forging an "all-Soviet" nationality, itself of course merely a euphemism for the fusion of national cultures with the Great Russian. But the contradictory tendencies of integration and rejection, assimilation and discrimination, that operate in Soviet society at large have hit the Jews more cruelly than any other religious or national group, preventing them from living either as Jews or as non-Jews.

The treatment of Jews as a special case has all along had the dual effect of at once suppressing and stimulating a sense of Jewish identity. There is no doubt, however, that the years since 1967 have witnessed a profound resurgence of ethnic solidarity (though not necessarily of religious sentiment) and an unprecedented defiance of the authorities among a large number of Soviet Jewish youth. . . .

Clearly it is the intention of the Soviet regime to wield the political instrument of anti-Semitism with calculated moderation rather than, as did Stalin, with uncontrolled fury. But the danger is that the fantasies produced by systematic lying may under certain circumstances become a political force that can sweep up a divided leadership worn out by constant crisis. . . . In Czechoslovakia we are still witnessing the effects of a Moscow-sponsored operation to channel hatred for Soviet domination into hatred for Jews. Faced with colonial or internal political-social crises that demand symbolic scapegoats, the besieged and embattled men in the Kremlin invariably fasten upon the traditional suspect: the Jews. The conjunction of old and "new" anti-Semitism in moments of acute crisis transforms the officially nonexistent Jewish problem into the single most important catalyst for all the strains and tensions within the system. This is the recurrent pattern and the "lesson" of Communist history for the Jews, no matter what they themselves may or may not have done throughout

---

*Free (literally "clean") of Jews, a term used by the Nazis who planned to make all of Europe judenrein—Editor.

that history and no matter where they may now happen to live within the Soviet sphere of influence.

* * * * *

Herbert Aptheker, holder of a Columbia University doctorate in history, director of the American Institute for Marxist Studies, and a member of the Communist Party of the United States, represents the pro-Soviet, Western Marxist point of view. Writing at a time when Nikita Khrushchev headed the Soviet Union's Communist Party and government and George Lincoln Rockwell, self-proclaimed leader of the American Nazi Party, led anti-Semitic demonstrations in the United States, Aptheker denies, in no uncertain terms, all Western charges of a state policy of "Soviet anti-Semitism," although he does not dispute the existence of lingering anti-Semitism among some elements of the Soviet population. Not only is there no such state policy, but, on the contrary, holds Aptheker, ever since 1917 the Soviet Union has made an all-out effort—and an extremely successful one at that—to combat anti-Semitism within its borders, has, from the very beginning treated Jews in all respects as equals of all other Soviet citizens, and alone among the world's major nations saved large segments of Europe's Jewry during the era of the Nazi holocaust.

Some of the renowned Jews of the Khrushchev era mentioned in Aptheker's article reprinted below have changed jobs, have retired, or are no longer living, while others have since then risen to prominence; some of the figures and percentages reflective of conditions in the early 1960s have obviously changed. Yet, Aptheker's piece is of more than historic value, for his and his Party's basic position has remained essentially unaltered and so has his contention that what has really happened to Soviet Jews remains "a signal achievement of the Revolution and a powerful tribute to the Marxist answer to the question of racial and national oppression."

THE FRAUD OF "SOVIET ANTI-SEMITISM"

Herbert Aptheker

For many months a concentrated campaign has been conducted in the United States by every means of communication having as its object to portray the Soviet Union as a land and a government drenched in anti-Semitism. Via radio and television, from the mouths of leading

---

From Herbert Aptheker, The Fraud of "Soviet Anti-Semitism" (New York: New Century Publishers, July 1962. Reprinted by permission.

politicians—like Senators Javits and Keating of New York and Dodd of Connecticut—and in the pages of publications whose circulation amounts to many millions—such as Life, Look, Saturday Evening Post, N.Y. Herald Tribune, N.Y. Post, Reader's Digest—this charge, with more or less circumstantial details, has been hurled against the U.S.S.R. It has also come from organizations with considerable influence—such as the Workman's Circle, the American Jewish Committee and the (Orthodox) Rabbinical Council.

As part of the necessary effort to get at the truth, and as part of the effort to liquidate the Cold War, let us turn to an examination of the present reality concerning this charge of anti-Semitism hurled against the Soviet Union.

Who Is Guilty?

The Soviet government is not guilty of anti-Semitism; on the contrary, it is one of the few governments in the world—there are several others now, since there are several Socialist states—which illegalizes all expressions or manifestations of anti-Semitism or any other form of racism. It is one of the few governments on earth which not only illegalizes anti-Semitism and all forms of racism, but also conducts a vigorous and sustained campaign of denunciation of such poisons and of education in human brotherhood in accordance with its socialist morality and law.

Would, as an American, that I could say the same about the United States. . . .

No discussion of the position of Jews in the Soviet Union should begin without bringing to the fore two basic facts. Firstly, Czarist Russia was the prison-house of nations, and among its most awful features was the thorough and official policy of anti-Semitism. The ghetto and the pogrom were regular features of czarist life; and in that society there existed the most widespread anti-Semitism among the populace, especially in the predominant rural areas. This was as wide and deep as is white chauvinism in the United States today.

The struggle against anti-Semitism by the Government and the Communist Party of the USSR has been one of the very important features of Soviet life since the Revolution; one of the most momentous successes of that Revolution is the cleansing from Soviet life of anti-Semitism. This does not mean that all its aspects and vestiges have been eliminated, and certain events since the Revolution—to which I shall revert—have tended to retard the cleansing. But the historic fact is that since and because of the Great Socialist Revolution in Russia that vast land has been transformed from one characterized by intense racism and anti-Semitism into one singularly devoid of both.

Secondly, there are only two European countries in which a substantial portion of the Jewish population managed to survive the Hitlerite holocaust; these were Bulgaria and the Soviet Union. The fifty thousand Jews of Bulgaria were saved by the struggles of the Left and by the very militant resistance therein by the Jewish people themselves. With the Soviet Union, however, one is not dealing with Jews by the thousands but by the millions, and while none of the nations of Europe—or the rest of the world, for that matter—intervened, as governments and states, with any effectiveness at all on behalf of Jewish survival, the Soviet Union did.

In the Soviet Union top priority was given to saving elements of the population especially threatened by the nazi beast. Among these elements were the Jews. Hundreds of thousands of Jews from Poland and Rumania and hundreds of thousands of Jews from the USSR were shipped east out of the path of the nazis. It is because of this—undertaken in the face of fantastic difficulties, when all priorities went to movement from the east to the west—that literally hundreds of thousands of Jews were saved by moving them from west to east. And it is because of this that there are living today—as full and equal citizens of the Soviet Union—about two and a half million Jewish people.

It will not be remiss to recall the words of Albert Einstein, spoken in New York City in December, 1945, before a Nobel Prize winner's banquet: "We do not forget the humane attitude of the Soviet Union who was the only one among the big powers to open her doors to the hundreds of thousands of Jews when the nazi armies were marching in Poland." Nor is it irrelevant to quote the publication of the Carnegie Peace Foundation, International Conciliation (April, 1943); "Of some,1,750,000 Jews who succeeded in escaping the Axis since the outbreak of hostilities, about 1,600,000 were evacuated by the Soviet Government from Eastern Poland and subsequently occupied Soviet territory. . . . About 150,000 others managed to reach Palestine, the United States, and other countries beyond the seas."

The Soviet Union has been the savior of the Jews of Europe. That is a fact, and it is a central and basic fact for any discussion of the attitude of the Soviet Government towards Jewish people and towards anti-Semitism.

What are some of the main charges leveled today against the Soviet Government by those who accuse it of pursuing an anti-Semitic policy? . . .

The So-Called "Quota System"

A common charge is that there exists a "quota" in the educational institutions of the Soviet Union, as there used to exist in old Russia—

and old Poland, Hungary, Rumania—and as exists presently in many educational institutions in the United States, where it is still applied against Jews, let alone the notorious and rigid discrimination against Negroes.

This charge is false. Merit in the Soviet Union—unlike in the United States—basically determines entrance into educational institutions and increasingly, since education is free—as facilities grow—everyone is receiving equally more and more education. Thus, as of December 1, 1960, there were 3,545,000 Soviet citizens in schools of higher education; of these, 2,070,000 were Russians, 517,000 were Ukrainians, 291,000 were Jews, 95,000 were Byelorussians, 88,000 were Georgians, 74,000 were Armenians, etc. Jews, though standing eleventh in terms of numbers among the nationalities within the USSR, stood third in the number of students attending higher institutions of learning; put another way, though Jews amounted to only 1.1 % of the population of the Soviet Union, they amounted to 8.2% of the number of students in institutions of higher learning in that country.

At this point it is sometimes objected—as by Senator Javits, for example—that while the percentage of Jewish students at such institutions may be beyond the percentage of Jews in the population, still the present percentage is below what it was in 1935. And that fact—it is a fact—is supposed to show some kind of quota system and to be explicable only on the basis of such a system, reflecting an alleged policy of anti-Semitism. First, if the percentage of Jewish students is about 8 times that of the Jewish population as a whole it surely does not reflect a quota system against Jews. Second, the fall in percentage in the past twenty-five or thirty years is explained by two things: (a) the casualty rate among Jews in World War II was higher than that for most other nationality groups in the USSR; (b) the literacy and cultural levels of other nationalities in the Soviet Union have leaped forward as a result of the Socialist revolution.

Additional data may be brought forward demonstrating the absence of any quota system and simultaneously going a long way to demolish the myth of "Soviet anti-Semitism." Specialists employed in the Soviet Union, possessing a higher education, number 427,000 Jews, 257,000 Byelorussians and 155,000 Georgians, yet both of the latter nationalities considerably outnumber the Jews. Among scientific workers in the USSR—in both the natural and the social sciences—Jews stand third: Russians, 230,000; Ukrainians, 35,000; Jews, 33,500. In fact, though, as we have noted, the Jews number but 1.1% of the Soviet population, they constitute today 14.7% of all doctors, 8.5% of all writers and journalists, 10.4% of all jurists; 7% of all art workers (actors, musicians, artists, sculptors, etc.).

These facts demonstrate conclusively that the charge of a quota system—while true in many countries of the "free world," including the United States—is not true as regards the Soviet Union.

In this connection, it is noteworthy that Jewish scholars are present in considerable numbers among the faculties of Soviet universities. Thus, several of the faculty members of the Moscow Institute of Foreign Languages are Jewish, including: Sophia Frey, Ilya Galperin, Elisa Rizel, Isaac Salistra, Israel Shekter. Forty members of the faculty of the Lenin Teachers' Center, in Moscow, are Jewish. The Dean of the Faculty of Music at the University of Moscow until his death early in 1962 was Jewish—the famous composer, Alexander Goldenweiser. At the Byelorussian State University in Minsk, 68 of the faculty members (out of a total of 300) are Jewish, and five departments at that University are headed by Jewish scholars, including Professor Grigori Starobinets, head of the Department of Analytical Chemistry, and Professor Lev Shneerson, head of the Department of Modern History.

"No Outstanding Jewish Leaders"?

It is frequently alleged, as part of the charges of anti-Semitism against the USSR, that there are no leading personalities, especially in government and in the foreign service and in the armed forces, who are Jewish. The facts demonstrate this to be as false as the charge of a quota system in education.

Who are some of the outstanding figures of Jewish nationality in the Soviet Union today?

They include:

M. B. Mitin, Chairman, All-Union Department of Political and Scientific Education, Communist Party of the Soviet Union.

Veniamin Dymshitz, Member, Central Committee, CPSU, Member, State Planning Commission of the Soviet Union, formerly chief engineer of the Bhilai Steel Mills Project in India.

Jacob Kreizer, Colonel-General in the Soviet Army, Member, Central Committee, CPSU, Hero of the Soviet Union, Member, Supreme Soviet, RSFSR, Commander-in-Chief of all Soviet Armed Forces in the Far East.

David Dragunsky, General in the Soviet Army, Twice Hero of the Soviet Union, Delegate XXII Congress of the CPSU; Commander, Southern District, European Front, Deputy from Armenia to Supreme Soviet.

It may be added that there are 400,000 Jews who are members of the Communist Party of the Soviet Union; and there are over 100 Jews who are Generals in the Soviet Army.

Among Jews holding very responsible positions in the foreign and diplomatic services of the USSR are: N. Tsarapkin, Chief of the Soviet Mission at the Geneva Disarmament Conferences; G. Mendelevitch, Secretary of the Soviet Mission to the United Nations.

Cabinet rank in several of the Republics of the Soviet Union is held by Jews; among others are Ilya Beliavicus of the Lithuanian Socialist Republic, and Leonid Paperny of the Byelorussian Socialist Republic. In many other cases positions of great political consequence are held by Jewish people, as in the instance of Genrikas Zimanas, Member of the Political Bureau of the Communist Party of Lithuania (and Editor-in-Chief of the Party's organ in Vilna); of Ilya Egudin, Chairman, State Collective Farm of the Crimea and Member of Supreme Soviet of the Ukrainian Republic; of Israel Kazhdan, Deputy Chairman, City Soviet of Minsk.

The editorial staffs of leading newspapers and journals almost always include Jews among other nationalities, and in not a few cases chief editorships are held by Jews. Thus, for example, the editor-in-chief of the very significant journal, Problems of World Economics and International Relations is Jacob Khavinson, while the editor-in-chief of Problems of Oriental Research is Professor Joseph Braginsky, also Jewish.

Outstanding research and administrative figures in scientific endeavor in the Soviet Union include Jews. Thus, the Chief of the Theoretical Section, Institute of Atomic Energy, is Savely Feinberg (a Lenin Prize winner), and the Chief of the Magnetic Laboratory of the Institute of Terrestrial Magnetism is Shmai Dolginov. Among the many outstanding medical institutions in Moscow, seven are headed by Jewish scientists; Professors Berlin-Chertov, David Vas, Nahum Altshuller, Mendel Vasserman, Zinovy Lurye, Liber Nisnevich and Yetim Pasnykov. The chosen President of the Society of the History of Medicine of the USSR is the revered scientist—a Jew—Professor Ilya Strashun. The Chief of the Physical and Electronic Optics Division of the Institute of Surgery (Moscow) is Dr. Eliazar Rosenfeld.

Among those announced in 1960 as having been awarded the Lenin Prize were 38 Jews, and their fields of accomplishment included physics, mathematics, medicine, history, economics, machine-construction, automation, metallurgy, chemistry, energetics, architecture, communications and agriculture.

One of the most distinguished physicists in the Soviet Union—and in the world—is Dr. Lev Landau, who is Jewish. A foremost psychologist, Dr. A. R. Luria—well-known in the United States, for his work has been published here and he toured this country, speaking before professional assemblies, in 1960—is Professor of Psychology at the State Institute of Experimental Psychology (Moscow); Dr. Luria is Jewish.

Directors of world-famous artistic and cultural organizations not infrequently are Jewish. Thus, the Director of the Russian Drama Theatre in Vilna is Lurye; of the Bolshoi Theatre in Moscow is Chaikin; of the Bolshoi Ballet is Feier; of the Maly Theatre in Leningrad is Rabinovich; chiefs of choreography with the Kirov (Leningrad) Ballet are Fenster and Yakubson.

Several of the Soviet artistic performers and literary figures whose genius has gained applause from the entire world are Jewish; Emil Gilels, David and Igor Oistrakh, Leonid Kogan, Vladimir Ashkenazi and Ilya Ehrenburg.

Yevtushenko's "Babi Yar"

Even the publication of the very moving poem, "Babi Yar," by Evgeny Yevtushenko, has been made into an attack upon the Soviet Union and some kind of "proof" of its being guilty of anti-Semitism.

But what is the truth of this matter? Yevtushenko is a splendid product of Soviet society; he is a Russian, a non-Jew, who has helped in the translation of the work of such Jewish writers as Feffer and Vergelis. He is a Communist.

His "Babi Yar" appeared, together with another poem from his pen hailing the Cuban Revolution (for some "unknown" reason the American press, so smitten with Yevtushenko's poetry, has ignored entirely his work on Cuba!), in The Literary Gazette. That journal is the central organ of the Soviet Writer's Union and has a circulation of over 700,000.

Yevtushenko has stated that the immediate inspiration for the poem was the publication of the Draft Program of the XXII Congress of the CPSU—a Draft envisioning the building of Communism in the USSR, and containing a very strong attack upon all forms of racism and explicitly against anti-Semitism. The poem memorialized the scores of thousands of Jews who, together with many Soviet Army officers, were slaughtered by the nazis near Kiev during World War II.

This stirring poem concludes:

> Wild grasses rustle over Babi Yar.
> The trees look sternly,
> like judges.
> Everything here cries out in silence,
> and doffing my hat,
> I feel
> how I suddenly become gray,
> And myself—
> like one entire soundless cry

over thousands and thousands of buried ones.
I am—
  each old man shot right here.
I am—
  each baby shot right here.
Nothing within me will ever forget it!
Let thunder the "International,"
  when forever buried shall be
  the last anti-Semite on earth.
  There is no Jewish blood in my blood.
  But hated vehemently I am
  By all anti-Semites.
  Just as a Jew
And therefore—
  I am a true Russian.*

This poem has been recited before thousands in the Soviet Union, in addition to reaching hundreds of thousands in printed form. It was passionately discussed—culture is a matter of universal interest in the USSR. In some cases it was criticized, justly (as failing to make any mention of the struggle against anti-Semitism that was characteristic of the best in the Russian revolutionary tradition; as failing to note the many non-Jews slaughtered with the Jews in the Soviet Union, and at Babi Yar, itself), and unjustly, too in a dogmatic and sectarian way.

But, basically, the poem and the poet reflect the health of the Soviet Union, the best in its younger generation, and the refreshment coming with the post-war purging of the rigidity, excesses and illegalities associated with the latter years of Stalin's power. While the first edition of Yevtushenko's collected poems was printed in 20,000 copies, the second edition recently issued numbered 70,000. He himself recently visited Great Britain, France, the United States and Cuba and has now returned home.

Yevtushenko's "Babi Yar" was written as news of the swastika paintings in West Germany and the United States, the attacks upon Jewish communities and people in many places of the "Free World," were horrifying all civilized mankind. It is a cry of outrage against such barbarism in all its forms and no matter how covert its vestiges, coming from one of the magnificent products of a socialist society. It reflects the finest values created and nurtured by that society.

---

*For a slightly different translation of the ending of this well-known poem, see page 20 above—Editor.

Economic Crimes Against Society

The Soviet Union is now consciously building a Communist society. This is the task set forth in the Program of the Communist Party adopted at its XXII Congress. It is the third Program that Party has so far adopted: the first, at its II Congress (1903) set the task of destroying Czarism; the second, at the VIII Congress (1919) set the task of building Socialism. Both those Programs were accomplished; the third also will be accomplished—if peace is preserved in the world. . . .

To accomplish this, economic crimes against society—such as large-scale and systematic stealing, speculating, black marketeering—must be eliminated, for they reflect the persistence of an ethic that is incompatible with socialism and communism and they constitute blows of a material character that intensify the difficulties of accomplishing the Program of the Party. Such crimes are few because the society has been transformed and with it its people have been transformed. Still such crimes do appear; under present conditions and in that kind of society they are the worst forms of criminality. Hence for them, in aggravated and repeated instances, severe penalties have been provided, including even execution.

Since these laws were passed, several score people have been found guilty—among the 210,000,000 people of the USSR—of these crimes and perhaps as many as twenty or twenty-five have been executed. Those jailed and executed make up many nationalities of the USSR and include Jews; the press of the West, and especially of the United States—but not of the USSR—has made much of the fact that Jews appear to be among the criminals arrested and/or executed in these cases. These laws and their enforcement have nothing at all to do with anti-Semitism. They are laws aimed against criminals; they severely punish the forms of crimes held to be most awful in a society that is socialist and that is consciously struggling to build communism. They are applied to those guilty, and their nationality has nothing whatsoever to do with the cases.

Professor Harold Berman, of the Harvard Law School, was in the Soviet Union for several months in 1962 lecturing on American Constitutional Law as a Visiting Professor in the University of Moscow. Himself Jewish, Professor Berman had the following to say about this matter:

> In the past months I have read reports in American newspapers that anti-Semitism is supposedly growing in the Soviet Union. To my mind there is a large element of subjectivism and inaccuracy in these reports. I know they are often connected with the recent trials in the

> USSR of big speculators, thieves and embezzlers. However, this in my opinion, does not mean that any policy of discrimination is being pursued against the Jews. My Jewish friends in the Soviet Union with whom I discussed this question, confirmed this. For among those convicted are not only Jews but individuals of other nationalities.

On the general question of the existence of anti-Semitism in the Soviet Union, it is worth quoting Professor Berman again:

> I have been in the Soviet country for almost a year and have not seen any manifestation of anti-Semitism. I have attended many meetings and conferences of Soviet lawyers among whom there were quite a few Jews. At these meetings there were often heated, even sharp, arguments on the questions under discussion. But I have never felt any element of national or racial hostility in these arguments. (Vochenblatt: Canadian Jewish Weekly, May 10, 1962.)

The "Banning" of Matzoh

Much capital for the Cold War was made as a result of the order in 1962 by the Soviet Union banning the baking of matzoh (unleavened bread) in State Bakeries; this also was played up in the Western press as evidence of anti-Semitism. The fact, however, is that the same decree which banned the use of State Bakeries for the making of matzohs also banned them for the making of wafers used in the religious services of the Greek Orthodox Church. In neither case was the baking of the product forbidden, or its use in any way prohibited; as a matter of fact, both products were made in homes and in private religious institutions and were used during the appropriate holidays. But they are no longer to be produced by the State; this has nothing to to do with being anti-Semitic (or anti-Greek Orthodox), but is rather part of the continuing effort to divorce absolutely and completely the state and the church—the secular from the religious—within the Soviet Union.

Revival of Yiddish Culture

For the last several years a process of the revival of Yiddish culture has been going forward in the Soviet Union. Among the crimes, illegalities and excesses associated with the repudiation of collective leadership and Leninist principles of Party and government functioning, during the last years of Stalin's life, measures were taken against the cultural life of the Jewish people. In addition, among the many peoples victimized in that period were Jews. Related to this was the corrupting impact of years of nazi occupation in considerable areas of European USSR, as well as the incorporation within the Soviet Union of areas that had been dominated by quasi-fascistic governments in Poland and in Rumania. These harmful and anti-Marxist and anti-Soviet acts and policies—organically tied to preparing for World War II and then the worst years of the Cold War—have been utterly repudiated and stern measures of correction and of renovation have been undertaken.

In the recent period scores of thousands of copies of the works of Sholem Aleichem, Mendele Moishe-Seforim, I. L. Peretz, David Bergelson, Osher Swartsman, have been published, in Yiddish, in the Soviet Union. The bi-monthly magazine, Soviet Homeland, in Yiddish, has been issued since August, 1961; it is published in 25,000 copies and during the first year carried the creative writings of 112 Soviet Yiddish authors, poets and dramatists.

Concert tours, recordings, plays, theatre groups, choruses—all performing in Yiddish—have been seen or heard by millions and millions of Soviet citizens in the past six or seven years. These individuals or groups have toured every major city in the Soviet Union; their appearances have been advertised in both Yiddish and other languages (on billboards of various Republics) and their audiences are made up of every nationality in the vast country.

As a few examples: A Soviet Yiddish revue, "Zol zein Fraid" (Let There by Joy) has been performed, in 1961, in Zoporozhe, Dniepropetrovsk, Yalta, Sinferepol, Evpatoria, Kislovodsk, Yesentuki, Piategorsk, Moscow and other cities. In Riga, Latvia, the Distributive Workers formed a Yiddish Dramatic Group—and it has given many performances not only in Latvia but in other Republics. The Pensioners' Council of Lithuania also formed a Yiddish Theatre Group which performs regularly at the Kovno State Theatre. The Trade Unions of Lithuania have formed a Yiddish Amateur Theatre Ensemble (52 members) which has presented Yiddish plays in Vilna, Minsk, Moscow and Leningrad in the past few months. A concert ensemble was formed in Czernowitz and this has carried classical and modern Yiddish culture to Moscow, Leningrad, Kiev, Tashkent, Vitebsk, Gomel and Odessa in the recent past. There are many other examples of collective—and individual—cultural performances in Yiddish everywhere in the USSR today, and they are witnessed by literally millions of people each year.

Other forms of activity directly related to Yiddish cultural activity may be instanced. Thus, in December, 1960, an exhibit of the life and works of the great theatre personality, Solomon Mikhoels, was offered at the Central Actors' House, in Moscow. In July, 1960, in Czernowitz, the Writer's Union held a literary evening, attended by 1,500 people, at which Ukrainian, Russian and Yiddish literary figures read from their works—Moishe Altman and H. Blushstein, reading from the Yiddish. In April, 1961, a Warsaw Ghetto Memorial Meeting was held in Vilna, under the auspices of the Trade Union Cultural Council of that city; the Vilna Yiddish Chorus sang partisan songs, a Russian survivor of nazi imprisonment spoke (in Russian), a Lithuanian spoke, in his language, and a Jewish survivor, Mendel Deitch, spoke in Yiddish.

The rehabilitation of those victimized in the "Bad Years" includes Jews, of course, as well as non-Jews. The works of Mikhoels, of Feffer and of Kvitko have been issued in hundreds of thousands of copies; records of reading of the writings of Feffer and others, in Yiddish and in Russian, have been produced by the scores of thousands. Late in 1959 a monument to Mikhoels in Moscow was unveiled in a very impressive public ceremony attended by outstanding political and artistic figures; the sponsor of the monument was the All-Russian Theatrical Association. On the suggestion of the Soviet Writer's Union, the city of Rogochev, birthplace of the famous Yiddish poet, Shmuel Halkin, named a main street after him. (The city already has a street named in honor of Sholom Aleichem.) It is worth adding that the city of Vitebsk, in the Ukraine, named a street, in 1960, after Morris Winchevsky, the Lithuanian-born Yiddish socialist poet and editor, who lived in the United States from 1894 until his death in 1933.

Of perhaps even greater consequence, in terms of the evidence concerning anti-Semitism, than the renaissance of Yiddish cultural expression which is again in the process of development in the USSR, is the really impressive evidence of the bringing of the best in Yiddish culture to the vast masses of the non-Jewish population of the Soviet Union, in forms understandable by them.

Literally millions of copies of classical and modern Yiddish literature have been published in recent years in the Russian, Ukrainian and other languages of the USSR. Thus, in 1957, in the Russian language, David Bergelson's poetry was issued in 75,000 copies; L. Kvitko's in 300,000 copies; the books of Sholom Aleichem in 700,000 copies, and many others.

In 1959, the centenary of Aleichem's birth, millions of copies of his works were issued—including a six-volume collection in 225,000 sets. A general commemoration-day was held with outstanding figures of the governmental and literary world participating. The government issued a postage stamp carrying Sholom Aleichem's face and name. In 1961, the All-Union Group Publishing House issued an exquisite book of lithographs on Aleichem themes by the Jewish artist, Anatoly Kaplan.

In 1960, there was issued a "Collection of Jewish Songs" with texts in Russian and Yiddish, and musical scores by the prominent Soviet Jewish composer, Kampaneyetz. In that year and in 1961, there were performances and recordings of Shostakovich's "From Jewish Poetry," the record containing the voices of outstanding Soviet artists, as Zara Dolukhanova and Mark Reisen.

Plays by Jewish artists having themes exposing the horrors of anti-Semitism, either in Czarist days or in fascist countries, have been produced in many Soviet cities and witnessed by tens of thousands. A feature movie on Biro-Bidjan ran for several months in Moscow theatres in 1961; in 1960, an East German film based on the Ann Frank diary ran for weeks in various Soviet cities; the Youth Theatre of Riga, in 1961, performed its own version of the Ann Frank story.

In the latest issue of Soviet Homeland (June, 1962) figures are published showing that from 1955 through 1961 there were published in the Soviet Union 187 different books by 80 Jewish writers, in printings totalling almost twelve million copies, in all languages, including Yiddish. Sholem Aleichem's works, during that period, were published in the USSR in seven languages (including Yiddish) in 3,062,450 copies.

Just as it is a fact that the Soviet Union was the savior of the Jews of Europe, it also is a fact that no country in the world approaches the Soviet Union in its systematic effort to bring the riches of Yiddish thought and culture and the realities of Jewish life to its entire population.

Education in Communist Outlook

Furthermore, there is, of course, in the Soviet Union continual education in the Communist world outlook—i.e., materialist, scientific, humanist, anti-religious, anti-mystical. As part of this, there is repeated reference, including from the highest level of government, to the abomination of anti-Semitism, its sources and the necessity to combat it. This appears not only in terms of the publication, in millions of copies and in the languages known by the masses of people, of the greatest classics of Yiddish writings; it appears positively, as in Boris Polevoi's best-selling novel, The Story of a Real Man, and in the beautiful film made from that book.

It appears, too, in specific and unequivocal condemnations of anti-Semitism. Thus, for example, the Prime Minister of the USSR, Nikita Khrushchev, in addressing the Supreme Soviet, January 14, 1960, noted the upsurge of anti-Semitic outrages in the West, especially in West Germany, and went on to say:

> The current fascist anti-Semitic incidents in many cities of West Germany are a characteristic sign of the

upsurge of reaction, whose evil maneuvers have long since been widely known to the world community. Many decades ago, during the period when Czarist reaction was rampant, anti-Semitic pogroms had been organized by the "black hundred" [gangs] from time to time. Lenin, the Bolsheviks and all progressives, decisively combatted that ignominious manifestation.

> In Germany Hitler aggressively fanned the flames of anti-Semitism. He suppressed all freedoms, ruthlessly crushed democratic rights. And he perpetrated all that in order to launch his bloody cause—to spark war.

It would be well if a President of the United States would some day favor the Congress with such a lesson.

In New Times, November 4, 1961, as another example—and New Times is a weekly magazine published in Moscow in seven languages in addition to Russian with a circulation of many hundreds of thousands—one finds a leading historian, Zinovy Sheinis, quoting Lenin on the Jewish question. Sheinis writes:

> It is not the Jews who are the workingman's enemies. The workers' enemies are the capitalists of all countries. Among the Jews there are workers, toilers, they make up the majority. They are our brothers in oppression by capital, our comrades in the struggle for socialism. . . . Shame on accursed Czarism, which has tormented and persecuted the Jews. Shame on those who sow enmity for the Jews, who sow hatred for other nations.

Professor Sheinis then continues:

> In the Soviet Union, whose Jewish population is half as large again as that of Israel, Jews are working devotedly, with all our other peoples, in the building of communist society. In the war years they fought and laid down their lives for the Soviet homeland; many were honored with the title of Hero of the Soviet Union, and tens of thousands were awarded decorations. Now, in peacetime, they are active in all branches of our economic, scientific, and cultural life.

With such statements coming from a nation's Prime Minister made before its Parliament, and from a nation's leading historian published in one of its most widely circulated publications, it is difficult not to believe that those who persist in spreading slanders about "Soviet anti-Semitism" are engaged in this effort not because of concern for Jewish people, but because of a desire to condemn Socialism and to worsen international relations.

There is great complexity on the whole question of Jewish culture, and much room for honest disagreement and fraternal seeking of the best possible approach. The general trend, especially in the USSR, but also in most advanced societies, is toward full integration of Jew and non-Jew. The Jews of the Soviet Union have features of a nationality, but are not a nation; and in the United States—where anti-Semitism . . . is sharp and deep and widespread—integration also has gone far. There are now, for example, in the United States only three Yiddish-language daily papers, and 110 English-language papers devoted largely to Jewish people's affairs. The Yiddish-language theatre has all but disappeared, and publication of creative works in Yiddish is done in editions that may total about 1,000 copies. Real integration has gone much further, and is on a much higher level, in the Soviet Union. But the tendency there, very definitely, is away from the decision of post-World War II and towards rebuilding Yiddish cultural activities and expressions in Yiddish itself. This process undoubtedly received a boost when the census returns in 1960 showed that about 450,000 Soviet citizens stated that their first language was Yiddish.

Of course, the general long-term commitment of Marxism-Leninism towards human integration as a whole should be borne in mind; it is reiterated in the Program of the XXII Congress of the CPSU, laying out the road from Socialism to Communism.

It is basic to understanding the Soviet Union to keep in mind its commitment to a materialist philosophy and its principled opposition therefore to religious ideology. This is reemphasized in the present period with the planned move to a communist society. The number of churches—and synagogues—has been declining and will continue to decline, as has the number of seminaries—and yeshivas. They all still exist and are maintained privately by those who feel the need for them, but the long-term commitment of the building of communism is away from religious ideology, practices and institutions. This has nothing to do with anti-Semitism; it is opposition to superstition and to the idealistic philosophical outlook—to obscurantism and mysticism. It is aimed not at Judaism *per se*, but at all religious outlooks.

Anti-Capitalism Is Not Anti-Semitism

It is necessary, also, to bear in mind the anti-capitalist commitment of Marxism and of the Soviet Union. This is relevant to the kind of attitude reflected in certain upper-class Jewish circles, where hostility to the bourgeoisie is confused—more or less deliberately—with anti-Semitism, or hostility to Jews per se.

Dr. Nahum Goldmann, for example, the President of the World Zionist Organization, speaking in Jerusalem, May 27, 1962, according to the N.Y. Times, "declared that Jewish communities abroad, while not seriously threatened by anti-Semitism, were facing dangers of a different nature. He noted the revolutionary atmosphere prevalent in many areas of the world and the fact that social upheavals could ruin Jews of the prosperous middle and upper classes. 'The classic example,' Dr. Goldmann said, 'is Castro's Cuba where a flourishing Jewish community was ruined overnight, not because of any anti-Semitic tendencies of the Castro regime but because of the social revolution he brought about.' "

If this is ruination, then many Jewish communities—not only in Cuba, but in Atlanta and Miami, too—are in for "ruination" in time. But the Jewish community under Batista and the Jewish communities in the midst of systematized Jim Crow do not live as real Jews, and do not live as full human beings. And in both cases, also, of course, the anti-Semitic poison is not absent.

Refutations of "Soviet Anti-Semitism"

Denials of the charge of anti-Semitism brought against the Soviet Union have come from several eminent sources that cannot be suspected—if that is the right word—of being Communistic. We have already quoted Professor Harold J. Berman of the Harvard Law School to that effect. Dr. Goldmann himself, in the above-cited speech, said that the Soviet Union "does not deny equal human and civil rights to Jews"; he differed with its approach to the matter of religion and of nationality—as one would expect from the head of World Zionism—but this is not a charge of anti-Semitism. On the contrary, Dr. Goldmann specifically denied its existence in the USSR; this denial, made in May, 1962, was a reiteration of what Dr. Goldmann had said earlier at the 25th World Zionist Congress, held in Jerusalem.

In October, 1961, André Blumel, a prominent French attorney, and former head of the Zionist Organization in France, having returned from his fourth visit to the USSR, said:

> After carefully studying the situation there, I found no anti-Jewish discrimination.
>
> The cultures of the various Soviet nationalities are reaching ever newer heights and the USSR is determined to fight every manifestation of anti-Semitism.

> Besides the Jewish paper in Biro-Bidjan and the Moscow journal, Soviet Homeland, and besides the books that have appeared in Yiddish, there are in the Soviet Union fifteen performing groups in the Yiddish language.
>
> Jews are to be found holding various official posts, including high military posts and prominent positions in the sciences. Jews are heads of such a vital ministry as atomic energy.
>
> Jews in the Soviet Union are not ashamed of their Jewish origin. Jews must not be dragged in as pawns in the cold war. (Vochenblatt, November 2, 1961).

These are the findings, as of the end of 1961, by the former President of the Zionist Organization of France. They are in accordance with the vast body of evidence. It is clear that the Soviet Union is a remarkably cleansed country so far as anti-Semitism is concerned and that, most certainly, the Government of the Soviet Union is not guilty of anti-Semitism. On the contrary, the truth is that the Soviet Government is one of the few governments in the world committed to the extirpation of that fascistic poison.

The Ultra-Right and the Cold War

In the United States today, the rise of the ultra-Right and the accentuation of the danger of fascism are clear. The intensification of anti-Semitism, including violent assaults upon the property and the person of Jews, is a fact in our country at the present time and this certainly is related to the threat from the Right.

Parties such as the National States Rights Party, the American National Party, the American Nazi Party, and the whole collection of Right-wing vermin from the White Citizens Council to the (so-called) Christian Anti-Communist Crusade are saturated in anti-Semitism and some of them put out literature openly calling for a policy of genocide so far as Jews are concerned. Here, for example, before me as I write these lines is the February, 1962 issue of The Stormtrooper, a lavishly illustrated magazine published by Rockwell's Nazi Party, in Virginia. On the cover, in color, is a Streicher-like caricature of what is labeled "A Miami Beach Kike"; inside are offered for sale, such choice objects as the "Jew Zoo—A portfolio of 20 brutal caricatures of some of the top Hebrews in our national life—plus Eleanor herself," and "Ann Frank Soap Wrappers—Look absolutely genuine and guarantee soap is 100 percent kosher. Put it on regular cakes and delight your friends."

This is what is printed in the United States and goes through the mails; and the editor of this magazine is not troubled by the McCarran Act!

In the face of menaces real and awful as these are; in the face of the realities of the Cold War today and what a Hot War would mean with modern weaponry, the concocting of a frantic campaign denouncing the alleged "official Soviet anti-Semitism" is a service to no one except atom-maniacs and George Lincoln Rockwell.

Among the greatest achievements of the Great October Socialist Revolution of 1917—despite fantastic difficulties and awful setbacks and fearful human failures—stand the building of Socialism, breaking Hitler's back, creating a society with the lowest death rate in the world, the lowest illiteracy rate in the world, the lowest crime rate in the world, the second mightiest industrial capacity in the world, and the least racism in the world.

Remembering what Czarist Russia was—the prison-house of nations and the land of institutionalized anti-Semitism, of the pale, the ghetto and the pogrom—and seeing what the Union of Soviet Socialist Republics is today—a land where racism is outlawed, where anti-Semitism is considered barbarism, and where scores of nationalities live in equality and fraternity, one must hold this to be a signal achievement of the Revolution and a powerful tribute to the Marxist answer to the question of racial and national oppression.

Americans must labor not to intensify hostility towards the Land of Socialism but to develop a sense of friendship for that country and its more than two hundred million peoples. What is needed by all Americans—and most certainly, what is needed by Jews in America—is not the freezing of the Cold War, but the ending of that War. The truth about the two and a half million Jews now living in the USSR will serve to enhance Soviet-American friendship, and so play its part in preventing world war.

* * * * *

In the brief selection below, taken from two recently published official Soviet sources, the Western "bourgeois" press and Zionist leaders respectively are accused of distorting facts in a vain attempt to prove that the USSR is a hotbed of anti-Semitism. To this end, the Soviets hold, the "falsifiers" label justifiable denunciations of Zionism in the Soviet press as anti-Semitic and try to convey the impression that the Soviet state pursues anti-Semitic policies, while in reality Soviet nationality policy has outlawed anti-Semitism from the very outset and has waged an unrelenting struggle against chauvinist and national prejudices.

ANTI-ZIONISM IS NOT ANTI-SEMITISM

For many years now, bourgeois propaganda in the West, especially spokesmen for Jewish bourgeois organizations in the United States and Great Britain have used the press and other mass media to put over the idea that there is anti-Semitism and discrimination against Jews in the USSR. This propaganda campaign was intensified in connection with the Soviet Union's position regarding Israel's aggression against the neighbouring Arab states in June 1967.

Lacking evidence of official anti-Semitism in the USSR, bourgeois propaganda resorts to outright distortions and garbled facts. To make their allegations ring true bourgeois propagandists refer to articles in the Soviet press which expose the reactionary nature of Zionism, denounce the adventurist position of the Israeli extremists torpedoing efforts to arrive at a military and political settlement of the acute crisis in the Middle East. The bourgeois press bemoans the alleged growing Soviet anti-Semitism, persecution of Jews, etc. Attempts are made to draw a parallel between Zionist ideology and Israeli extremists on the one hand, and Soviet Jews, on the other.

The anti-Soviet, anti-Communist propaganda of the bourgeois press and Jewish organizations in the West, purposely overlooks the simple fact that in the 50-odd years of Soviet government more than one generation of Jews have been brought up on the communist ideals. Hundreds of thousands of Soviet Jews are members of the Communist Party of the Soviet Union. Nine out of every ten young Jews between 14 and 28, i.e. at least one third of all Soviet Jews, are members of the Young Communist League. The loyalty of non-Party and religious Jews to their socialist homeland has never been questioned. . . .

Subversive activities against the Soviet Union, other socialist countries and the international communist movement are important instruments of Zionist policy. Zionist leaders are guilty of slander when they say that anti-Semitism flourishes in socialist society. Their purpose is to prove that socialism is unable to solve the Jewish problem and elimate anti-Semitism. Yet, the experience of socialist countries shows that in socialist countries there are no social classes interested in anti-Semitism or in the discrimination against any other nationality because the social and political roots of anti-Semitism have been eliminated.

This does not mean that in one or another socialist country there are absolutely no persons with anti-Semitic or other nationalist

---

From Soviet Jews: Fact and Fiction (Moscow: Novosti Press Agency Publishing House, 1970), pp. 5-6 and Zionism: Instrument of Imperialist Reaction (Moscow: Novosti Press Agency Publishing House, February-March 1970) pp. 71-72 and 74.

prejudices. The reasons for these prejudices, which are not typical of socialist states, lie in the fact that there are still people influenced by views of the old bourgeois society and the capitalist world. Such influences are also exerted through ideological work by imperialism from the outside which is trying to instil nationalist prejudices and sow seeds of discord among peoples and thus undermine socialist countries from within.

The elimination of the survivals of anti-Semitism and other nationalist prejudices in the minds of people in socialist society is not an isolated question, but part of the general question of overcoming the vestiges of the ideology of capitalism in socialist society. . . .

* * * * *

The selection below, authored by a prominent Soviet journalist, is typical of recent Soviet attacks against Zionism. Zionists are accused of having cooperated to the fullest with White Russian anti-Semitic leaders, with Mussolini, and with Hitler for the double purpose of combating socialism and the Soviet system and of creating circumstances conducive to attracting Jewish immigrants to the "promised land." After the end of World War II, the Soviets charge, Zionists became the tools of U.S. imperialism and played a major role in the attempt to overthrow the socialist system in Czechoslovakia and to lead that country back into the fold of Western imperialism. In recent years, Zionists have allegedly conjured up an imaginary monster of Soviet anti-Semitism in the hope that it will damage the image of socialism and of the Soviet Union abroad and create dissent among Soviet citizens. Zionists, the Soviets maintain, are greatly disturbed at the lack of anti-Semitism in the USSR, for anti-Semitism is the catalyst that induces Jews to emigrate to Israel.

ANTI-COMMUNISM: MAIN LINE OF ZIONISM
Vladimir V. Bolshakov, USSR

Zionism: A Tool of Imperialism

The logic of the development of the two world systems—capitalist and socialist—is such that, because of their historical confrontation, the ideological struggle between them is becoming increasingly acute.

From V. Bolshakov, Anti-Communism: The Main Line of Zionism (Moscow: Novosti Press Agency Publishing House, 1972) pp. 1-57 passim, 75, 78, and 82. Reprinted by permission.

The bourgeoisie have been carrying on this struggle against scientific communism and the theory and practice of socialist construction for a long time.

While it builds up its military potential, imperialism is at the same time putting increasing numbers of new detachments of "ideological saboteurs" into the field. At the present time international Zionism is operating energetically as one of these detachments.

"Zionism," the 16th Congress of the Communist Party of Israel stressed in a resolution headed, "About the Jewish Question and Zionism in Our Days", "serves as one of the tools of imperialism in its global struggle and its work of ideological and political subversion against the USSR and the entire world socialist system, with the aim to shake the socialist regimes from within."[1]

That Zionism is synonymous with anti-communism and anti-Sovietism is borne out by its entire history and everything it is doing at the present time.

Zionism joined imperialism's pay-roll not out of tactical considerations but because its class character is the same, Present-day Zionism is an ideology coupled with an extensive system of the organisations and policies of the Jewish big bourgeoisie, who are tied up with the monopolists in the USA and the other imperialist countries. What underlies it is bellicose chauvinism, anticommunism and anti-Sovietism.

Over the years, as it developed together with its bourgeois founders, Zionism accumulated connections and money, becoming a large international concern. The international Zionist body [as represented by the World Zionist Organization (WZO), together with its adjunct, the World Jewish Congress (WJC), and its other numerous branches] is at the same time one of the largest amalgamations of financial capital, an intelligence network and a well-organised propaganda and slander service for international Zionism. . . .

The Zionist ideology, being a mixture of Judaistic mysticism, nationalistic hysteria, shameless social demagogy and racialist concepts of the superiority of "the God's chosen people" over all other peoples, affects primarily the religious, the ideologically unsound and the politically naive. The Zionist leaders appeal first to the emotions, not the mind. . . .

Hand in Hand with Pogrom-Makers

At a secret conference in Moscow on May 2, 1918, Zeire Zion, one of the widely ramified Zionist organisations of that time, adopted a programme that was really a concrete plan for fighting communism and which specifically stated: "Socialism stands in Zionism's way, which means that they are not only two opposite, repelling poles but also two mutually excluding elements."[2]

From its very inception Soviet power fought the underground Zionist movement, which was working hand in hand with counter-revolution. This policy that the Soviet Government adopted did not of course spring from "Bolshevist anti-Semitism," although the Zionists accused it of being anti-Semitic just as they accuse it today. In fact the Zionists badly wanted the Bolsheviks—that is, Soviet power—to display anti-Semitism, and they were very frustrated to find that the nationalities policy espoused by the Bolsheviks was fundamentally opposed to anti-Semitism. As early as 1905, Jabotinsky observed that, "As an excuse for Zionist agitation, anti-Semitism, especially when 'elevated to principle,' is naturally most convenient and useful."[3] This explains why Jabotinsky collaborated so closely with Petlura during the Civil War and why Zionists were members of the governments of Denikin, Hetman Skoropadsky, Petlura and Wrangel, and why they formed armed Zionist detachments to fight the Soviet republic.*

"I still remember the day Jabotinsky arrived in the Ukraine," Haim Davidovitch Okner, today residing in Dushanbe, relates. "In Kamenets Podolsk he was welcomed by Petlura and Vinnichenko with bread and salt in true Ukrainian fashion. They knew that they would be able to come to terms. Jabotinsky cared nothing for the Jewish poor, in whose murder he was a direct accessory, as he helped Petlura to engineer pogroms. They had one common concern which was to destroy Soviet power, even at the price of hundreds of thousands of Jewish lives."

During the rule of Petlura's "Directory," there were several Zionist parties, such as the Bund, the Paolei-Zion and the United Jewish Socialist Party represented in the government of the so-called Ukrainian People's Republic. The representatives of these parties, according to the Ukrainian historian, A. Likholat, "looked on impassively at the extermination of the Jewish working population by Petlura's monsters. The ministers for Jewish affairs preoccupied

---

*Generals Anton Ivanovich Denikin, Pavel S. Skoropadsky, Peter Nikolaevich Wrangel, and Symon Petlyura were all leaders of the White Russian forces that attempted to prevent the Bolsheviks from retaining power in Russia and continued fighting against them for some three years after the 1917 Revolution. As regards Jews, the policies of the White Russian forces and leadership were extremely anti-Semitic and numerous appalling pogroms took place in territory occupied by them. "Hetman," the word before Skoropadsky, means commander in chief; it is a military title formerly in use in Poland and introduced from there into the Ukraine—Editor.

themselves exclusively with registering the number of ransacked towns and villages and the number of victims. Meanwhile the Zionist leader, Jabotinsky, even proposed to Petlura that he form Jewish regiments to fight the Bolsheviks."[4]

The panic into which the Jewish big bourgeoisie were thrown by Bolshevism and their fear that they would lose, not only their money, but also their power over the Jewish workers made the Zionists applaud the most rabid of Petlura's pogrom-makers. . . .

Petlura organised appalling pogroms in Zhitomir and Berdichev in retaliation for the attempt made by the factory workers and mutinous soldiers to restore the Soviets and retake power. Large numbers of Jews were massacred also in Proskurov (now Khmelnitsky) and in Felshtin during suppression of a revolt against the Directory. "The quashing of revolutionary action," Likholat notes, "was accompanied by pogroms in Ovruch, Vasilkov, Radomysl, Dombrovitse, Korosten, Korostyshev, Poltava and many other places in the Ukraine."[5]

The pogroms were part and parcel of Petlura's programme and, as subsequent events showed, of all other counter-revolutionary programmes. It is characteristic that, during the Proskurov massacre, all workers' and trade union organisations were smashed and all Communist party and trade union functionaries were annihilated regardless of nationality, "The Petlura men massacred about a thousand persons in the poor Jewish neighbourhoods along the banks of the River Bug," the Ukrainian collective farmer G. U. Pavlik, an eyewitness of the pogrom, relates. "However, not a single Jewish merchant family living on the main Alexandrovskaya Street was touched. . . ."

According to incomplete statistics, during these pogroms 164,000 people were killed, 34,000 were injured and another 8,000 beaten up and crippled. These were the results of the Zionist deal with counter-revolution in times about which the "benefactors of the Jews" from the international Zionist cartel now prefer to say nothing. . . .

The Zionists conceal the fact that they needed the anti-Semitism of counter-revolution to compel working Jews to rush for refuge from pogroms into the bosom of Zionism and emigrate to Palestine, where colonisation was then proceeding in full swing according to the plans of the international Zionist organisation. Nor do they say anything about the fact that it was only Soviet power which saved the Jews from these torments, when it evicted from Soviet territory the White Guard and nationalist gangs along with their Zionist hangers-on. . . .

A Deal with the Devil

The American journalist, I. F. Stone, who for a long time co-operated with the Zionists, noted with more bitterness than pride that,

"Zionism grows on Jewish catastrophe."[6] This is certainly true of the dark days of fascist domination in Europe.

"The Zionists," the West German newsman, Heinz Höhne, observed in a series of articles under the general title of Under the Jolly Roger published in Der Spiegel in December 1966, "received the Nazi advent to power in Germany, not as a national disaster, but as a unique opportunity to carry out their intentions."[7] . . . We know only too well that Zionism had always looked upon anti-Semitism as an ally in achieving its ends. . . .

The Zionists were quite familiar with the Nazi party (NSDAP) programme of February 1920, which said in black and white that "no Jew can be a member of the German race," and consequently a German citizen, let alone a civil servant. They were just as familiar with Hitler's Mein Kampf, which contended that the Nazis, to discharge their mission, must treat the Jews as deadly enemies.[8] Still, realising the force that fascism represented, the Zionists immediately tried to curry favour with its leaders.

On November 13, 1934, Mussolini gave an audience to Nahum Goldmann who had come to Rome to gain the backing of "one of the most powerful personalities of the Western World" for his plan of setting up a World Jewish Congress to work among Jews unreceptive to Zionism. (Subsequently Goldmann was for a long time—between 1956 and 1968—at the head simultaneously of both the World Zionist Organisation and the World Jewish Congress), Mussolini approved of the idea and promised support.[9]

Zionist contacts with Hitler date back to about the same time. Chaim Arlozoroff, the head of the Political Department of the Jewish Agency, made a deal with Nazi Germany for planned Jewish resettlement in Palestine.[10] The so-called Palestine Office set up in Berlin began to "sort out" refugees with the direct participation of the late Israeli premier, Levi Eshkol. As John and David Kimche, authors of the book The Secret Roads, pointed out, Palestinian emissaries "had not come to Nazi Germany to save German Jews . . . They were looking for young men and women . . . prepared to pioneer, struggle, and, if necessary, fight for it [Palestine]."[11]

With the approval of the Nazi authorities, special "indoctrination camps," where young Jews were trained for work in the kibbutzim,* were set up outside Berlin and other big German cities. As Heinz Höhne notes on the basis of documentary evidence, the Nazis and, more specifically, chief of the Division for Jewish Affairs . . . of Intelligence H.Q., von Mildenstain, who "did all he could to assist Zionist organisations,"[12] kept a close eye on this Zionist activity.

---

*Israeli (formerly Palestine) collective farms—Editor.

How did it come about that dyed-in-the-wool anti-Semites and instigators of pogroms from among the Nazis reached such an understanding with the Zionists who pretended to be the "saviours" of the Jews? We find the answer in the class character of Zionism and its pathological anti-communism and anti-Sovietism. The Zionists looked upon fascism as the force which they believed could achieve what the Entente, the White Guards, and the nationalist bands—in short, everyone they had served in their time—had failed to achieve, namely, the destruction of Soviet power and the crushing of the international communist and working-class movement. Though one cannot say that the Zionists were directly interested in the wholesale annihilation of Jews, they were prepared, however monstrous this may appear, to sacrifice, just as during the Civil War in Russia, hundreds of thousands, even millions, of Jewish lives in order to save the representatives of the Jewish big bourgeoisie and to destroy communism. . . .

Today, when an unremitting Zionist anti-Soviet campaign is being conducted in many Western countries and when international Zionism, flying in the face of the obvious facts, is shouting about "persecution of Jews" in the USSR, many people, Jews and non-Jews, both inside and outside the USSR, note that the Zionists never showed such concern for the Jews in Nazi Germany, although then there was more than enough reason for it. . . .

Heinz Höhne in his Der Spiegel series says, "since the Zionists and Nazis had made race and nation the yardstick of everything they were bound to build a common bridge"[13] which rested on the anti-communism and anti-Sovietism of both. As for the theories about "racial purity" and deliberations about "the Ubermensch" and "Untermensch,"* the Zionists indeed had much in common with the Nazis, even to the point of using the same terms. "Zionist doctrine," Israeli Communists observe, "as well as anti-Semitism derive from the same premises: the Jews are in all countries a foreign element, different from the rest of the population."[14] In his well-known book The Other Side of the Coin, the American journalist, Alfred Lilienthal, speaks of the other aspect of Zionist activity in Germany: "In the early months of the Hitler regime the Zionists were the only Jews to associate with German authorities, and they used their position to discredit anti-Zionists and assimilation Jews. . . . The result was an agreement between the Jewish Agency for Palestine and Nazi authorities to assist in the Zionist plans for illegal immigration into the Holy Land. Even the Gestapo and the SS were helpful."[15]

---

*Literally "superman" and "inferior person," "Übermensch" and "Untermensch" refer to a member of a "superior" (master) and an "inferior" race, respectively—Editor.

It stands to reason that Nazi-Zionist understanding arose and was sustained on more than just an "idealistic" foundation. Hitler tried to make use of Zionism in his fight against Britain. In 1939, when it was decided to set up in Germany the Reich Centre for Jewish Emigration, the British Government published the so-called MacDonald White Paper, which, says the American historian, Alan R. Taylor, "imposed severe restrictions on Jewish immigration" into Palestine. The 1939 Zionist congress called this White Paper "invalid."[16]

Britain, which had always supported the Zionists, had imposed these restrictions on immigration for a number of reasons. Zionism was already escaping from British control. It was now no longer the servant of just one master, British colonialism, but of three. US capital was rapidly infiltrating the Middle East and was coming to hold an increasing portion of the controlling shares in the international Zionist Concern. Zionism's flirting with fascism had resulted in greater German intelligence activity in Palestine and neighbouring British possessions. The German Information Bureau operating in Palestine served as a front for Nazi intelligence. Chief resident agent of the Nazi secret service in Palestine and Syria was Feivel Polkes, a commander of the "self-defence forces," a semi-guerrilla organisation of the Jewish colonists that was known as the Haganah. According to Nazi documents, this man was responsible for "the administration of the entire security apparatus of the Palestinian Jews." As Eichmann's agent, he maintained direct contact with the German intelligence service through the agent Reichert, who was on the staff of the German Information Bureau.[17] The Haganah's leaders, more specifically Golomb, openly opposed Britain's new attitude to Jewish resettlement. The Irgun, Haganah and Stern Gang were the organisations that worked still more actively for Germany. Incidentally, from these gangs have come many of the leaders of Menahem Begin's present-day Zionist Herut Party, which has branches in many capitalist countries where Zionist organisations are active. The most conspicuous among these are the Zionist storm-troopers of Kahane's so-called Jewish Defence League.

Heinz Höhne tells us that the Zionists from these terrorist organisations had no compunction in availing themselves of Nazi help for purposes of resettlement. . . .[18]

The "Crystal Night" was a Nazi measure "to legally remove Jews from German territory,"* (the Gestapo term.-V.B†). This Nazi

---

*The Crystal Night was a pogrom, allegedly in retaliation for the assassination of a German diplomat in France. It was carried

†V.B. stands for V. Bolshakov, author of the booklet from which this selection has been reprinted—Editor.

programme fitted in well with the schemes of the international Zionist organisation. The Mossad, in the person of its agents, Ginzburg and Auerbach,* proposed expediting the Zionist programme for the indoctrination of "healthy non-elderly" Jews desirous of going to Palestine.[19] By March 1939, Ginzburg had the first party ready, and it was soon delivered to Palestine. This clandestine immigration was resolutely opposed by the British, but, as Heinz Höhne notes, "the more rigorous the British countermeasures, the more willing Heydrich's headquarters to help the Zionists. By the mid-summer (of 1938.—V.B.) ships were allowed to go to Emden and Hamburg to transport Jews straight from Germany."[20] To be fair, one must note that although Britain obstructed immigration into Middle East countries after 1939, these restrictions were not imposed on other British territories. However, the Zionists insisted exclusively on Palestine.

In short, German Jews were faced with the dilemma of either going to Palestine via the "indoctrination camps" or of being herded into concentration camps. . . .

In 1952, Jerusalem was venue of the trial of Rudolf Kastner, one of the top men in the Mapai party, to whom Ben Gurion, Golda Meir and other Zionist leaders belong. Monstrous facts attesting to the criminal complicity between the Zionists and the Nazis were revealed in the course of the trial. During the Second World War Kastner had been the Jewish Agency's representative in Hungary, where he headed the Committee for the Salvation of Hungarian Jews. His name first came to light during the Nuremberg trial when Eichmann's agent, Wisliceny, testified that in March 1944, Kastner had had negotiations with Himmler's agent Standartenführer Becher (at the trial Kastner perjured himself in Becher's favour.—V.B.) and with Eichmann himself. Wisliceny confirmed that, at their first meeting, Kastner had given Eichmann the large sum of 3,000,000 Horthy pengos. Wisliceny said nothing about Kastner's real role, though he did mention that as the upshot of negotiations with Eichmann some 3,000 Jews were "released from Germany."[21]

---

out throughout Germany and Nazi occupied Austria from November 9-11, 1938. Hundreds of Jewish-owned shops, homes, and synagogues were destroyed; tens of thousands of Jews were arrested and sent to concentration camps; and an unknown number were killed or injured—Editor.

*The Zionist Mossad le Aliyah Bet was the Committee for Illegal Immigration. On pages 30 and 31 of the Soviet booklet from which this selection has been taken, Pino Ginzburg and Moshe Auerbach, agents for the committee, are reported to have established contact with the Gestapo and to have arrived in Germany during the "Crystal Night"—Editor.

The Jerusalem trial revealed new details about Kastner's connections with the Gestapo. Hannah Arendt writes that Eichmann had come to an agreement with Kastner that "he, Eichmann, would permit the 'illegal' departure (to Palestine via a neutral country.-V.B.) of a few thousand Jews (the trains were in fact guarded by German police) in exchange for 'quiet and order' in the camps from which hundreds of thousands were shipped to Auschwitz. The few thousand saved by the agreement, prominent Jews and members of the Zionist youth organisations, were, in Eichmann's words, 'the best biological material.' Dr. Kastner, as Eichmann understood it, had sacrificed his fellow-Jews (about half a million.—V.B.) to his 'idea.' "[22] Wisliceny testified that the half a million had all been shipped to Auschwitz, where they died in the gas chambers of this death camp.[23]

The Zionist leaders tried to make Kastner the lone scapegoat for the deal with Eichmann, in order to keep themselves out of the limelight. However, nothing came of that. In his authenticated book Perfidy, about the Kastner trial, the writer, Ben Hecht, one well familiar with Zionism's backstage manipulations, demonstrated that the Zionist ringleaders were fully aware of all the Jewish Agency's negotiations with the Nazis, including the Kastner talks, and that although they had known in advance when and how half a million Hungarian Jews would be exterminated, they had not lifted a finger to warn them about it. Ben Gurion and Mosche Sharett, two of Israel's future presidents, had known of Kastner's vile deal. In his book Ben Hecht speaks of one Hungarian Jew who, though doomed by Kastner and Eichmann, had been able by superhuman efforts to escape. The unfortunate man wasted several weeks in an attempt to see Weizmann, the then president of the World Zionist Organisation, and subsequently head of the State of Israel but was nevertheless not granted an audience. Could it have ever crossed his mind that Weizmann was aware of the Kastner-Eichmann talks?[24]

The trial also disclosed that Kastner and his Zionist helpers had zealously acted as "appeasers" in Jewish ghettos and concentration camps. "Thus," an . . . Israeli Communist Party resolution emphasises, "they damped their vigilance (of the Jews.-V.B.) and made easy the work of the Nazis who sent them to the extermination camps. . . ."

"How are we to explain the fact," the newspaper Herut, one of the most reactionary in Israel said when attacking West Germany out of demagogic considerations, "that the leaders of the Jewish Agency and the chiefs of the Zionist movement in Palestine kept silent? Why didn't they raise their voices? Why didn't they shout about it over the whole wide world? Why didn't they appeal in broadcasts of their 'secret' Haganah radio station to Jews in ghettos, camps and villages to flee to the woods, to mutiny and fight, to try to save themselves?

By silence they collaborated with the Germans to no less an extent than the scoundrels who provided the Germans with the death lists, (from Nuremberg trial records we learn that the Nazis were furnished with these lists by the heads of the so-called Jewish Councils, the judenrats, who were, more often than not, Zionists.—V.B.). History will yet pronounce its verdict against them. Was not the very existence of the Jewish Agency a help for the Nazis? When history tries the so-called judenrat and the Jewish police, she will also condemn the leaders of the Agency and the leaders of the Zionist movement. . . ."[25]

The New Master's Bidding

Fascism was smashed. The Soviet army had saved millions of Jews from extermination. Paradoxically enough, the Zionists could not forgive socialism that. Their loud claims to be "the saviours of the Jews," and their wide-spread self-publicity paled into insignificance when compared with the exploit of the Soviet fighting men who extinguished the incinerators in Hitler's death camps.

After the war US Big Business became the patron of the Zionists. On August 5, 1952, shortly after the establishment of the State of Israel, the Israeli newspaper Al Hamishmar published a commentary on a statement made by Sharett, then Foreign Minister in Tel Aviv, which said: "The active contribution of American Jews to the effort to build up our state depends on the degree to which Israel's foreign policy is integrated with Washington's global policies. Our Jewish brothers across the ocean will not help unless we submit to their government's bidding."

The subordination was total. The branches of the international Zionist cartel in Israel and elsewhere in the so-called "free world" became active vehicles of the USA's reactionary foreign policy, conspicuous in the "cold war" years for its manifestly aggressive character of the Dulles-type and for its open anti-communism. . . .

In the new ideological offensive that imperialism mounted against the USSR and other socialist countries, and against the international communist and working-class movement, the Zionists were allotted the role of "deathwatch beetles," to "erode" communist convictions. This line of action proceeded from theories of the "erosion," "undermining" and "emasculation" of communism, that had been evolved, with Zionist help, in the anticommunist laboratories of ideological warfare in the USA and other imperialist states.

The Zionists now returned to the so-called "socialist" edition of Zionism, the idea put forward by Ber Borochov, Nahum Sokolow, and others. In their resolution "About the Jewish Question and Zionism in Our Days" Israel's Communists have thus most aptly described in true Marxist style, the "socialist" Zionist organisations of today: "There never was, nor could there be, a socialist Zionism. . . . But in ideological as well as political respects, also the 'socialist-Zionist' organisations have sided in all decisive struggles, in all tests of the times, with imperialism, against socialism and the movements for national liberation." Lenin's thesis that bourgeois and proletarian ideologies cannot co-exist is confirmed also in the case of the "socialist-Zionists."[26] . . .

Zionists try to convince every Jew, regardless of where he lives, that his enemies are non-Jews, not the imperialists, whom the international Zionist cartel so zealously serves. "Anti-Semitism is eternal" the Zionist leaders preach, echoing Theodor Herzl. They urge the Jews to self-isolate themselves and retire to psychological ghettos, and at the same time they encourage animosity towards the peoples among whom Jews live and work. In capitalist countries the aim of these preachings is to detach working Jews from the class struggle and from involvement in revolutionary movements along with the representatives of other nations and nationalities. In the socialist countries Zionist propaganda attempts to alienate Jews from the ideology and practice of socialist and communist construction.

This was frankly stated by Nahum Goldmann, back in March 1964, when he was president of the World Zionist Organisation: "We have to conduct a face to face fight against the non-Jewish world and even within the Jewish community itself for our right to live as a separate minority, as a minority that does not identify itself with any regime or any country. We have to direct the Jewish people in our efforts and our struggle for our specific right to remain the same Jewish people as we have been for thousands of years, a people united round our creative centre in Israel."[27]

All the Zionist propaganda beamed at the socialist countries is subordinated to this aim. It goes further than Kol Israel broadcasts in the languages of these countries and in Yiddish and Hebrew or the publication of anti-communist magazines such as Jews in Eastern Europe and other rubbish of this type.

In 1966 and 1967, Zionist organizations, on both regional and world-wide levels, took an active part in hatching a counter-revolutionary situation in some of the socialist countries of Eastern Europe. In conformity with the designs of imperialist strategists, drafted with an eye to the defeat of the counter-revolutionary insurrection in Hungary, it was planned to strike first at Poland and Czechoslovakia. In the guise of tourists, businessmen, diplomats, students, scientists, writers and artists, carrying various Western passports, Zionist emissaries began to frequent Eastern Europe countries, bringing in for anti-socialist elements and incorrigible enemies of socialism who had gone deep into hiding, money, instructions, forged documents, weapons and Zionist literature. They set up special underground letter-drops and contacts, spun webs of espionage and recruited men from lurking counter-revolutionary elements and duped Jewish citizens of these countries. In the words of Gus Hall, General Secretary of the US Communist Party, "the bridge-building" policy amounted in practice, to a means of "digging" ideological underground "tunnels." The attempt made to exploit these "tunnels" for counter-revolutionary action in Poland was absolutely abortive. But in Czechoslovakia, in early 1968, the "quiet" counter-revolution enjoyed temporary success.

How did international Zionism operate during these developments?

"Considerable influence in the struggle against socialism in Czechoslovakia," says the document entitled "The Lessons of the Crisis Development in the Communist Party and Society of Czechoslovakia after the 13th Congress of the Communist Party of Czechoslovakia," which this party's Central Committee adopted at its plenary meeting in December 1970, "was exerted by forces coming out actively from positions of Zionism, which is one of the instruments used by international imperialism and anti-communism. Among their prominent representatives in our country were F. Kriegel, J. Pelikan, A. Lustig, E. Goldstücker, A. Liehm, E. Loebl and K. Winter."[28] The Zionist centre active in Czechoslovakia received energetic backing from abroad.

Here is a brief list of Zionist organisations, which, in league with other persons, associations, groups, societies and imperialist intelligence services "concerned," took part in subversive activity in Czechoslovakia and subsidised and advised the counter-revolutionaries, who pretended to be "liberalising" socialism: the World Zionist Organisation, the World Jewish Congress, the Zionist Youth Organisation, the Congress of European Zionists, the Co-Ordinating Board of Jewish Organisations, the International Council of Jewish Women, the World Sephardi Federation, the Women's International Zionist Organisation, the World Council of Jewish Workers, the World Union of Jewish Students, the Jewish Telegraphic Agency and the World Congress of Jewish Journalists. . . .

In conformity with the libretto for the "quiet" counter-revolution that had been prepared in the USA by the Hudson Institute, international Zionism was allotted an important role in the Czechoslovak events. Its principal task was to seize the press and other mass media. . . .

The Zionists seized the leading executive posts in virtually all the mass media in Czechoslovakia, and, with the assistance of this powerful lever for influencing public opinion, carried on rabid propaganda against the Communist Party of Czechoslovakia, the USSR, the CPSU, and the Communist parties of the fraternal socialist countries. . . .

After the troops of the five Warsaw Treaty countries, at the request of thousands of Czechoslovak Communists, including members of the Central Committee of the Communist Party of Czechoslovakia and of the Czechoslovak Government, came to the assistance of the fraternal people of Czechoslovakia in their struggle against counter-revolution, the Zionist underground movement turned to illegal methods of struggle. The many secret radio stations that were active in Czechoslovakia in disseminating anti-socialist slanders were staffed by rabid Zionists, including "advisers" from among Israeli citizens.

The collapse of the plot of international reaction in Czechoslovakia upset the far-reaching schemes of US imperialism and its Zionist agents. The "bridge-building" policy was scathingly criticised even by people who had once supported it. . . . The Zionist organisations were ordered to abandon all "moderation" with respect to the USSR and to mount an "offensive campaign." . . .

Under the Flag of Anti-Sovietism

International Zionism particularly intensified anti-communist activity during the preparations for, and after, the June 1967 war against the Arab countries. During 1966-68, the Zionists switched to a policy of outright interference in the affairs of the socialist countries, firstly Czechoslovakia and Poland.[29] In early 1969, when all hopes of successful counter-revolution in Czechoslovakia had been completely dashed, the international Zionist corporation decided to declare a "psychological war" against the USSR. This was started under the repeatedly discredited pretext of "defending Soviet Jews." . . .

Zionism's anti-Soviet campaign reached a truly hysterical pitch as soon as the news broke of the trial of a gang of criminals, including Jews, who had tried to hijack a plane near the Soviet-Finnish border. Speaking in the Knesset in this connection, Meir Vilner, General Secretary of the Communist Party of Israel, strongly criticized the Zionist supporters of this gang of criminals then on trial in a Soviet court of law. "All this talk," he said, "about Jews being tried (in Leningrad—V.B.) just because they are Jews is nothing but slander, as should be quite apparent from the simple fact that there are Russians among the would-be hijackers. All this talk about Jews being tried just because they asked for permission to go to Israel is nothing more than slander, because many have been allowed to go to Israel from the Soviet Union. Anti-Soviet hysteria has always been an element of the global cold war against the Soviet Union and it still is. One of its aims is to try to divert world public attention away from the grievous plight of the Arabs in the occupied (by Israel.-V.B.) territories and away from the condition of Negroes in the USA."[30]

In the "cold war" against the USSR the Zionists have always clubbed together with the US imperialists—as we well know.

It stands to reason that it is not concern for their "blood brethren" that causes Zionist lamentations over the "persecution" of Soviet Jews. The Zionists are infuriated precisely because there is no anti-Semitism in the USSR, which would stimulate a mass emigration of Soviet Jews to Israel. The British Guardian has said that, "Russia is the last real reservoir of potential immigrants since there is considerable evidence that the Jewish communities of Western Europe and the United States, mostly comfortably off and subject to no persecution, have lost the urge to go and dig the desert for Zionism."[31] International capitalism gives Zionism unreserved support because of Zionism's hatred for and ideological sabotage of socialism. In imperialism's war of ideas against socialism, the Zionist leaders have been set two main objectives. The first is to try to discredit socialism's image and ideas in the eyes of the working class in the capitalist countries, and the second is to erode as far as possible the communist convictions of the working people in the socialist countries. And, indeed, all of Zionist propaganda beamed at the USSR and the other socialist countries is dictated by these aims. But Zionist activities are not restricted to the broadcasts of "Free Europe," a station where Zionists are most active, and of the "Voice of Israel" in Russian, Yiddish or Hebrew or to the publication of cheap anti-Soviet magazines such as Jews in Eastern Europe and other publications of that nature. On the contrary, along with its provocatory terroristic activities, international Zionism's main concern is attempting to organise acts of outright interference in the USSR's internal affairs and carry on espionage and subversion.

In recent years, with the help of tourists, certain Western journalists accredited in the USSR, visiting businessmen and exchange students, the international Zionist concern has been endeavouring to organise the illicit delivery to the USSR of Zionist literature in Russian and to start a Zionist underground movement in this country. For example, printed in neatly got-out pocket-sized booklets on airmail paper is a gross slander against the policies of the Soviet Government. The anonymous "well-wishers," taking upon themselves the right to speak for "all Jews," attempt to blacken the socialist system. They do more than that. They also instruct. For instance, the Zionist rag, Home!, which says: "The war must be fought by every means ranging from anonymous letters westward to open statements." They try to recruit more followers, never letting the opportunity pass to explain their views to the uninitiated. "The underlying principle of the Zionist's day-to-day work," says one Zionist booklet, "is very simple. It is that a Zionist must be a Zionist at every step in life. He must stop to think over everything in his life, whether it be a major event or a trifle, and consider whether it cannot be used for the good of our cause. Not a single chance must be lost."32

It is not difficult to guess what the Zionists mean by "the good of our cause." . . . The Soviet people will not let Zionist agents operate in their midst and provoke hostility in the monolithic multi-national family, which for over fifty years now has successfully been creating a new society. This new society has no room for the exploiting class that nourishes Zionism: nor will it tolerate anti-Semitism or any of the forms of racialism that flourish and are legalised in the Israel of the Zionists.

In the Soviet Union these forms of discrimination have been rooted out and prohibited by law. . . .

References

1. Information Bulletin, Communist Party Israel (IB CPI) Tel Aviv, 3/4-69, p. 202.
2. Central State Archives of October Revolution, file 11, part 2, "B," 1898.
3. Jabotinsky, Critics of Zionism. Odessa, 1905.
4. A. V. Likholat, Defeat of Nationalist Counter-Revolution in the Ukraine (1917-1922). Moscow, 1954, p. 168.
5. Ibid., p. 167.
6. New York Review of Books, 3.8.1967.
7. The Trial of German Major War Criminals, Proceedings of the International Military Tribunal Sitting at Nuremberg,Germany. London, 1946, Part 2, p. 380.
8. Ibid.
9. Yuri Ivanov, Caution: Zionism! Moscow, 1970, p. 82.
10. IB CPI, 3/4-69, p. 196.
11. John and David Kimche, The Secret Roads. London, 1954, p. 27.
12. Der Spiegel, 19.12.1966.
13. Ibid.
14. IB CPI, 3/4-69 pp. 190-191.
15. Alfred Lilienthal, The Other Side of the Coin. New York, 1965, p. 19.
16. A. R. Taylor, Prelude to Israel. Beirut, 1970, p. 55.
17. Der Spiegel, 19.12.1966.
18. Ibid.
19. Ibid.
20. Ibid.
21. The Trial of German Major War Criminals, Part 3, p. 287.
22. Hannah Arendt, Eichmann in Jerusalem. New York, 1965, p. 42.

23. The Trial of German Major War Criminals, Part 4, pp. 723-724.
24. V. Prakhie, Truth About "Promised Land." Odessa, 1969.
25. Herut, 25.5.1964.
26. IB CPI, 3/4-69, pp. 209-210.
27. Ibid., p. 191.
28. The Lessons of the Crisis Development in the Communist Party and Society of Czechoslovakia After the 13th Congress of the Communist Party of Czechoslovakia. Moscow, 1971, p. 27.
29. Yuri Ivanov, Caution: Zionism!, pp. 156-157.
30. The Communist Party of Israel in the Knesset About the Leningrad Trial, Press Release IB CPI, 22.12.1970, pp. 1-3.
31. The Guardian, 28.12.1970.
32. Pravda, 19.2.1971.

CHAPTER

6

SOVIET JEWS TESTIFY

No books on the position and treatment of Soviet Jews, and surely no book of readings on the subject, could ever be complete without giving due consideration to the testimony of Soviet Jews themselves. As is to be expected, such testimony runs the gamut from charges of anti-Semitism, emanating predominantly from some of those who either want to emigrate or who have emigrated already, to highly approbatory testimonials by "loyal" Soviet citizens of Jewish extraction. The testimony of the former has been challenged by some as "Zionist" or "imperialist" inspired or as an attempt to ingratiate themselves with authorities in their newly chosen domicile, usually Israel; the testimony of the latter has been denounced by others as dictated from above. Yet, neither the denunciations nor the endorsements may be so meaningless as one might suspect since the former group, after all, could have chosen to remain in the Soviet Union and the latter to look for greener pastures abroad. Hence, the reader should not assume a priori that one or the other group is intentionally deceitful. Contradictory though their statements may be, they might well reflect the experiences, the views, and the feelings of those who made them.

In the first five sections of this chapter, present or former Soviet Jews who, in varying degrees, are critical of the Soviet treatment of Jews speak out; in the last six sections, other Soviet Jews present their case, taking a strongly pro-Soviet stance.

* * * * *

In the following selection, Alla Rusinek, a Jewish woman now living in Israel, tells what conditions were like for her in the

Soviet Union, how she became aware of being a Jew, and how she responded to her situation.

"HOW THEY TAUGHT ME I WAS A JEW"

You ask me how I came to the idea of leaving the Soviet Union and going to Israel. I think that though I heard about Israel only four years ago my whole life was the way to it. You can see it yourself.

I was born in Moscow in 1949 and was the most typical Soviet girl. I studied well, was a young Pioneer-Leninist. My classmates thought me very ambitious. But they were wrong. My family was very poor. Mother brought us up, two daughters, without a father and on a very low salary. We never had new clothes. I never thought about our poverty. I was sure that everybody lived this way, at least the families of engineers, because my mother was an engineer.

I gave all my time to my school, my Pioneer organization and later the Young Communist League—the Komsomol. I worked hard. And I was happy coming home late after school. According to Communist ideals, "the individual must sacrifice his own personal interests for that of the socialist society at large." And I loved my country, my Soviet people.

My? Yes, I thought it was mine. But there was something that made me different from other people. I happened to be born a Jew. I didn't know what it meant but it was written in my identity card: Yevreika. My Russian classmates insulted each other with this word. I saw it written in chalk on the walls of the houses. It was written very distinctly in my identity card and legalized by a round seal of the government. At the beginning of every school year the teacher asked everybody: "Your name and nationality." I answered in whispers.

Little by little I began to understand what it meant to be Jewish. In 1961 I was not admitted to a special English high school. In 1966 I was not admitted to the Institute of Foreign Languages. I thought it was my personal failure and couldn't understand why the examiner, looking at my identity card, said that I didn't speak good Russian.

Well, in other words, I understand at last. They don't want me. I am a stranger, this is not my country. But where is a place for me? I began to be proud of being Jewish.

When I heard about Israel in 1967, about "an aggressive, capitalist state, an agent of U.S. imperialism in the Middle East," I didn't fail to understand it was my home, my people, defending their young

---

state. I understood that to be Jewish meant to belong to the Jewish nation with its history, culture, religion.

I began to study Hebrew. In some old books I learned the first facts about Jewish history: the Maccabees, the Warsaw ghetto. For the first time in my life I went to the synagogue, the only synagogue in Moscow, where I saw thousands of people who looked like me and thought like me. We sang Jewish songs, we danced Israeli dances. It was wonderful but it was dangerous. Secret police entered my life. They followed me, they searched me, they called me in for "frank talks" and threatened me. What did I think then about Communism? I didn't think. I was tired and frightened. For two years I applied for an exit visa and was refused. I applied alone. Mother had died after eight years of dreadful disease.

I was not alone in this struggle. There were thousands of us in Russia who came to the synagogue to sing. And among them was one, the most handsome boy in the Soviet Union at least. A year after we met at a Chanukah party we married. We were in a hurry, any of us could be arrested then in the summer of 1970. Most of our friends were arrested then in Leningrad and Riga. We didn't want to lose each other.

A week after our marriage I was informed that I had to leave the country within six days and alone.

Please, don't ask me what I felt. I don't remember. Perhaps I was in a deep shock. No, I didn't cry. His family paid for me the sum the Soviets demanded for "renunciation of Soviet citizenship"—900 rubles [nearly $1,000]. I never thought I owned such an expensive thing or I would have sold it and bought something nice. All these months I have hoped they would allow him to join me. We are husband and wife. One family. But he has not been allowed to leave.

You ask me what I think about Israel now that I live there. It is difficult to answer this question. It's the same as if you ask me what I thought about myself. I can't praise myself. Israel is me and I am Israel.

P.S. I have just learned today (Wednesday) after my article was written that my husband has been granted permission to leave the Soviet Union and join me in Israel. I wish to express my thanks to everyone who has helped, and particularly to the American people.

* * * * *

On October 14, 1970, police officers searched the apartment of Raiza Palatnik, a young Jewish woman born in 1936 in Odessa, and found there "slanderous, anti-Soviet Zionist literature." After several interrogations by the KGB, Raiza Palatnik, on November 20, 1970, wrote the open letter reprinted below in which she explains how she became aware that there was no future for her in the country of her birth. In subsequent questioning, she refused to cooperate in any way; although she was trained as a philologist in Russian literature and had full command of the Russian language, she even refused to answer her interrogators in any language other than Yiddish and demanded a translator. In June 1971, she went on trial in the Odessa provincial court and was sentenced to two years in a detention camp, reportedly on charges of "planning to slander the Soviet Union."*

"I HAVE NO FUTURE IN THE COUNTRY IN WHICH I WAS BORN"

I was born in a small town of a Jewish family. Yiddish and Jewish traditions were taught me at home. There was no Jewish school and therefore I attended a Russian one. In childhood I felt myself Jewish and consciously sought for ways to express a personal, national identification.

In the eighth grade my refusal to learn Ukrainian and insistence that my mother tongue was Yiddish confounded the school authorities. I was 14 when the unbridled anti-Semitic campaign known as the struggle against cosmopolitanism—*bezrodny cosmopolity*—began. I remember the atmosphere of fear and trepidation in the family, awaiting something terrible, frightful and unavoidable. During that period I kept a diary. Now that I reread it before destroying it so that it will not fall into the hands of the KGB, I again relive the pain and bitterness, anger and resentment of those days. Even then I could not understand why it was enough to be a Jew in order to be ostracized and persecuted.

Then Stalin died. The doctors were rehabilitated. Beria and his henchmen were executed. With childish naivete I exulted and believed that justice had triumphed. I enrolled in the Institute for Librarians in Moscow. I remember the enthusiasm with which I learned of the condemnation of the personality cult of Stalin by the 20th Congress of the Communist Party. But why did they not give so much as a hint of the physical destruction of the finest representatives of the Jewish intelligentsia from 1949 to 1952? Why did they not condemn

---

From an open letter by Raiza Palatnik in Richard Cohen, ed., *Let My People Go!* (New York: Popular Library, 1971), pp. 69-72. Reprinted by permission.

---

*Cohen, ed., *Let My People Go!* p. 73.

anti-Semitism, which had been raised to the status of national policy? Why did they not open Jewish schools, theaters, newspapers, magazines? These questions and others like them puzzled me.

That my belief in the liquidation of anti-Semitism was only an illusion I began to understand when I finished at the Institute and began to look for work. No one was interested in my knowledge and capabilities. The fact that I belonged to the Jewish nationality shut out all opportunities for work in a major library. With difficulty I managed to find a job in Odessa in a small library, where I work to this day.

With renewed intensity dozens of questions came to me to which I found no answers in official literature. I began to read Samizdat.* The sentencing of Joseph Brodsky I perceived as part of a new stage of Soviet anti-Semitism. The poet was condemned on the evidence of patent anti-Semites who did not even know him personally, while the efforts of Marshak, Tshukovski, Paustovski and others who cried out in his defense were of no avail. After this came the trial of Daniel and Siniavsky. . . .

In search of a solution I began to think more and more of Israel. The prelude to the Six Day War shocked me to my very roots. It seemed to me that the whole world looked on apathetically while well-equipped armies prepared to finish Hitler's work, to annihilate the small Jewish nation of 2,500,000, to erase from the face of the earth the State of Israel reborn after 2,000 years. On the eve of the war, when the Strait of Tiran was closed, the UN forces were expelled and the Arab armies approached the borders of Israel; while Fedorenko was cynically declaring in the UN, "Don't over-dramatize events," I was close to nervous exhaustion. I wanted to shout to humanity, "Help!"

Then I understood that I could have no future in the country in which I was born, and that I had no alternative save reunion with my people who had suffered so much, in my ancestral homeland.

I remember the unbounded pride and happiness when the reborn David again conquered Goliath. The flood of anti-Semitic curses and hysteria from the Soviet press, radio and television forced me to feel even more strongly my unbroken bond to Israel and my personal responsibility for her. I began actively to interest myself in everything connected with Israel. Friends who felt as I did discussed the possibility of leaving for Israel.

The press conference [March 1970] † organized by the authorities in which the "loyal" Jews slandered Israel in the name of all Soviet Jews, meaning also in my name, aroused a deep bitterness. How to

---

*Literally "self-publish," Samizdat refers to underground literature published clandestinely in the USSR—Editor.

†See pages 204-206 below—Editor.

shout out that they are just a tiny group and that the majority thinks otherwise? And then I heard over the radio the letter of the 39. How sorry I was that I could not also sign that letter! I typed this letter so that my friends could also read it.

I applied to P.O.B. 92 with a request to locate my relatives in Israel. And then the KGB began to show an interest in me. They searched my apartment and that of my parents. I am constantly summoned for questioning. My friends and relatives, the people I work with, are interrogated and pressured to give witness to my anti-Soviet activity. I understand that arrest and maybe years of imprisonment await me. But I know one thing positively: my fate is tied irrevocably to Israel. No imprisonments in Leningrad, Riga and Kishinev can halt the struggle for repatriation to Israel.

To my regret I do not know my people's tongue, Hebrew, but in my trial I will cry out against all anti-Semites in the Yiddish I was taught by my mother and father.

* * * * *

In February 1968, an anonymous letter addressed to A. Snietskus, first secretary of the Central Committee of the Lithuanian Communist Party, voiced bitter complaints about conditions for Jews in Lithuania. The authors, claiming to be 26 "representatives of the Jewish intelligentsia" but stating they had decided not to sign their surnames, charge that anti-Semitism has not only persisted but has actually been on the rise in Lithuania since the end of World War II. Excerpts from this letter are reprinted below.

RISING ANTI-SEMITISM IN LITHUANIA

We, Communist and non-Party representatives of the Jewish intelligentsia who have discussed and signed this document, address ourselves to the Central Committee of the Lithuanian Communist Party because of our great anxiety about the rising wave of anti-Semitism in Soviet Lithuania. . . .

We realize that the anti-Israel propaganda conducted by the Soviet press is not intended for internal consumption and is not directed at Jews who live in the Soviet Union. However, we should not ignore the fact that, despite all the stylistic nuances, the anti-Israel propaganda,

---

From Moshe Decter, ed., REDEMPTION! REDEMPTION! REDEMPTION!: Jewish Freedom Letters from Russia (New York: American Jewish Conference on Soviet Jewry and Conference on the Status of Soviet Jews, 1970), pp. 10-14. Reprinted by permission.

and especially the cartoons in the central press, have revived anti-Semitic passions in a certain part of the Lithuanian (and not only Lithuanian) people. Therefore we can not be silent at a time when in the present tense situation new notes emerge that give a local character to the entire matter. We can not be silent when the press publishes material that nourishes local judeophobia. . . .

We would like to point out that, because of the onesidedness of our propaganda, objective conditions have been created for the flourishing of anti-Semitism. Individual leading personalities, Communists, are quite openly promoting it and are personally willingly expressing it. Here are several facts out of many:

When the Deputy Minister of Trade, Kazbaras, was reproached for not observing the Leninist principle of selecting cadres on the basis of their political and technical qualifications, he replied publicly: "To be a Lithuanian in Soviet Lithuania is a political qualification."

The Deputy Chairman of Television, Kuolelis, openly criticized a correspondent in a meeting for his Jewish mannerisms on the screen.

The President of the Pedagogical Institute, Uogintas, bluntly told one of the instructors: "It matters little that today you excel others in the German or English languages, in physics or mathematics, chemistry or music. We will develop our own cadres so that tomorrow Lithuanians will be more qualified than you." All Uogintas did was to give public expression to a principle that has been in force for a long time in cadre [employment] policy.

Here are the facts. During the entire postwar period, not a single Jewish student living in Lithuania (except for a few children of privileged persons) was given a state scholarship to continue his studies at institutions of higher learning in Moscow or Leningrad. Not a single Jew originating from Lithuania has taken post-graduate courses in the institutes of Moscow or Leningrad. Not a single Jewish Communist has attended the Academy of Social Sciences or the Party University of the Soviet Communist Party's Central Committee (except M. Bordonaite).

And here are the facts about the distribution of cadres. Ten percent of the inhabitants of Vilnius are Jews. Until now not a single Jew has ever been elected chairman, deputy chairman or secretary of the city or of the city's four regional executive committees. Since the dismissal of Atamukas, not a single Jewish Communist has ever been elected secretary of a Party city committee or a city-region committee, nor have any been appointed department heads by the corresponding plenums.

Not a single Jew has been elected judge of a people's court. Not a single Jew has been elected to any higher position in the trade unions. During the entire postwar era, not a single representative of Jewish youth has risen to a leading position in the state, party or trade union activity—while at the same time the mass of Lithuanian cadres has been educated and promoted during the postwar years. In fact, only a handful of meritorious Jewish revolutionaries of the older generation are still merely tolerated in higher positions, and they are now being hurriedly pushed out to pension as soon as possible. . . .

As for the protection of Jewish cultural monuments, it must be stated that not a single synagogue structure that survived the Occupation [by the Nazis] has been declared an architectural monument under state protection; whereas a considerable number of Catholic churches-architectural monuments are protected by the state and repaired at its expense. Moreover, one of the most outstanding architectural monuments of 16th century Lithuania, the underground synagogue of the Gaon of Vilna (at the intersection of Muziejus and Rudininkai Streets), was deliberately destroyed and desecrated during the doctors' trial in Moscow in 1952.

Local authorities, with the obvious connivance or even silent consent from above, are destroying Jewish cemeteries, while the cattle of the townspeople graze on those that remain. . . .

We do not wish to over-state the case. By no means. We know that the situation of the Jews is considerably better in Lithuania than in other parts of the USSR; especially terrible is the discrimination against our compatriots in the Ukraine. . . .

We highly value the Lithuanian Communist Party, the traditional internationalism of its Central Committee, and the national tolerance of the Lithuanian people. Nevertheless, as the chairman of the state security committee, Petkevicius, stated at the plenum of the Lithuanian Communist Party's Central Committee—emigrational tendencies are increasing among the Jewish inhabitants. It is known that if the borders would be opened for emigration today, some eighty percent of the entire Jewish populace would leave Soviet Lithuania and depart for Israel. These people would leave everything here—despite the unsettled conditions in the Near East, despite the fact that our people in this country are used to a damp climate and would find it difficult to acclimatize there, despite the fact that almost no one among the Lithuanian Jews knows Hebrew anymore or observes religious traditions, despite the fact that their present qualifications (most economically active people are employed in service occupations) would not make it easy for them to become integrated into Israel's society.

We are confronted with a paradox here. We are not wanted here, we are being completely oppressed, forcibly denationalized, and even publicly insulted in the press—while at the same time we are forcibly kept here. As the Lithuanian proverb goes, "He beats and he screams at the same time." . . .

The authors of this document are appealing to you and your colleagues' universal human, democratic convictions. Do all in your power to put down the menacingly rising wave of anti-Semitism. It is not too late yet. If that is not done now, Lithuania will again "adorn itself" with new Ponars and Ninth Forts.*

It has been decided not to make public the surnames of the twenty-six signers of this document. . . .

* * * * *

Soviet Army Major Grisha Feigin, World War II hero of the Soviet Army, twice-wounded participant in the liberation of Warsaw and Berlin, recipient of seven decorations, returned his medals to Soviet authorities in protest against this country's treatment of Jews.† For this act of defiance, he was committed to an insane asylum. Eventually released, he was finally given permission to emigrate to Israel. The statements below were made by Major Feigin before and after he left the USSR,

"I CAN NO LONGER WEAR YOUR MEDALS"

From a letter by Soviet Army Major Grisha Feigin, addressed to the Supreme Soviet, USSR, and written while he was still in the Soviet Union.

I hereby declare that I do not consider it possible to wear the distinctions granted to me by a government which does not honor my rights and which is hostile in its policies towards my own country. I ask you to deprive me, in accordance with the relevant procedure, of all distinctions I have been awarded and I appeal to you: Let my people go home!

---

*Ponar, located on the outskirts of Lithuania's capital Vilna, is the site where tens of thousands of Jews from the city and surrounding areas were slaughtered by the Nazis; the Ninth Fort located in a suburb of Lithuania's second largest city Kovno (Kaunas) was a military structure where a similar massacre took place—Editor.

†This description is based on Western accounts and on Major Feigin's own statements. Pro-Soviet sources have described him as a man "who had served time as a counterfeiter and a confidence man and who invented a fictitious record of 'war heroism.'" (Hyman Lumer, "The Truth About the Lies at Brussels," Daily World, Magazine Section, March 20, 1971, p. M-5.)

From Richard Cohen, ed., Let My People Go! (New York: Popular Library, 1971), pp. 48 and 128. Reprinted by permission.

From an address by former Soviet Army Major Grisha Feigin (now an emigré in Israel) to the World Conference of Jewish Communities on Soviet Jewry, Brussels, February 23, 1971.

I left a country where 500,000 Jews fought against Nazi Germany, where 240,000 of them fell in battle, where Jews live as loyal and active citizens—but where Jews are the only people deprived of their rights as a people. Here all Jewish learning is annihilated, all Jewish activity considered Zionist plotting. Here the science of anti-Semitism flourishes, here the notion of the unity of the Jewish people is denied and the rebirth of the ancestral state condemned. In this country full of terror, oppression and fear, tens of thousands of Jews claim their right.

* * * * *

Since the Israeli victory in 1967, increasing numbers of Soviet Jews have applied for exit permits to go to Israel. Prior to 1971, few such permits were granted. Some of the rejected applicants began to write letters to Soviet leaders or to international organizations or open letters to the general public, stating their reasons for wanting to emigrate and asserting their right to leave. Some of these would-be emigrés level bitter charges of anti-Semitism against the Soviet Union, others merely complain about religious or cultural discrimination, while yet others express gratitude to the Soviet people for having saved them from the Nazis, explaining that they want to go to Israel for reasons other than discrimination, reasons such as the desire to live in their "own" land, to raise their children in a more "Jewish" environment, or to join relatives abroad. The excerpts reprinted below comprise a representative cross-section of such letters.

"WE WANT TO GO TO ISRAEL BECAUSE . . ."

(1) From a letter by 7 Vilna Jews addressed to U Thant, secretary general of the United Nations, to the chairman of the U.N. Commission on Human Rights, and to Mrs. Golda Meir, prime minister of Israel, February 1, 1970.

After the catastrophy that befell the Jews of Lithuania in the years of the fascist occupation, the surviving Jews believed that the

---

From Moshe Decter, ed., REDEMPTION! REDEMPTION! REDEMPTION!: Jewish Freedom Letters from Russia (New York: American Jewish Conference on Soviet Jewry and Conference on the Status of Soviet Jews, 1970), *passim*. Reprinted by permission.

day had come when this "eternal" question would be solved and there would be once and for all an end to anti-Semitism and that we, the Jews, had at last acquired true defenders of human rights.

However, all the time that has passed has shown how deeply mistaken we were. There is no country except Israel that can solve our problem. The events in the U.S.S.R. in 1948-53 . . . testify to this. . . . They killed our singers, our poets, our writers and artists and scientists with world-famous names. And only because they were Jews.

Where is there the guarantee that the tragedy . . . will not repeat itself? And what about the pogrom in the small Lithuanian town of Plunge in the sixties? And how little there lacked for a pogrom to be launched in Vilnius when the charge was made against us of ritual murder before Passover. Thank God it transpired that the murderer was a Lithuanian, Petrila, who had strangled a little girl. But what would have happened had this been a mentally ill Jew? Who would have defended us from the enraged crowd?

Today we, citizens of the U.S.S.R., pray for only one thing—we want to live in our own land. Let us go!! Let us go Home! We hear the voices of the ancient prophets, we are called by the Messiah of freedom, we are called by our Homeland!

(2) From a letter by a 21-year-old Soviet citizen addressed to the Supreme Soviet, USSR, Moscow, May 20, 1968.

I am a Jew, I was born a Jew, and I want to live out my life as a Jew. With all my respect for the Russian people, I do not consider my people in any way inferior to the Russian, or to any other, people, and I do not want to be assimilated by any people.

As in the Soviet Union there are no conditions for the existence of the Jewish nation, Jews who wish to leave the USSR should be given the possibility to do so (just as this is done in other countries: Rumania and Poland, for example).

I am a Jew, and, as a Jew, I consider the State of Israel my Fatherland, the Fatherland of my people, the only place on earth where there exists an independent Jewish State, and I, like any other Jew, have the indubitable right to live in that state.

The Jewish people has a right to its own, independent State and every Jew, no matter where he lives and no matter where he was born, has the right to live in the Jewish State. . . .

It does not matter what the political regime in Israel is, what is the internal or the foreign policy of Israel. It is our country. Israel is a Jewish State, and only we, the Jews, have the right to change anything in that country, if we consider it necessary. This depends upon us, and only upon us.

I do not wish to be a citizen of the USSR, of a country that refuses to the Jews (and to other nations, too,) the right of self-determination.

I do not wish to be a citizen of a country where Jews are subjected to forced assimilation, where my people is deprived of its national image and of its cultural treasures, of a country where, under the pretext of a struggle against Zionism, all the cultural life of the Jewish people has been eradicated, where the dissemination of any literature on the history of the Jewish people or on the cultural life of Jews abroad in our times is persecuted.

I do not wish to be a citizen of a country that conducts a policy of genocide toward the Jewish people. If the fascists exterminated us physically, you are exterminating Jews as a nation. I do not wish to collaborate in this additional crime of yours against the Jewish people. . . .

I also know about the clearly anti-Semitic policy waged in 1948-53, when the best representatives of Russia's Jewry were annihilated, and I also know that this anti-Semitic policy is being carried out at present, even though in a somewhat changed form and by less barbaric methods.

I do not want to live in a country whose government has spilled so much Jewish blood. I do not want to participate with you in the extermination of the Jewish nation in the Soviet Union. I do not wish to live in a country in which have been re-established (even though in secret) limitations concerning Jews (concerning admittance to a number of educational institutions, establishments, enterprises, etc.). I shall not enumerate it all: you know this better than I do.

I do not wish to be a citizen of a country that arms and supports the remaining fascists and the Arab chauvinists who desire to wipe Israel off the face of the earth and to add another two and a half million of killed to the six million who have perished. I do not want to be a collaborator of yours in the destruction of the State of Israel because, even though this has not been done officially, I consider myself to be a citizen of the State of Israel (the more so as I possess an invitation for permanent residence in the State of Israel).

On the basis of the above, I renounce Soviet citizenship, and I demand to be freed from the humiliation of being considered a citizen of the Union of Soviet Socialist Republics.

I demand to be given a possibility of leaving the Soviet Union.

(3) From three identical open letters signed respectively by 25 Jews from Moscow, 22 from Riga, and 4 from Georgia, all addressed to U Thant, secretary general of the United States and Miss Angie Brooks, president of the 24th Session of the General Assembly, 1969.

We the signatories to the present appeal, are persons of various ages, occupations, education, and tastes and are not connected with one another in anything except the wish to leave the USSR for Israel, in order to reunite there, in our own land, with our relatives. . . .

All of us have been refused [exit permits]. . . . We are being kept forcibly. WE ARE NOT ALLOWED TO GO. . . .

Such treatment is an act of lawlessness, it is an open violation of the rights of man.

We consider that to hold us forcibly is against the elementary concepts of humanity and morality.

We Demand Free Exit From The USSR!

(4) From a letter by 11 Jewish women, addressed "To you, Women," 1969 (no information is available about where this letter was published).

According to some law—more barbaric and amoral than lawful—we are not allowed to leave the USSR. . . . We are kept forcibly, by the law of the stronger.

. . . they proclaim loudly that there ARE NO persons desirous to go to Israel. . . .

This dream of ours did not come suddenly; it emanates naturally from the 2,000-year-old history of the dispersion of our people. The desire for national reunification on the land of Israel is the inevitable end to the many centuries of the wanderings of the Jews. This is our right, just as it is the right of the Armenians to live in Armenia, or the Poles to live in Poland . . . and it must be understood rightly.

We are sincerely grateful to the people of the Soviet Union . . . but today, in the second half of the 20th century, we have our own JEWISH state. Whether it is good or bad, it is OUR OWN country.

And we appeal to the Soviet Government: "Let us go in peace! Don't keep us by force." . . .

(5) From a letter by 9 Leningrad Jews representing 9 families or 24 individuals, addressed to the United Nations Commission on Human Rights, February 1, 1970.

We wish to explain the reasons for our decision to emigrate to Israel for permanent residence.

1) We want to live in Israel, together with our relatives from whom we have become separated as a result of the tragic historical fate of the Jewish people and other circumstances. . . .

2) For us, the unassimilated and the refusing-to-assimilate Jews, the satisfaction of our cultural-national needs in the Soviet Union is practically impossible due to the absence of proper national-cultural institutions, Jewish schools, etc.

This factor is of greater importance for those of us who have children . . .

We were born Jews, and we continue to be Jews, and this is why we want to unite with the Jewish people in Israel.

3) Some of us are religious. The observing of religious rites . . . will of course be much easier for us in Israel than in the USSR.

Among us are persons of various ages and professions. All of us, during our entire lives, have been loyal citizens of the Soviet Union . . . we possess no information that can be considered state secrets.

The granting to us of a permit to go to Israel is not contrary to the laws of the Soviet Union. Emigration to Israel means only that we wish to be together with the Jewish people, and to live a national life with all its particularities, just like any other people. . . .

(6) From a letter by Moscow Jew Ch. Sh. Rabinovich addressed to the editorial office of Pravda, January 26, 1970.

Of course, we the Soviet people—both Jews and non-Jews—would like that there should be a socialist system there, that there should be peace between the Jews and the Arabs, between all the States of that region. But in the Soviet Union, in Russia, not everything was done all at once. . . .

I was born in the Soviet Union, I grew up and studied in a Soviet school, a Workers' Faculty and an Institute, I lived all these years having contacts with the Russians and nobody could ever accuse me of [Israeli] nationalism. . . .

Why do I want to go to Israel with my family?

1) I was born into a religious Jewish family and I cannot observe here all the traditions and the holidays of my people.

2) I have two daughters. They are growing up and they do not know the history of their people and have no possibility of studying the Jewish language (there are no schools, no newspapers, no theater).

I cannot refuse my gravely ill wife her last wish—to live among her relatives and to die there. . . .

(7) From a letter by 18 religious families in Georgia, to Mrs. Golda Meir, prime minister of Israel, in late summer 1969 and transmitted by Yosef Tekoah, representative of Israel in the United Nations, to the UN Commission on Human Rights.

Everybody knows how justly national policy, the theoretical principles of which were formulated long ago by the founder of the State, V. I. Lenin, is in fact being carried out in the USSR. There have not been pogroms, pales, or quotas in the country for a long, long time. Jews can walk the streets without fear for their lives; they can live where they wish, hold any position, even as high as the post of minister, as is evident from the example of V. Dymshits, Deputy Chairman of the USSR Council of Ministers. . . .

Therefore it is not racial discrimination that compels us to leave the country. Then perhaps it is religious discrimination? But synagogues are permitted in the country, and we are not prohibited from praying at home. However, our prayers are with Israel, for it is written: "If I forget thee, O Jerusalem, may my right hand forget its cunning." . . .

They say there is a total of twelve million Jews in the world. But he errs who believes there is a total of twelve million of us. For with those who pray for Israel are hundreds of millions who did not live to this day, who were tortured to death, who are no longer here. They march shoulder to shoulder with us, unconquered and immortal, those who handed down to us the traditions of struggle and faith.

That is why we want to go to Israel.

(8) From a letter by Soviet Jewish poet Joseph Borisovich Kerler to his friend Nehama Lifshitz, famous Soviet Jewish singer, who had emigrated in early 1969 from the USSR to Israel. November 18, 1969.

I am a Jewish poet and as such I am utterly superfluous in the Soviet Union. Surely no one can any longer deny that, because of certain historical developments there is absolutely no future for Jewish culture here. . . .

Our passionate yearning to go to Israel is natural, lawful, just and very human.

Does this mean that we are disloyal to the Soviet Union? Absolutely not! Like my wife, I fought actively in the Great Fatherland War, and was wounded several times in battle against the German fascists. The earth, soaked in blood and sweat, is dear to me, is my own. The great culture of Russia is dear to me, is my own. I was reared in its revolutionary, freedom-loving spirit. I love Russian poetry, and the Russian landscape. We will never forget the extraordinary sacrifices by which the Soviet people saved humanity in general and the Jewish people in particular from the Brown Plague and extermination.

And yet—we must leave Russia. Better to remain friends from afar. . . .

I go with heavy heart,
With leaden steps
With each step
I tear away
Pieces of earth
Soaked with my blood
I wrench my eye away

I wrench my heart away
And wish you: Let all be well with you!

* * * * *

In a letter published in Pravda on April 10, 1971, 70 veteran Bolsheviks of Jewish extraction who joined the Communist Party between 1903 and 1907 remember their struggle against the Czar, the war against the Nazis, and the benefits they say all nationalities have reaped under Soviet rule; and they admonish the Israeli Zionists to stop their "dirty solicitations."

"WE HAVE NOT FORGOTTEN"

Many of us experienced the pogroms. We have not forgotten that the wealthy Jews were protected from the pogroms by the tsarist autocracy, which sent soldiers and police to guard their homes.

We have not forgotten, either, how Russian workers, risking their own lives and the lives of their families, hid poor Jews from the Black Hundred thugs. They voluntarily took up arms and defended the Jewish population against the brutalities of the pogrom-makers.

We have not forgotten the fight of our party against the Zionists, Bundists and other Jewish nationalists, who opposed Jewish workers uniting with the Russian workers and workers of other nationalities in their struggle against the autocracy and capitalism.

We all fought for the overthrow of the tsarist autocracy and for the victory of the Great October Socialist Revolution.

Side by side with all the citizens of our multi-national motherland, we fought against the nazi barbarians and defended our Soviet motherland.

We still have vivid memories of the horrors of fascism, which brought incalculable suffering to our entire people, including citizens of Jewish nationality.

We likewise have not forgotten that more than 20 million of our compatriots perished on the battlefields, on the gallows, in gas chambers, in fascist prisons, in concentration camps and in fascist slavery.

. . .

The Soviet Union has granted all nationalities, including Jews, every right and possibility to work, to enjoy all the benefits of science, culture, education and art, the right to take part on a broad scale in

---

From Soviet News, April 21, 1970, p. 29. Reprinted by permission.

all aspects of the running of the state and the right to elect and be elected to all organs of government.

This country is our only dearly beloved mother country!

To the Israeli Zionists we say: stop your dirty solicitations! You won't find a single traitor among the Jewish working people of the Soviet Union!

* * * * *

On numerous occasions in recent years, groups of renowned Soviet Jews have issued joint statements backing their country's policies in regard to Israel, denouncing Zionism and Zionist charges of discrimination against Jews in the USSR, and extolling life in their native land. Parts of three such statements are reproduced below.

"WE REJECT ZIONIST LIES"

(1) At a press conference for Soviet and foreign correspondents held in Moscow on March 4, 1970, 50 of the Soviet Union's most prominent Jewish citizens released a statement in which they branded the Israeli leaders as aggressors and Zionism as a tool of "international imperialism," and in which they rejected as totally untrue Zionist charges of mistreatment of Jews in the USSR. Among those who signed the statement were high government officials, generals in the Soviet Army, newspaper editors, members of the Soviet Academy of Sciences, and university professors—some of them state prize winners, others holders of high honorary titles such as Hero of the Soviet Union and Hero of Socialist Labor.

Parts of the statement dealing specifically with the situation in the Middle East have been omitted; the rest of the statement is reprinted below.

Acting at one with Zionist centres in the United States and some other Western countries, Zionist quarters in Tel Aviv allege that in the Soviet Union citizens of Jewish nationality lead a miserable life, are subjected to houndings, etc. They say that for this reason they ought better go to Israel.

The boundless cynicism and provocational methods used by the Zionists are illustrated by statements made by the former Israeli head

---

From Zionism: Instrument of Imperialist Reaction (Moscow: Novosti Press Agency Publishing House, February-March 1970), pp. 22-24; and from Soviet News, March 17, 1970, p. 115, and January 18, 1972, p. 18. Reprinted by permission.

of government, one of the leaders of Zionism, Ben Gurion. He urged sending people to various countries specially to whip up anti-Semitism and thereby cause a growth in emigration.

We know that Israeli rulers cannot be embarrassed even when confronted by facts and logical reasoning. And it is not to them that we address ourselves. We make this statement to open the eyes of gullible victims of Zionist propaganda in the whole world.

Our Motherland is the Soviet Union.

In the 240-million-strong closely knit Soviet family, the Jews of our country live shoulder to shoulder with the other fraternal peoples. Living now are the children and grandchildren of those Jews who after the October Revolution acquired the only and inimitable Motherland in the Soviet socialist state created by the Party of the great Lenin.

In landlord-capitalist Russia, the overwhelming majority of the Jewish population was subjected to terrible oppression—economic, spiritual and national. The capitalist Jews squeezed dry all the labouring Jews, just as oppressors of other nationalities did. An end was put to this forever by the Great October Socialist Revolution, accomplished under the leadership of the Communist Party.

Under the guidance of Lenin's Party Russia's entire proletariat, including working Jews, acquired genuine freedom in the struggle against the hated tsarism, against exploitation and national strife.

In the difficult days of the fascist invasion all the peoples of the Soviet Union rose to defend the socialist homeland. Soviet Jews also donned army greatcoats. They defended freedom and independence, the socialist system that brought genuine equality and friendship to the peoples.

Working together with all the peoples of the USSR are the Jews—equal citizens of the Soviet Union, workers and engineers, collective farmers and agronomists, nurses and doctors, professors and academicians, officers and generals, writers and actors, public figures and statesmen. About eight thousand of them have been elected deputies to district, city, regional Soviets of Working People's Deputies and the USSR Supreme Soviet.

For successes in labour and participation in the Great Patriotic War nearly 340,000 Jews have been awarded orders and medals of the Soviet Union, 117 won the title of Hero of the Soviet Union and 71—the title of Hero of Socialist Labour, including nine who won this award a second and third time.

The great Soviet Union merits eternal gratitude for having saved millions of people of many nationalities, including Jews, from racist annihilation, for its decisive contribution to the rout of hitlerite Germany and for having saved mankind from fascist slavery.

Lenin's national policy, unswervingly and consistently promoted by the Communist Party and the Soviet Government, has won respect and appreciation in the whole world. It serves as a source of inspiration for working people of all nationalities and all countries. Irrespective of their nationality, men of labour have only one road—the road of international unity, social progress and socialism. . . .

Being Soviet patriots and internationalists, we scorn the ludicrous claims of the rulers of Israel and their Zionist accomplices in other countries to speak on behalf of all Jews.

(2) On March 9, 1970, Jewish religious leaders in the Soviet Union signed a statement condemning Israel's policies in the Middle East and denying charges of discrimination against Soviet Jews. The statement, from which excerpts are reprinted below, was signed by the late Rabbi Levin of the Moscow Synagogue, Rabbi Lubanov of the Leningrad Synagogue, Rabbi Mizrahi of the Baku Synagogue, Rabbi Shvartzbladt of the Odessa Synagogue, Rabbi Oppenstein of the Kuibyshev Synagogue, Rabbi Livshytz of the Novozybkovo Synagogue, and other Jewish religious leaders.

We are religious leaders, not politicians, but we realize that the activities of the Zionists have nothing in common with religion. They are a screen to conceal the interests of the most extremist reactionary circles. . . .

The Israeli rulers have no right to speak on behalf of all Jews. . . .

The real motherland of Soviet Jews is our mother country, the Soviet Union.

Like citizens of other nationalities, Jews in the Soviet Union enjoy all the rights and freedoms guaranteed by the constitution, including freedom of religious worship. The peoples of our country live as brothers and no one will be able to sow discord among them.

(3) At a public meeting held in Moscow on January 13, 1972, Soviet Jews who attended approved the text of an "open letter to the public of all countries" to "protest against the crimes of Zionism and against the Zionist congress being held in Jerusalem, which sets itself the aim of propagating anti-Soviet slander and mobilizing Jews in all parts of the world against the policy of peace and progress." Among the signatories to the letter were the composer Oscar Feltsman, the writer Genrich Gofman, Genya Beilina, a woman worker at the Isolyator factory in Moscow, academician Nikolai Dubinin, one of the Soviet Union's leading biologists, Yosif Goverman, head of Moscow's Autotransport agency, and the veteran woman communist Yelizaveta Barskaya. Excerpts from that open letter are reprinted below.

[Zionist] propaganda calls for anti-socialist action, fans the flames of chauvinism and nationalistic prejudice and manipulates for its own purposes such fantastic ideas, reeking with provocation, as the "problem" of the position of Jews in the Soviet Union, the aim being to slander the Soviet government and the Soviet way of life.

We angrily refute the malicious lies about our country. We protest against the provocations and slander and against the attempts of the Zionists to determine the fate of Soviet citizens and push them into betraying their country.

This year marks the 50th anniversary of the Union of Soviet Socialist Republics. Its half a century of existence has confirmed the indestructibility of our state and of the bonds that unite its peoples. The anniversary reaffirms the wisdom of the Leninist nationalities policy of the Communist Party of the Soviet Union. Like all Soviet people, citizens of Jewish nationality are enthusiastically preparing to celebrate the anniversary of Soviet government.

They are contributing all their strength, all their knowledge and all their energy to the building of a communist society—the most humane and just society on earth. That and only that is the position of Jews in the U.S.S.R.

* * * * *

Readers of Soviet Life* have reportedly asked various questions about the status of Jews in the USSR. These questions have been referred to and have been answered by a number of loyal Soviet Jews who deny the existence of any kind of discrimination and comment favorably on conditions in the Soviet Union, on opportunities open to Soviet Jews, and on the treatment accorded them in the USSR. The questions and replies are reprinted below.

"IN ANSWER TO YOUR QUESTIONS"

Question: To what extent do Jews hold government or administrative posts or commands in the Armed Forces?

From "How Jews Live in the Soviet Union," Soviet Life, July 1971, pp. 36-37. Reprinted by permission.

---

*Soviet Life is a pictorial magazine, published monthly under an agreement between the government of the United States and the government of the Soviet Union whereby this magazine is distributed in the United States by the Soviet Embassy in Washington, while the U.S. Embassy in Moscow distributes a magazine called Amerika in the USSR.

Answered by Jewish Colonel General David Dragunsky twice Hero of the Soviet Union, deputy to the Supreme Soviet of the Georgian SSR: It would not be overstating the case to say that there is not a single area of political or economic activity in the Soviet Union in which Jews are not directly involved along with representatives of other nationalities. Our first President, for instance, was Yakov Sverdlov, a Jew.

The person who asked that question would probably want a list of our statesmen of Jewish nationality. But to name even only those I know personally would make a long list. So I'll mention just a few. [Now follows a list of names of prominent Soviet Jews with whom General Dragunsky is personally acquainted. Most of their names appear on pages 55-58 above.]

I head one of the Soviet Army's military academies. I was promoted only recently: I was a Lieutenant General, now I'm a Colonel General. I know quite a few generals, colonels and other officers of Jewish nationality in the professorial staff of Moscow's military academies. Some of them were schooled on the battlefields of World War II, others come from the young galaxy of Soviet military leaders.

Question: Why are there no Jewish schools in the USSR?

Answered by Riva Vishchinikina (Jewish), chairman of the Executive Committee of the Valdheim Rural Soviet, Jewish Autonomous Region: Immediately after the Revolution the Soviet state set up a wide network of Jewish schools, because at that time the children of the Jewish poor usually knew only one language—Yiddish. The task of the Jewish schools was to make culture and knowledge accessible to the younger generation of Jews, to draw them into the country's new life.

The years went by. Life changed. In due course the Russian or Ukrainian or Byelorussian language imperceptibly and inevitably became the native tongue of Jewish families. Attendance in Jewish schools naturally began to drop. Parents preferred to send their children to a Russian school. In view of historically established conditions, Russian became the second language in all the republics, a vitally necessary language for international relations.

Although I, in my day, attended a Jewish school, I sent my children to a Russian one. Why? Well, judge for yourself. Besides Jews in our village of Valdheim, there are Russians, Ukrainians, Byelorussians, Tatars and Bashkirs. The children play together, are brought up together in the kindergarten, make friends. It would be cruel to separate them from each other, isolate them. Wouldn't sending them to a Jewish school, when all the rest of the children of other nationalities are studying together in a Russian school, isolate and hurt them irreparably?

But I didn't send my children to a Jewish school because of one other, no less important, reason. On finishing a Russian school, they will be able to continue their education in Khabarovsk, Moscow, Leningrad or any other big city—in other words, in the educational institutions of large centers, which have absorbed the very best of Russian and foreign scientific thought. Those are the lines along which not only Jewish mothers reason, but Tatar, Armenian, Uzbek and others living in the Russian Federation. It may sound paradoxical, but it is a fact: Jewish mothers closed the Jewish schools. However, all those who wish to learn Yiddish can study it at home, privately, in courses, or by joining amateur Jewish theater groups. The monthly magazine Sovetish Heimland has Yiddish language lessons in every issue.

Question: Is it true that admission of Jews to institutions of higher learning is limited?

Answered by Nelli Goz, Jewish fifth-year student at Moscow University: No, it's not true. I know from my own experience that an applicant's nationality plays absolutely no part in admission to the university. The main thing is knowledge. Pass the competitive examination, and you get your student pass. Several of my girl friends took the entrance exams with me. Some of them, Russian by nationality, did not make it, and only because they did not pass the mathematics and physics exams.

I live in Moscow. Father is a highly skilled fitter, mother is an engineer-economist, and my brother, a university graduate, works in one of Moscow's design institutes. I'm a student of the Mechanics and Mathematics Department specializing in the theory of probability. I've been getting a state stipend from the very first year, and now, in my fifth year, I'm getting a larger grant for high grades.

Young people of every nationality are studying at our university, including Jews. I know many of the Jewish young men and women in my field of study. I know Jewish teachers, too. For instance, Professors Samari Halperin and Aaron Vainstein, and Doctor of Engineering Mark Freidlin, who is only 32, have the respect of the entire faculty. . . .

Question: Is Judaism persecuted in the USSR? Why are there so few synagogues? Are prayer books published? Where are rabbis trained?

Answered by the late Rabbi Yehuda Leib Levin, former head of the Moscow Choral Synagogue: Judaism is not persecuted in the Soviet Union. The Jewish religion has equal status with every other religion. This is ensured by the Constitution of the USSR: In our country the church is separated from the state. A Soviet citizen is free to profess any religion or be an atheist. Religious belief is the private affair of each individual.

As for Judaism, I'll cite a few facts, and let readers judge for themselves.

We have three synagogues in Moscow, besides a synagogue in Malakhovka, a Moscow suburb. Services are conducted regularly everywhere, and no one interferes with the activities of the congregation. From 50 to 100 people, mainly elderly and pensioners, pray daily, morning and evening, at the Choral Synagogue. Our congregation on Saturdays and especially during big holidays is much larger—no less than a thousand. For services on these days we have a cantor and choir.

Why are there few synagogues? What is meant by few or many? Synagogues function wherever believers want them, where the local congregations are able to maintain them and cover all expenses. To my knowledge, there are some 100 synagogues in the Soviet Union. Besides that, there are no less than 300 minyans in various populated areas, large and small, where religious Jews live.

Concerning prayer books. Our congregation recently issued a new prayer book. We had it printed by one of Moscow's state printing houses. Besides, every year we publish a religious calendar for the New Year.

Concerning the training of rabbis. For many years now a Yeshivah (a Talmudic academy) for the training of rabbis has been functioning under our synagogue.

Question: Is it possible to see a Jewish play in the Soviet Union? Hear a Jewish song?

Answered by Maria Kotlyarova, Jewish actress: Certainly it is! Come visit us. See and hear for yourself.

I, personally, am a member of the Moscow Jewish Dramatic Ensemble, which is headed by Honored Artist of the RSFSR Veniamin Shvartser. Our company numbers over 20 actors, and our repertoire includes Shalom Aleichem's *Tevye the Milkman* and *200,000* Lermontov's *Spaniards*, Goldfaden's *Witch* and Gordin's *Overseas*.

We prepare and rehearse every performance in Moscow. All the expenses of direction, scenery, costumes, stage requisites and premises are covered by the state. By the way, the actors all receive fixed and steady salaries regardless of the number of performances we give. When touring, we get additional pay (traveling expenses, hotel accommodations, a daily allowance, and so on).

Our company performs not only in Moscow, but in different cities of the Soviet Union, and everywhere to full houses.

Besides our ensemble, Anna Guzik's and Sidi Tal's musical variety ensembles are very popular in Moscow, as are the talented reciters Emmanuel Kaminka, Joseph and Leah Kolin, Sofia Saitan and Dina Roitkop, singers of Jewish songs Mikhail Alexandrovich, Clementina Shermel, Anna Sheveleva and others.

I attended a concert not long ago given by Ethel Kovenskaya, an actress of the Mossoviet Academic Theater in Moscow. Her program was made up of folk and contemporary Jewish songs. I was enchanted by her masterful renderings. No wonder every one of her songs evoked general applause.

I had occasion to attend performances of the Kishinev Jewish People's Theater. The company has many talented young people. All of them act with great enthusiasm and a strong sense of responsibility to their art and the audience.

I also know that the Jewish people's theaters in Vilnius and Birobidzhan are very popular with their audiences. Their repertoires include classical and contemporary plays.

Question: Is Jewish culture really being suppressed in the Soviet Union?

Answered by Abraham Gontar, Jewish poet: Why should Jewish culture be suppressed? What points to that?

Jewish poets, prose writers, critics and literary scholars live and work in Moscow and Kiev, in Birobidzhan and Vilnius, in Kishinev and Minsk, in Chernovtsy and other Soviet cities. Their writings appear regularly in Sovetish Heimland, a literary magazine published in Yiddish in Moscow. In the 10 years of its existence this magazine has carried scores of novels, hundreds of novelettes, thousands of stories, poems, songs, essays, literary critiques and historical studies that mirrored the many-sided life and creative effort of the peoples of the Soviet Union and, in particular, the country's Jewish population.

We publish our writings in Yiddish. A one-volume collection of my poetry, Pigeons on the Roof, came off the press not long ago. It's made up of lyrical and philosophical poems and poems about my early childhood, about loyalty and friendship. On my bookshelves are friends—poets Itsik Fefer, Lev Kvitko, Samuel Galkin, Aaron Vergelis, Girsh Osherovich, Yevsei Driz, Matvei Grubian, prose writers Eli Shekhtman, Nathan Lurie, Joseph Rabin, Samuel Gordon and many others. Alongside of the above are new editions of the Jewish classics—Sholem Aleichem, Mendele Mocher Seforim and I. L. Peretz. I edited the last two.

Our books are also translated into Russian and other languages of the Soviet Union. Some 10 years ago a six-volume edition of Sholem Aleichem in Russian came out in Moscow in 225,000 copies. Four volumes of the same writer's selected works were published some time later in Kiev in Ukrainian, with a preface by Mikola Bazhan, a well-known poet-academician. A new enlarged six-volume collection of Sholem Aleichem is now being prepared for publication in Moscow. It will probably be printed in an edition of 300,000 copies.

One hundred and seventy-five books by 72 Jewish writers, and seven collections and anthologies (each containing from 10 to 50 authors) have been published in the Soviet Union in the last five years—1965-1970—in editions totaling over 20,354,000 copies in the Yiddish, Russian, Ukrainian, Byelorussian, Lithuanian, Latvian, Moldavian, Georgian, Kazakh, Uzbek, Turkmenian, Kirghiz, French, English and Spanish languages.

A collection of new Jewish songs edited by Dmitri Shostakovich, the eminent composer, was released recently in Moscow, and a richly illustrated album of works by well-known artist Samuelis Rozinas, entitled Jewish Folk Songs, was published in Vilnius. The latter series was very well received at exhibitions of the artist's work in many cities.

To the above I'll add that the Melodiya Company in Moscow regularly releases long-playing records with Jewish songs rendered by prominent Soviet performers. They can be bought in any music store in Moscow.

Question: What professions are open for Jews in the Soviet Union?

Answered by Mikhail Dulmanas (Jewish), Lithuanian deputy minister of Construction: The Constitution of our country unequivocally states that "any direct or indirect restriction of the rights of, or, conversely, the establishment of any direct or indirect privileges for, citizens on account of their race or nationality, as well as any advocacy of racial or national exclusiveness or hatred and contempt, are punishable by law."

I must say I do not know of a single instance of violation of this law. And if such a thing had occurred, the culprits would definitely have been severely punished as criminals.

I myself was born in Lithuania and lived there back in the days of bourgeois rule. I remember very well the fascist coup in 1926. And I must say I was very quickly made to feel I was a Jew. I felt if both studying at the university and when I tried to get a job. Jews were hired most reluctantly.

Now I occupy the post of Deputy Minister of Construction of Lithuania and in no way at all feel myself an object of discrimination. But perhaps I'm an exception? Let's see. I'm naturally best acquainted with the field I'm working in. Our republic borders on Byelorussia, Latvia and the Russian Federation. The Deputy Minister of Construction of Latvia is Comrade Barran, a Jew by nationality. And in Byelorussia this same post is occupied by a friend of mine and colleague, Comrade Paperno, also a Jew by nationality.

I frequently come to Moscow on business. We naturally maintain close contact with the capital's research and designing institutes which draw up the technical documentation for many of our major construction projects. For instance, we are now completing the construction of a big cement works. Its chief engineer is a Jew. He heads a large body of engineers and scientists who are responsible for a huge amount of research and planning. He is entrusted with major construction projects, and no one would ever think of asking him whether he is a Jew, a Lithuanian, an Armenian, a Russian or a Byelorussian.

So I can, in general, say with absolute confidence that there is no branch of the Soviet economy to which people of Jewish nationality have not contributed their knowledge, experience and ability. So-called "Jewish professions" have long since ceased to exist. In addition to doctors, lawyers, shoemakers and tailors, there are today in the Soviet Union builders and metallurgists, fitters and lathe operators, mechanics and drivers, engineers and miners, pilots and teachers, government employees and artists, architects and party functionaries, geologists and ship captains, professional soldiers and men of letters, professors and academicians of Jewish nationality.

Question: Can Soviet Jews travel freely throughout the country? Must they live in Birobidzhan, or do they have a free choice of place of residence?

Answered by Samuel Gordon, Jewish member of the Writers' Union of the USSR: This question was probably asked by a very old person, someone who left Russia before the Revolution. Under czarism Jews were indeed restricted in their choice of residence to the so-called Pale of Settlement.

In those days, if the police found a Jew in Moscow or St. Petersburg, he was immediately shipped back home. Very few Jews, only merchants of the first guild, highly qualified artisans and those with a higher education, were allowed to live anywhere outside the Pale of Settlement.

The October Revolution, once and for all, put an end to the discrimination of Jews, as well as other nationalities in Russia. All Soviet citizens, irrespective of nationality, can live wherever they please, and Jews are no exception.

I'm a Jewish writer. I grew up in a little town in the Ukraine. Later, after graduating from Moscow University, I went on living in the capital. The same is true of many of my peers.

My friends say I'm a footloose person. That's because I'm always traveling around the country searching for characters for my novels, stories and essays. Today Jews live all over the country. I have met them in the capitals of the different republics, in Kazakhstan's virgin land area, on new construction sites in the Urals and Siberia, in the Jewish Autonomous Region and in the Crimea, in cities beyond the Arctic Circle and in the Ukraine.

A book of mine titled Spring was recently published here in Yiddish. Its characters are our contemporaries—workers, engineers, farmers, scientists and students from all parts of the country.

Question: Is it true that Soviet Jews are being forcibly assimilated?

Answered by Professor Joseph Braginsky (Jewish), corresponding member of the Tajik Academy of Sciences, editor in chief of the magazine Peoples of Asia and Africa: Nothing of the kind. There is not and cannot be any forced assimilation of Jews in the Soviet Union. It would run counter to the entire national policy of the country, which is based on friendship, mutual aid and mutual respect. What is happening is a natural process, the voluntary merging of different nationalities in the Soviet Union, with national traditions preserved and national cultures encouraged. It is an absolutely realistic and inevitable process under conditions of national and racial equality. And it should be noted that Jews aren't the only ones affected. Take my experience as a cultural worker among the peoples of Central Asia. In Uzbekistan, for instance, there are several hundred thousand Tajiks. They speak both the Tajik and Uzbek languages and, as you might expect, a considerable fraction of Uzbekistan's intellectuals are Tajiks.

Other nations and peoples, irrespective of race, who live beyond the confines of their national republics, are also subject to this historically objective law. Thus, only 80 percent of the country's Russians live in the Russian Republic. Russians also live and work in the Ukraine, in Kazakhstan, in Uzbekistan and in other union republics.

Of the Soviet Union's total Ukrainian population, a little over 86 percent live in the Ukraine proper. Large groups of Ukrainians live and work in the Russian Federation, Kazakhstan and Moldavia. Only 56 percent of the country's Armenians live in Armenia, most of the rest live in the neighboring republics and the Russian Federation. This factor serves to bring peoples and their cultures together, to shape common traditions.

Here is an example: Suleimanov, a young talented Kazakh poet, writes his poetry (usually on Kazakh themes) in Russian, while poet Nadezhda Lushnikova, a Russian by nationality (born in Kazakhstan in 1942), writes her poetry in the Kazakh language. Or take Alexander Belousov, a young Russian from Kuibyshev, who, having found Yiddish to his liking, writes his poetry in Yiddish and is published in the magazine Sovetish Heimland. One could cite many examples of such merging of cultures.

Testifying to the ever increasing rapprochement of nations and peoples in the Soviet Union is the multinational composition of workers in our factories and offices, of the students in all types of educational institutions, and the joint rearing and schooling of children of different nationalities and races in our nurseries and kindergartens. The mixed marriages of people of different nationalities is also very convincing evidence of the way national barriers and prejudices are breaking down.

Question: Why is the nationality of Soviet Jews listed in their passports? Isn't that discriminatory?

Answered by Grigori Lapidus, Jewish miner from the city of Gorlovka, Donetsk Region: Our miners' team of 25 men, for instance, is made up of Russians, Ukrainians, Jews, a Tatar, an Uzbek, a Kazakh, a Chuvash and a Mordvinian. Each one's nationality is listed in his passport. My wife Victoria is a Russian. And that's what it says in her passport. And why not? I believe that recording a person's nationality in his passport is a sign of respect for the holder's nationality. Besides that, nationality is indicated in passports for statistical purposes (so that proper planning can be done for the publication of literature, educational aids, etc.).

Is this notation in passports discriminatory? No. All Soviet people, irrespective of the nationality indicated in their passports, enjoy equal rights guaranteed by the Constitution. Included are the right to vote and be elected, the right to work, to free medical service, to free education and to rest and leisure.

There are quite a few Jews among my friends and acquaintances in Gorlovka: Vladislav Vinov, a foreman blaster; Mikhail Feingold, assistant chief engineer of the mine; Isaac Portnoy, chief mine technologist; Isaac Epstein, chief of a mine section; and Mark Braslavsky, chief of the mine planning department.

As for me, I'm 33 years old. My father was a miner. I followed in his footsteps and earn 270 to 300 rubles a month. I also study at an evening mining technical school. My wife, a mining engineer, is also well paid. We have two children and are expecting a third. We live in a comfortable apartment.

Question: What is the attitude of the Soviet Jewish people to Zionism?

Answered by Isaac Mints (Jewish), historian, member of the USSR Academy of Sciences, twice USSR State Prize winner: Our attitude to Zionism? I'll give it to you in two words: very negative. In my country, not only the young, but the old Jews have nothing in common with Zionist ideology, which is alien to our views, minds, psychology and way of life. There are, of course, exceptions. But it is not at all typical of Soviet Jews, to whom national narrow-mindedness and exclusiveness are repugnant. They have learned from their own experience that the road to a new life lies only through the consolidation of friendship among peoples.

I must say that Zionism, in general, was never popular with the working Jews of Russia. This is not surprising. The struggle against czarism, against poverty, inevitably led to the rallying of people of the same class, who were defending common interests. Zionism, however, propagated undisguised nationalism and racism, attempting to isolate the working Jewish masses from their class brothers of other nationalities.

Lenin, the founder of the Soviet state, said: "Among the Jews there are working people, they form the majority. They are our brothers, who, like us, are oppressed by capital; they are our comrades in the struggle for socialism. Among the Jews there are kulaks, exploiters and capitalists, just as there are among the Russians and among people of all nations. . . . Rich Jews, like rich Russians and the rich in all countries, are in alliance to oppress, crush, rob and disunite the workers."

Lenin was highly critical of Zionism, no matter what toga it donned. He was particularly critical of the idea of an exclusive Jewish nationality and of so-called national cultural autonomy. Lenin saw them as a reflection of the aim of the upper Jewish bourgeoisie—namely, to isolate the Jewish working people from their brothers in the class struggle.

I'm a historian. I've been studying the history of the shaping and development of the Soviet socialist state for many years now (I'm 75 already). And I know that the victory of the 1917 October Revolution was the result of the joint struggle of peoples of different nationalities. The October Revolution was profoundly international, both in spirit and in the humane tasks it set itself. A crushing blow was delivered to age-old national oppression. So it was not surprising that the masses of Jewish toilers, who had been subject to double suppression and oppression, joined the Revolution. . . .

In conclusion I want to join my voice to the voices of those who say: "The Soviet Jews will manage perfectly well without the outside help of uncalled-for champions." We are being cared for by Soviet power, by the power of the working people, which in the grim years of World War II saved millions of Jews, not only in my own country but all over the world, from the bloody hand of fascism.

Question: What is the basis of the relations between the peoples of the Soviet Union?

Answered by Aaron Vergelis, Jewish poet and editor in chief of the Yiddish literary magazine Sovietish Heimland:* As a result

---

*The parts of the answer not relevant to the position of Soviet Jews have been omitted.

of the October Revolution all nationalities in our country were proclaimed free and equal. . . .

During World War II the Soviet Government found ways of evacuating great numbers of people who would have inevitably been exterminated on entry of the Nazis. Hundreds of thousands of Jews from the Ukraine, Byelorussia, Moldavia and the Baltic republics found safety in Bashkiria, Kirghizia, Tajikistan, Uzbekistan, Kazakhstan, Siberia and in the Urals. More than 300,000 Jews who fled from nazi-invaded Poland found shelter in the Soviet Union.

The savage reprisals and massacres the Jewish population suffered in the occupied areas evoked deep pain in the hearts of the Soviet people. The Ukraine's most distinguished poets, Pavlo Tychina and Maxim Rylsky, wrote burning lines, describing with deep compassion and pathos the tragedy of the Jewish people. The poem "I'm a Jew" by Uzbek poet Gafur Gulyam, published in the Soviet press in 1942, made a tremendous impact. Hitler's program for the complete extermination of the Jewish people intensified the Soviet people's hatred of the enemy, roused them to fight harder. The communist underground and partisan forces in occupied Minsk, Kiev and Vilnius made truly heroic efforts to free as many people as possible from the ghettos and send them off to the woods to the partisans. Hundreds of thousands of Jews were saved that way.

One could cite many instances when Russians, Ukrainians, Byelorussians, Lithuanians and Latvians risked their own lives to come to the aid of doomed Jews. . . .

* * * * *

In efforts to discredit Western allegations of discrimination against Jews and to offer proof that "the Zionists hunt up all sorts of 'problems' and 'questions' and raise a hullabaloo about a 'Jewish question' in the U.S.S.R. which they themselves have invented,"* the Soviet press frequently publishes letters of interviews in which Soviet Jews attest to the good life they have been living and the equal opportunities they have had under Soviet rule.

Reprinted below are examples of such testimonials from three Soviet Army officers (one of them a retired general), a veterinarian,

---

*Brahye, Deceived by Zionism, p. 27.

a collective farm chairman, a doctor, a civil aviation pilot, a food store manager, and a scientist.

"WE LIVE AND WORK IN THE USSR"

I consider it my civic duty, the duty of a Soviet citizen, a Communist and a Jew to address people in the West who may have been misled by bourgeois propaganda. I declare in no uncertain terms that there is absolutely no ground whatsoever for inferring anti-Semitism in the Soviet Union or the unjust treatment of any other nationality.

L. Tseitlin, Soviet Army officer

The question of my nationality never worried me. I graduated from a military school, joined the Communist Party, and have been entrusted with the most honorable post: to stand on guard of my Homeland.

D. Heifman, lieutenant colonel, Soviet Army

I have lived a long life. I was born in Minsk in a Jewish working-class family. In October 1917 I volunteered for the Red Guard right at the factory where I worked as a fitter; I was ready to pursue a military career. All in all, I have served 44 years in the ranks of our glorious Armed Forces. I joined Lenin's Party in August 1919. Throughout, I have held command posts in active service. I was wounded six times. I was with the army in the field from the very outset of the Great Patriotic War. From February 1942 I was six years artillery commander and member of an army military council. I still well remember the appalling atrocities the fascists perpetrated in the occupied territories. I can never forgive them that.

In the regiments and brigades under my command there fought officers and men of various nationalities inhabiting our country. . . .

Soviet Jews have but one homeland. They have nothing to look for in distant parts beyond the seas. "We once again categorically tell all unasked-for intercessors for Soviet Jews that our Motherland is the Union of Soviet Socialist Republics. The cream of the Soviet people, among whom were many Jewish wo rking people of our region,

---

From B. Brahye, Deceived by Zionism (Moscow: Novosti Press Agency Publishing House, 1971) pp. 26-28; from Joseph Braginsky, "Jews in the U.S.S.R.—Equals Among Equals," Soviet Life, June 1973, p. 49; from "Soviet Jews Protest Against Israeli Aggression and Zionist Slanders," Soviet News, March 1970, p. 115; from Zionism: Instrument of Imperialist Reaction (Moscow: Novosti Press Agency Publishing House, February-March 1970) pp. 33-34 and 68-69, and March-May 1970, pp. 46-47. Reprinted by permission.

gave up their lives and shed their blood for its honour and independence. The present and future of all of us, of our children and grandchildren, are bound up with it alone, with our one and only motherland—the Soviet Union." All Jews in our country subscribe to these feelings as expressed in a resolution adopted by the regional aktiv of the working people of Jewish nationality in the Jewish Autonomous Region which has been awarded the Order of Lenin. Indeed it cannot be otherwise, for the Soviet Motherland, which Jews too, along with people of other nationalities defended from its enemies, has given them a life of which the finest representatives of the Jewish working folk have dreamed. In our country, where the nationality question has been settled, Jews feel that they are free citizens enjoying equal rights with all others.

Indeed, could I, a son of poor Jewish parents have become a general, or my brother an officer in tsarist Russia? A thousand times no! The lot of my brother and myself is no exception. In the Soviet Union there are no small number of Jews who are heroes of labour and war, statesmen, front-ranking factory workers and peasants, scientists and artists. This has become possible only because under Soviet government Jews, like the other national minorities of our country, have all civil rights, all the conditions for achieving material well-being and comprehensive cultural development.

Lieutenant-General G. Plaskov, retired

Anti-Semitism compelled me to flee from bourgeois Lithuania. I knocked around the world for a long time, lived in different countries, but nowhere did I find a home, nowhere did I feel free and needed. It was only at the end of 1939 that I finally found a Homeland—the USSR. Here in the Soviet land, I found work, got a secondary and then a higher education, and became a respected member of society. I live among splendid people, the Don Cossacks, and occupy the post of head veterinarian on a big state farm. For all this I am endlessly grateful to my government, to my people.

B. Shklyar, veterinarian

I am a son of the great Soviet people. I am a Soviet Jew, and I have children and relatives. About twenty-five members of our family were killed by the nazis at the time of World War II. I lost my elder brother, sister and three of my children. What is Golda Meir talking about? Who of us Soviet Jews living in friendship with the great Russian people, with whom we shared the last crust of bread, would want to go to Israel and become cannon fodder there at the grace of that country's leaders?

About our collective farm. I have been elected chairman 11 times. For 22 years I have been managing a diversified economy. Among our 10,000 farmers are representatives of nine nationalities. For a number of years, they have entrusted me with its management. Russians, Ukrainians, Byelorussians, Jews, Estonians and representatives of other nationalities of our country have placed their trust in me. I am a deputy to the Supreme Soviet of the Ukrainian SSR, member of the Budgetary Commission of the Supreme Soviet of the Ukrainian SSR, holder of three Orders of Lenin and a Gold Star of Hero of Socialist Labour. I am a member of the All-Union Council of Collective Farms.

My children have acquired an education. My elder son is a graduate of an agricultural institute; his junior graduated from a pedagogical institute; and the younger boy graduated from a special secondary school. He did not go to an institute, because he did not feel like it. What talk can there be of the inequality of Jews? We believe our elder brothers, the Russian people, and, together with them, we are a part of the great Soviet nation.

Our collective farm was recently visited by L. I. Brezhnev, General Secretary of the CPSU Central Committee. The General Secretary of the Central Committee of our Party dined in my Jewish home, at my Jewish table. I received in my home D. S. Polyansky, First Vice-Chairman of the USSR Council of Ministers. And recently we received G. I. Voronov, Chairman of the Council of Ministers of the Russian Federation. We also had a guest from Sweden: Erlander. There were 40 news correspondents with him and you may ask them about our life. We live wonderfully in our country and we shall not go anywhere.

I. A. Egudin, collective farm chairman

Could I, a poor Jewish boy, have dreamed of becoming a doctor, of doing scientific work, of becoming a D.Sc. and a professor of a medical institute?

All this has been given me by the Soviet system. What breaches of legality, what oppression is Golda Meir talking about? Who has given her the right to speak on behalf of the Soviet Jews, who are fully-fledged citizens of their great motherland which saved the world from the horrors of fascism?

Raifal Shub, doctor, D.Sc., professor at a medical institute

I am a Jew. My father was a cabby. I am a civil aviation pilot, first grade, with a three-million-kilometer flying record behind me. I was born in Siberia and, after demobilization from the Soviet Army in 1947, returned to my native parts. Today I live in Krasnoyarsk. I have a fine modern apartment and own a car. I am married and have two children—a son and a daughter—both of whom are learning music and belong to the figure-skating class of a sports school. Neither my children nor I ever feel we are treated any differently from the people of other nationalities. I'm happy to be a citizen of the Soviet Union, of our multinational Motherland.

G. Friedmanovich, civil aviation pilot

My biography is that of an ordinary Soviet man. I was born in the Zhitomir region into a poor Jewish family. I grew up in Soviet times. The Soviet Union is my beloved motherland which I defended in the Great Patriotic War. I do not have, and do not wish to have, any other motherland. Now Israeli Prime Minister Golda Meir is "inviting" Soviet Jews to Israel, claiming concern over their fate. . . .

I often ponder over the question: What would have become of me had I not lived under Soviet rule? Most likely, I would have become a small town shoemaker like my father whose family hungered seven days a week. Soviet Government provided me with the opportunity of finishing Baku military school. After the army I returned to Azerbaijan where I went to a trade school and then graduated from the Institute of Soviet Commerce in Moscow. I have been the director of foodstore No. 3 for many years now and have received due credit for my work. I have been elected deputy to the Nasimin District Soviet.

M. Shakhnovich, foodstore manager

A word about my many relatives. My indefatigable father, who was an office worker in the Baku oilfields for over half a century, could neither get a higher education nor use his talents and abilities to the full under czarism. He was happy to have lived to Soviet times and seen the miraculous changes that took place in the lives of his family.

Here is a picture of these changes. All four of my children have a higher education. One is a Doctor of Physics and Mathematics, a Lenin Prize winner; another is a Candidate of Philology.

There are engineers, doctors, teachers, factory workers, economists, students among my relatives. They live and work in Minsk (Byelorussia), Kiev (the Ukraine), Tbilisi (Georgia) and other cities. Some have married Armenians and Russians.

There is nothing exceptional about this picture—it is very typical.

We Soviet Jews live in peace and security. We have no worries about the future of our children or grandchildren.

Joseph Braginsky, corresponding member, Soviet Academy of Science, authority on the literature of the Near East and Hebraic languages, translator from Hebrew into Russian of Isaiah, Ruth, and other books of the Bible

* * * * *

Soviet emigrés to Israel do not find it easy to adjust to the new life. Climatic conditions they are not accustomed to, a language they do not understand, customs, traditions, ways of doing things in everyday life that are unfamiliar to them—all these add up to severe culture shock for the newcomers. There are reports that virtually all of them sooner or later sense a dreadful loss, "a treasured motherland no longer theirs, the new fatherland not yet fully theirs either," as one Western observer phrased it.* Some immigrants from the Soviet Union cannot make the adjustments at all, come to regret so bitterly their decision to leave the country of their birth that they actually attempt to go back. Israeli sources hold that out of some 45,000 Soviet Jews who arrived in Israel in 1971 and 1972, fewer than 100 fall into this last category. Soviet figures are larger but still modest: As of May 1972, they report having received several hundred letters from disillusioned emigrés who requested reentry permission. These letters, they tell us, "reflect the anguish and despair of people who have made a terrible mistake, people who are repentant and homesick for their Motherland, the Soviet Union. From their pages," the Soviets contend, "emerges the truth about the life of immigrants in Israel."†

The letters from which excerpts are reprinted below have been taken from a recently issued Soviet booklet. To check on their authenticity, this editor wrote to seven of the individuals in Israel whose names (and addresses) were given as signatories. Three responded, all affirming that they had indeed written the letters to Soviet authorities.

"WE WERE DECEIVED. ALLOW US TO RETURN"

(1) Please have my open letter published in the press, if possible. I appeal to every Jew in the Soviet Union. It does not matter what age he is, or what his occupation, it does not matter if he is religious or an atheist.

Jews! Sit tight in the USSR, kiss our Russian soil three times a day, and pray to your ancestors, thanking them you have not made my mistake, you have not left your home and your Motherland, your

---

*Herbert Gold, "The Soviet Jews Come Forward," Atlantic, May 1973, p. 103.

†The Deceived Testify, 2d ed. (Moscow: Novosti Press Agency Publishing House, 1972), p. 6.

From The Deceived Testify, 2d ed. (Moscow: Novosti Press Agency Publishing House, 1972), pp. 6-35 passim. Reprinted by permission.

friends and your work, your freedom and your right to be a man, the right to an education and to medical treatment.

I took my children to the Israeli land only to see them wounded by shell splinters, to see my son become an illiterate "goy" without an education. . . . My mother died and we could not bury her until I, like a fishwife, had bargained down the price of the grave, because I did not have much and the little I had was not enough. . . .

All those who want to return to their Motherland (and 99 percent of those who have come do want to return) are dragged to the Betakhon. My neighbours, Rosenberg from Riga, Vekris from Romania, Maikin from Riga, Benasher from Vilnius—all of them rue the day when they came to Israel and all of them are petitioning for a return. And when we ask for anything we always hear the same words: "What did you come for in the first place?"

There is an organisation called Sokhnut, which is supposed to look after the immigrants. But all the money that comes from America for the immigrants is spent on villas for Sokhnut officials and their mistresses.

Jew! Don't be an ass. Stay in your home and listen to the voice of Moscow and not to "Kol Israel."

Benedicta Tskavzaradze, 8/21, Izhak Sade, Natania, Israel

(2) I, Rosa Israilevna Rosenberg, born 1912, and my husband, Kurt Emilievich Rosenberg, born 1913 (Latvian by nationality), came to Israel on November 9, 1966. On arriving here we realised that we had made a serious mistake in leaving our mother country. We wanted to join my brother (my other brother died under Hitler), but he has turned out not to be our sort of person.

It is only in Israel that we have seen at first hand how the working class is humiliated and exploited. . . . We are prepared to go through any kind of difficulty, for we do not for a minute lose hope that we shall be forgiven and allowed to return to our homeland. . . .

Israel has brought us great misfortune. I feel guilty before my husband; he did not want to go and I have ruined his life. . . .

I beg of you and entreat you to give us permission to return to our homeland, because it is only in the Soviet Union that the working man enjoys human rights.

Respectfully yours, Rosa Rosenberg, Kurt Rosenberg, 9/12, Rehov Simhoni, Natania, Israel

(3) My husband, my son, my 12-year-old daughter, and I left the USSR for Israel on April 16, 1971. This was the darkest day of our life. My husband's father, Boris Seltzer, had been living in Israel and kept asking us to join him. A few years ago he died and was buried in Jerusalem. The thought that his father's last wish was to see him

would not leave my husband, even after the old man had died. And so, April 16, 1971 became our day of misfortune. It was like a nightmare.

On April 18, from the moment we found ourselves in this strange land, we realised that we had made a big mistake by leaving our motherland. It was only then that we became conscious of the deep roots we had in the Soviet Union where we had lived all our lives, where we raised our children and a grandson as well.

Our son and daughter-in-law and their child, my sister and her family all live in Chernovtsy. My brother-in-law and his family live in Kiev. We've written to our son in Chernovtsy and told him that he should kiss the holy land where he lives three times a day, something we are unable to do now.

Anyone who was born and was had lived under socialism cannot feel at home under the capitalist system.

We turn to you, Russia, as to a mother. A mother has the right to punish her bad children. We've been fully punished for our mistake. And now we beg for forgiveness. Take your prodigal sons back again.

Hannah Volfovna Seltzer, Iskok Berkovich Seltzer, son Edi and daughter Judith, B 718/34, Merkas Klita, Nazareth Illit, Israel

(4) Almost eighteen months have passed since I, my wife, and our only son left our country, the USSR. Our country had given us nothing but what was good: work, education, a flat to live in, and, what is most important, it saved us from death at the hands of the Nazi invaders. I have explained this to many people and will remember it all my life with gratitude.

As soon as we arrived in Israel we understood the difference between socialism and capitalism, and felt that we were not needed here. The country is in the grip of unemployment. It has no constitution. The factory owner is lord and master. The workers have no rights. There is enmity among the people, between the sefards (blacks) and the ashkenazis (the whites). The people here are very selfish, and have no respect for the elderly. Tickets for movies and concerts are expensive, and there is in fact very little cultural life here.

We ask to be allowed to return home. We are ready to go anywhere you send us.

D. Ya Vase, 11/1, Shikum Khadash, Gane-Tiqva, Israel

(5) On April 18, 1971, I left my country, my family, my relatives and friends and went to Israel. As soon as I set foot on this land I realised and felt the full extent of my mistake. I knew about the world of capitalism from books and stories. Now living in Israel I see and understand how despicable and cruel this world is, especially for us, ordinary Soviet people. Religious fanaticism and obscurantism, fierce hatred not only of the USSR but also of us, Soviet people, the

humiliating, shameful work we have to do for these cruel masters, all this has made me realise my guilt and my mistake.

I am ready to take any punishment for my crime so as to be able to see again all that was once so dear to me, all that I have left behind.

I ask you to give my wife hope that she will not be a widow. And give me hope that I may return home.

Cursed be that Zionism which has brought me and my family, and scores of Soviet people, great suffering and torment.

I implore you, my people and my family: please let me come—and leave this den of beasts.

Iosit Markovich Fleischer, 1020, 1 Malzgasse, Flat 27,
Vienna

* * * * *

The selection below is from a written protest, reportedly delivered to the Israeli Embassy in Austria by representatives of a large group of former Soviet citizens of Jewish extraction who had emigrated to Israel, subsequently left Israel, and, at the time this book went to press, were staying in Vienna.

"WE, FORMER SOVIET EMIGRÉS IN ISRAEL, PROTEST ZIONIST DECEPTION"

We, former Soviet emigrés in Israel, consider it to be our duty to lodge a protest with the Israeli government against the continued deception of Soviet citizens of Jewish nationality and the entire world public. This deception is practised daily by Israeli propaganda organs and international Zionist organisations.

Under the pretext of being concerned for the fate of Jews, they are recruiting them into Israel while conducting an unbridled anti-Soviet campaign.

We, a group of former Soviet citizens who were taken in by the promises of Zionist propaganda, left for Israel and lived there for about two years, have seen for ourselves the tragedy of thousands and thousands of families, emigrés from the Soviet Union, men and women, the aged and children.

The overwhelming majority of Soviet Jews who arrived in Israel have seen from their own experience that no other country can replace their Soviet homeland for them and that psychologically, culturally

---

From Soviet News, May 8, 1973, p. 196. Reprinted by permission.

and ideologically, they have nothing in common with the population living in the territory of Palestine in general and Israel in particular.

Israel turned out to be quite the opposite of the picture created in our imagination with the help of Zionist propaganda. . . .

All the vices of the infamous Zionist ideology and practices were manifested in the tragedies of Soviet Jews who found themselves in new conditions quite unacceptable to them.

Even the reactionary Israeli press does not conceal today that Soviet Jews have not accepted Israel. A morally decaying society which lives by the law of the jungle, broken and divided families, unemployment, financial dependence, alien surroundings, the need to struggle from the very first day for one's human and social rights, the humiliating position of women—all this affects people morally and is the cause of grave diseases, murders and suicides.

This is the price to be paid for the mistakes of people who have grown up in the conditions of Soviet society and who have found themselves in a backward eastern country, living in many respects under medieval laws. . . .

Immediately upon arrival, most of the emigrés become heavily indebted for many years to come and only very few of them succeed in shaking off this burden.

Most of the emigrés from the Soviet Union would willingly return to the Soviet Union. But, unfortunately, many of them who have already upset their well-adjusted lives, do not have enough strength, will, courage and means now to leave Israel and return to the Soviet Union.

The tragedy of the Soviet people who have found themselves in an alien country, transcends the bounds of a national problem and is being exploited by certain imperialist circles for political and ideological aims. Although these Soviet people have not accepted Israel and, on the other hand, Israel cannot receive most of the emigrés and provide them with jobs, western countries could not care less about the Soviet emigrés who, as soon as they leave the Soviet Union, become refugees whom no one needs, with all the consequences resulting from this. . . .

We, people who have seen all this with our own eyes and experienced all this ourselves, say to the Zionists: Hands off Soviet citizens! Hands off the Soviet Union!

We appeal to international public opinion to do everything possible to bar the way to Zionism, as was the case with fascism, and not give it an opportunity to ruin people's lives.

We urge the Israeli government to end the anti-Soviet campaign and stop enticing Soviet citizens into Israel. We demand that the Israeli government stop its campaign of pressure on persons who are willing to leave Israel and call off financial and administrative measures preventing their departure from Israel.

* * * * *

Some of the Jewish Soviet emigrés to Israel who regretted their decision and asked Soviet authorities to forgive them their "terrible mistake" have been readmitted to the USSR; others are reported even to have crossed Soviet borders illegally to return to their Soviet "homeland." In letters published in Soviet newspapers, in interviews, and at press conferences, these former emigrants, now back in the Soviet Union, talk about their disillusionment and warn other Soviet Jews not to be "deceived" by the talk about a "Jewish state" and a "promised land." Five statements by such former emigrants, slightly abridged, are reprinted below.

"WE HAVE RETURNED FROM ISRAEL TO OUR SOCIALIST HOMELAND"

(1) From the APN round table discussion

A few months ago I returned to the Soviet Union from Israel. Before I left the USSR I had applied four or five times for an exit visa so that I could see the land of my forefathers. Nobody could dissuade me from going, I would not listen to the warnings of good people and blindly believed the Zionist lies. I asked my wife to go with me, but she flatly refused. My son, Grigory, who was in the Soviet Army at that time, wrote: "You are going to a strange land. Why? You don't even want to think about the future of your children. . . . I, your son, have always been proud of you, of the fact that you've lived an honest working man's life. Please, sit down and think over the matter carefully before you decide."

But there were others who kept telling me: "Pack up and go. Don't listen to all this stuff. . ."

So finally I went. I was glad when I first got to Israel. I somewhat expected a "brass-band" type of welcome. . . Suddenly there was a commotion nearby. I asked an Israeli officer what it was all about, and he said that all the newly arrived immigrants wanted to go to Tel-Aviv, and that nobody ever wished to go to the desert.

I spent about an hour waiting for my relatives to come and fetch me. Then I telephoned my brother and he came to meet me.

He said hullo and kissed me, but it was a joyless sort of welcome. Then he said to me: "So you're here! Why did you come?" I looked at him and suddenly felt a chill running down my spine though it was very hot at the airport. I said: "But you kept asking me to come and our sister and nephews too. I had a letter of invitation from them."

From The Deceived Testify, 2d ed. (Moscow: Novosti Press Agency Publishing House, 1972) pp. 36-64 passim. Reprinted by permission.

"Then go to them," said my brother, putting 12 Israeli lires into my hand. "Don't expect any more from me!"

After he left I approached a Sokhnut* official and said: 'I am a working man, and don't need to go to Tel-Aviv. Just give me some work to do, so I'll have something to live on."

The official put me on a bus, and several hours later we arrived at a point near the Jordanian border. On the first day I collected garbage, the second day I repaired gates and fences and the third took samples of excrement from public latrines to the laboratory.

Soon afterwards I went to Elath. My niece Malka received me very reluctantly, and I knew right away that she did not want to have me around either.

I worked like a slave and got a mere 16 pounds for it. Out of this sum I paid four pounds for water alone. I worked in scorching heat for 16-18 hours a day, and I did so only because I wanted to save up some money to come back to the Soviet Union. It is impossible to come straight to the USSR from Israel. There is none who could help in this matter, for all the immigrants from the socialist countries are closely watched. Nevertheless these people leave Israel, too.

There are thousands of people there who would gladly come home on foot if they could. But Sokhnut puts your head into a noose as soon as you are in Israel. It offers you loans and thus ties you down since you can't leave without first paying back the money you've borrowed. I had met there some of my unhappy countrymen: Shloim Schlesinger, Seilik Weiss, and others. Schlesinger, who is now 70, works as a house-porter, and Weiss washes bottles at a hospital.

I had also seen there Schul Maushkonf who used to work at a purveying organisation in Mukachevo. Now he sweeps floors in a synagogue.

Their relatives also didn't want them.

Once I got sick and my employer told me: "If you can't do any work, go home." Those words were spoken in a callous tone such as I had never heard in our country, the Soviet Union. When I got home my brother, with whom I was staying after I had lost the job on the Jordanian border, said: "This is no Russia. You are not thinking that people here are going to coddle you, are you? What will you do? I'm not going to support you. . ." I am ashamed and pained to tell you all this. The fact is that the Zionists lure people to Israel to make

---

*A Hebrew word that literally means "agency." In this context, it refers to the Jewish Agency, an international organization that, among other things, makes arrangements for immigration to Israel and is supposed to look after the immigrants once they have arrived—Editor.

servants out of them, and not to make them masters of their country. As for young people, they are needed to fight the Arabs.

I saw no "promised land," but a hot and barren desert. I found myself among people who have no respect for anyone but themselves. . . .

I should like to say that in Israel, which is ruled by fanatic Zionists and chauvinists, one can expect nothing but bitter disappointment, tears, despair and a feeling of inferiority.

I didn't believe the good people who tried to warn me about the rash step I was going to take, and I blindly believed the Zionist lie. . . .

I had had first-hand experience of the "joys" of the Israeli "paradise," and I can tell my children, grandchildren and great grandchildren all about it, so they too will know!

Mikhail Goldstein, who has returned to Mukachevo, Ukrainian SSR, from Israel

(2) From the newspaper Sovetskaya Kultura

Right from the first few days of our stay in Israel we realised that there is no such thing as "a state for all Jews." There is an Israel for the rich minority rolling in wealth and an Israel of the working class majority which huddles in the "maabars," or villages of tiny cardboard houses on the outskirts of large cities. In one of these houses the Zionist authorities gave us an "apartment" in which we lived for six long terrible years.

I wasted a lot of time wandering about the Mishkat Avade (labour exchange) in Tel-Aviv looking for a job. "An artist?" shrugged the job-owners, "who needs loafers?" These cynical words happened to be true, and I had occasion to see this many times.

On a central street in Tel-Aviv, an artist was drawing pictures on the pavement with coloured crayons. The few passers-by dropped small coins into his hat. Next to him another artist put up a display of his oils and water-colours. We fell to talking. The man complained that he had a hard time scraping together money enough to stay alive. His fondest dream was to collect enough money to go to Europe.

Vladimir Baturin, who has returned to Zaporozhye from Israel

(3) From the newspaper Pravda Vostoka

If a person is over 40 and has a "common" trade (tailor, shoemaker, car-driver) he has to apply to the Labour Exchange for a job. More often than not a skilled worker has to accept any low-paid job. Doctors, lawyers, economists who do not know Hebrew (the state language of Israel) also find it difficult to find a job. I knew one such lawyer. He was compelled to work as a night watchman, another lawyer was a hotel usher. . . .

There is one haven for job-seekers. These are the kibbutz, a kind of rural community. Both parties (the kibbutz and the workers) fulfil their commitments towards each other with no money involved. You eat in the kibbutz and live in their house and do not pay a cent for it. However, you get no pay either, not a piastre, for your work on the farm. It stands to reason that if a member of a kibbutz works hard for the privilege of not dying of hunger and not sleeping under the open sky, the kibbutz must be earning lots of money. This money, almost all of it, is turned over to the political party which dominates at that particular kibbutz. In other words, the kibbutz is a well-camouflaged system of exploitation of the Jews who could not find a job in the cities. If a person decides to quit the kibbutz he leaves it with just the clothes on his back and without a penny to his name. . .

I would not say that the people of Israel are very pious. I talked to many of them and they said that they go to the synagogue, not as believers, but because this is the faith of their ancestors. I was absolutely flabbergasted to hear a rabbi warn several worshippers that if they did not pay for their pews in the synagogue on time they would be sold to someone else. . . As a rule a synagogue belongs to a local community. I never saw Jews from Africa or Asia go to a synagogue where European Jews worship. . .

I was inordinately happy, when after many years of separation I returned to my homeland. Here I became really happy and felt myself a man again.

Albert Stern, who has returned to Tashkent from Israel

(4) The temptation was too great, and I started out for that "paradise" after I had received an invitation—a fake one, actually—arranged by Rafael Zande through the Russian Committee. There I was met by him, warmly greeted and welcomed. But where was the comfort and prosperity Rafael had written me about? The paint was peeling off the walls, the furniture was shabby. When I went to the bathroom to wash, Rafael warned me, "Go easy on the water, it costs money, you know," and pointed to the meter.

The next day, Rafael introduced me to a man and he asked Rafael bluntly. "Why did you get him out here? He'll have nothing but sorrow!"

I found this out after I had been there for a couple of weeks, and I immediately saw that Rafael had deceived me. He . . . suggested that I go to Ulpan, a place where they taught Hebrew. And so I began to tighten the noose around my own neck.

I was convinced after spending two weeks at Ulpan that I would get nowhere by continuing to stay there, so I dropped my studies and went to Dram-Zegalo, a kind of ghetto for people from the Baltic, where I hoped to get some advice and help from my countrymen. And there I saw the "beautiful apartments" Rafael had written me about. Instead of parquet floors, there was cement, floor which caused most of the people living there to have rheumatism. My friends from Riga spent all day and every day trying to get enough money to live on. It was at Dram-Zegalo that I understood what it meant to be from the Soviet Union. It meant being an "inferior" Jew who was the last to get a job and whose pay was always lower than that of "real" Jews, that is, those who were born in Israel.

I found that people in Israel were divided into four classes—the rich, the middle class, the poor and the paupers. The last two were the most numerous, and their number was being constantly swelled by the arrival of new contingents of fools like me, who fell for the Zionist fairy tales about the "classless" Jewish state where "everyone has a chance to build a wonderful future for himself."

To get away from this "island of suffering" where I had met with more trouble than I had had all my life before coming here, where we, caught in the net of Zionist propaganda, we "second-class" citizens, had no right to exist, where our children would have to die for the aggressive designs of the Zionists in their war against the Arabs—to get away was my only desire. And I did manage to get out of that hell.

I will never wish on anybody the kind of life I had in the "land of my ancestors."

Yakov Liebgott, who has returned to Riga from Israel

(5) From the magazine Ogonyok

I was born in Kishinev where I received a medical education and for 16 years worked as a medical nurse. My relatives lived in Israel. I was alone with a little son, and my relatives invited me to come over. I went there because I did not want to be alone. However, I could not get adjusted to the life in a capitalist country and realised that I had committed a crime against my son by taking him there.

The Soviet Government allowed me to return to my homeland, I returned and was given a flat to live in. My son goes to school, and I am working as a medical nurse again. I'm free from the fear of losing my job. I am grateful to the Soviet Government and want to warn anybody who might be planning to go to the "promised land"—don't be in a hurry! Think again, so as not to suffer what I suffered.

Riva Kalinskaya, who has returned to Kishinev from Israel

ABOUT THE AUTHOR

Harry G. Shaffer is Professor of Economics and of Slavic and Soviet Area Studies at the University of Kansas. He has traveled widely and carried on research in the Soviet Union and in East Europe.

Dr. Shaffer has published five books and over thirty articles in the general area of Slavic and Soviet studies. His articles and reviews have appeared in The American Economic Review, The Journal of Industrial Economics, The Quarterly Review of Economics and Business, Soviet Studies, Problems of Communism, The Russian Review, East Europe, Central Europe Journal, The Rocky Mountain Social Science Review, Osteuropa, Osteuropa Wirtschaft, Revue de l'Est, Antioch Review, Kansas Business Review, and Queens Quarterly.

Dr. Shaffer holds a Ph.D. from New York University.

RELATED TITLES
Published by
Praeger Special Studies

BLACK COMMUNITY CONTROL: A Study of Transition in a Texas Ghetto
Joyce E. Williams

ETHNIC IDENTITY AND ASSIMILATION: THE POLISH-AMERICAN COMMUNITY: Case Study of Metropolitan Los Angeles
Neil C. Sandberg

POLITICAL SOCIALIZATION OF CHICANO CHILDREN: A Comparative Study with Anglos in California Schools
F. Chris Garcia

THE NATIONALITY QUESTION IN SOVIET CENTRAL ASIA
edited by Edward Allworth